English-Portuguese
Portuguese-English

Word to Word®
Bilingual Dictionary

Compiled by:
C. Sesma M.A.

Translated by:
Suzana Santos

Bilingual Dictionaries, Inc.

Portuguese Word to Word® Bilingual Dictionary
2nd Edition © Copyright 2012

Published in the United States by:

Bilingual Dictionaries, Inc.
PO Box 1154
Murrieta, CA 92562
T: (951) 461-6893 • F: (951) 461-3092
www.BilingualDictionaries.com

ISBN13: 978-0-933146-94-5
ISBN: 0-933146-94-9

Preface

Bilingual Dictionaries, Inc. is committed to providing schools, libraries and educators with a great selection of bilingual materials for students. Along with bilingual dictionaries we also provide ESL materials, children's bilingual stories and children's bilingual picture dictionaries.

Sesma's Portuguese Word to Word® Bilingual Dictionary was created specifically with students in mind to be used for reference and testing. This dictionary contains approximately 19,000 entries targeting common words used in the English language.

List of Irregular Verbs

present - past - past participle

arise - arose - arisen
awake - awoke - awoken, awaked
be - was - been
bear - bore - borne
beat - beat - beaten
become - became - become
begin - began - begun
behold - beheld - beheld
bend - bent - bent
beseech - besought - besought
bet - bet - betted
bid - bade (bid) - bidden (bid)
bind - bound - bound
bite - bit - bitten
bleed - bled - bled
blow - blew - blown
break - broke - broken
breed - bred - bred
bring - brought - brought
build - built - built
burn - burnt - burnt *
burst - burst - burst
buy - bought - bought
cast - cast - cast
catch - caught - caught
choose - chose - chosen
cling - clung - clung
come - came - come
cost - cost - cost
creep - crept - crept
cut - cut - cut
deal - dealt - dealt

dig - dug - dug
do - did - done
draw - drew - drawn
dream - dreamt - dreamed
drink - drank - drunk
drive - drove - driven
dwell - dwelt - dwelt
eat - ate - eaten
fall - fell - fallen
feed - fed - fed
feel - felt - felt
fight - fought - fought
find - found - found
flee - fled - fled
fling - flung - flung
fly - flew - flown
forebear - forbore - forborne
forbid - forbade - forbidden
forecast - forecast - forecast
forget - forgot - forgotten
forgive - forgave - forgiven
forego - forewent - foregone
foresee - foresaw - foreseen
foretell - foretold - foretold
forget - forgot - forgotten
forsake - forsook - forsaken
freeze - froze - frozen
get - got - gotten
give - gave - given
go - went - gone
grind - ground - ground
grow - grew - grown
hang - hung * - hung *
have - had - had

hear - heard - heard	**ring -** rang - rung
hide - hid - hidden	**rise -** rose - risen
hit - hit - hit	**run -** ran - run
hold - held - held	**saw -** sawed - sawn
hurt - hurt - hurt	**say -** said - said
hit - hit - hit	**see -** saw - seen
hold - held - held	**seek -** sought - sought
keep - kept - kept	**sell -** sold - sold
kneel - knelt * - knelt *	**send -** sent - sent
know - knew - known	**set -** set - set
lay - laid - laid	**sew -** sewed - sewn
lead - led - led	**shake -** shook - shaken
lean - leant * - leant *	**shear -** sheared - shorn
leap - lept * - lept *	**shed -** shed - shed
learn - learnt * - learnt *	**shine -** shone - shone
leave - left - left	**shoot -** shot - shot
lend - lent - lent	**show -** showed - shown
let - let - let	**shrink -** shrank - shrunk
lie - lay - lain	**shut -** shut - shut
light - lit * - lit *	**sing -** sang - sung
lose - lost - lost	**sink -** sank - sunk
make - made - made	**sit -** sat - sat
mean - meant - meant	**slay -** slew - slain
meet - met - met	**sleep -** sleep - slept
mistake - mistook - mistaken	**slide -** slid - slid
must - had to - had to	**sling -** slung - slung
pay - paid - paid	**smell -** smelt * - smelt *
plead - pleaded - pled	**sow -** sowed - sown *
prove - proved - proven	**speak -** spoke - spoken
put - put - put	**speed -** sped * - sped *
quit - quit * - quit *	**spell -** spelt * - spelt *
read - read - read	**spend -** spent - spent
rid - rid - rid	**spill -** spilt * - spilt *
ride - rode - ridden	**spin -** spun - spun

spit - spat - spat
split - split - split
spread - spread - spread
spring - sprang - sprung
stand - stood - stood
steal - stole - stolen
stick - stuck - stuck
sting - stung - stung
stink - stank - stunk
stride - strode - stridden
strike - struck - struck (stricken)
strive - strove - striven
swear - swore - sworn
sweep - swept - swept
swell - swelled - swollen *
swim - swam - swum
take - took - taken
teach - taught - taught
tear - tore - torn

tell - told - told
think - thought - thought
throw - threw - thrown
thrust - thrust - thrust
tread - trod - trodden
wake - woke - woken
wear - wore - worn
weave - wove * - woven *
wed - wed * - wed *
weep - wept - wept
win - won - won
wind - wound - wound
wring - wrung - wrung
write - wrote - written

**Those tenses with an * also
have regular forms.**

English-Portuguese

Bilingual Dictionaries, Inc.

Abbreviations

a - article
n - noun
e - exclamation
pro - pronoun
adj - adjective
adv - adverb
v - verb
iv - irregular verb
pre - preposition
c - conjunction

a *a* um
abandon *v* abandonar
abandonment *n* abandono
abbey *n* abadia
abbot *n* abade
abbreviate *v* abreviar
abbreviation *n* abreviação
abdicate *v* abdicar
abdication *n* abdicação
abdomen *n* abdômen
abduct *v* abduzir, raptar
abduction *n* abdução, rapto
aberration *n* aberração
abhor *v* abominar
abide by *v* obedecer
ability *n* habilidade
ablaze *adj* flamejante
able *adj* capaz
abnormal *adj* anormal
abnormality *n* anormalidade
aboard *adv* a bordo
abolish *v* abolir
abort *v* abortar
abortion *n* aborto
abound *v* abundar
about *pre* acerca de
above *pre* sobre, acima
abreast *adv* lado a lado
abridge *v* abreviar, resumir

abroad *adv* fora, no exterior
abrogate *v* abrogar, anular
abruptly *adv* abruptamente
absence *n* ausência
absent *adj* ausente
absolute *adj* absoluto
absolution *n* absolver
absolve *v* absolvisão
absorb *v* absorver
absorbent *adj* absorvente
abstain *v* abster (se)
abstinence *n* abstinência
abstract *adj* abstrato
absurd *adj* absurdo
abundance *n* abundância
abundant *adj* abundante
abuse *v* abusar
abuse *n* abuso
abusive *adj* abusivo
abysmal *adj* abismal
abyss *n* abismo
academic *adj* acadêmico
academy *n* academia
accelerate *v* acelerar
accelerator *n* acelerador
accent *n* acento
accept *v* aceitar
acceptable *adj* aceitável
acceptance *n* aceitação
access *n* acesso
accessible *adj* acessível
accident *n* acidente

accidental *adj* acidental
acclaim *v* aclamar
acclimatize *v* aclimatar
accommodate *v* acomodar
accompany *v* acompanhar
accomplice *n* cúmplice
accomplish *v* executar
accomplishment *n* realização
accord *n* acordo
according to *pre* de acordo com
accordion *n* acordeão
account *n* conta
account for *v* prestar contas
accountable *adj* responsável
accountant *n* contador
accumulate *v* acumular
accuracy *n* exatidão
accurate *adj* preciso
accusation *n* acusação
accuse *v* acusar
accustom *v* acostumar
ace *n* ás
ache *n* dor
achieve *v* realizar
achievement *n* realização
acid *n* ácido
acidity *n* acidez
acknowledge *v* reconhecer
acorn *n* bolota
acoustic *adj* acústico
acquaint *v* informar
acquaintance *n* conhecido

acquire *v* adquirir
acquisition *n* aquisição
acquit *v* absolver
acquittal *n* absolvição
acre *n* acre
acrobat *n* acrobata
across *pre* através de
act *v* agir
action *n* ação
activate *v* ativar
activation *n* ativação
active *adj* ativo
activity *n* atividade
actor *n* ator
actress *n* atriz
actual *adj* real, efetivo
actually *adv* na verdade
acute *adj* agudo
adamant *adj* adamantino
adapt *v* adaptar
adaptable *adj* adaptável
adaptation *n* adaptação
adapter *n* adaptador
add *v* adicionar
addicted *adj* viciado
addiction *n* vício
addictive *adj* que vicia
addition *n* adição
additional *adj* adicional
address *n* endereço
address *v* endereçar
addressee *n* destinatário

adequate *adj* adequado

adhere *v* aderir

adhesive *adj* adesivo

adjacent *adj* adjacente

adjective *n* adjetivo

adjoin *v* juntar

adjoining *adj* contíguo

adjourn *v* adiar

adjust *v* ajustar

adjustable *adj* ajustável

adjustment *n* ajuste

administer *v* administrar

admirable *adj* admirável

admiral *n* almirante

admiration *n* admiração

admire *v* admirar

admirer *n* admirador

admissible *adj* admissível

admission *n* admissão

admit *v* admitir

admittance *n* admissão

admonish *v* admoestar

admonition *n* admoestação

adolescence *n* adolescência

adolescent *n* adolescente

adopt *v* adotar

adoption *n* adoção

adoptive *adj* adotivo

adorable *adj* adorável

adoration *n* adoração

adore *v* adorar

adorn *v* adornar

adrift *adv* sem rumo

adulation *n* adulação

adult *n* adulto

adulterate *v* adulterar

adultery *n* adultério

advance *v* avançar

advance *n* avanço

advantage *n* vantagem

Advent *n* Advento

adventure *n* aventura

adverb *n* advérbio

adversary *n* adversário

adverse *adj* adverso

adversity *n* adversidade

advertise *v* publicar

advertising *n* propaganda

advice *n* conselho

advisable *adj* aconselhável

advise *v* aconselhar

adviser *n* conselheiro

advocate *v* defensor

aesthetic *adj* estético

afar *adv* longe

affable *adj* afável

affair *n* negócio, romance

affect *v* afetar

affection *n* afeição

affectionate *adj* afetuoso

affiliate *v* afiliar(se)

affiliation *n* filiação

affinity *n* afinidade

affirm *v* afirmar

affirmative *adj* afirmativo

affix *v* afixar

afflict *v* afligir

affliction *n* aflição

affluence *n* abundância

affluent *adj* opulento

afford *v* ter recursos

affront *v* afrontar

affront *n* afronta

afloat *adv* à tona

afraid *adj* medroso

afresh *adv* novamente

after *pre* depois

afternoon *n* tarde

afterwards *adv* posteriormente

again *adv* de novo

against *pre* contra

age *n* idade

agency *n* agência

agenda *n* agenda

agent *n* agente

agglomerate *v* aglomerar

aggravate *v* agravar

aggravation *n* agravação

aggregate *v* agregar

aggression *n* agressão

aggressive *adj* agressivo

aggressor *n* agressor

aghast *adj* consternado

agile *adj* ágil

agitator *n* agitador

agnostic *n* agnóstico

agonize *v* agonizar

agonizing *adj* agonizante

agony *n* agonia

agree *v* concordar

agreeable *adj* agradável

agreement *n* acordo

agricultural *adj* agrícola

agriculture *n* agricultura

ahead *pre* à frente de

aid *n* auxílio, apoio

aid *v* auxiliar, apoiar

aide *n* ajudante

ailing *adj* doente

ailment *n* dor

aim *v* visar

aimless *adj* a esmo

air *n* ar

air *v* ventilar

aircraft *n* aeronave

airfare *n* tarifa aérea

airfield *n* aeroporto

airline *n* linha aérea

airmail *n* correio aéreo

airplane *n* avião

airport *n* aeroporto

airspace *n* espaço aéreo

aisle *n* corredor

ajar *adj* entreaberto

akin *adj* consanguíneo

alarm *n* alarme

alarming *adj* alarmante

alcoholic *adj* alcoólico

alcoholism *n* alcoolismo
alert *n* alerta
algebra *n* álgebra
alien *n* estrangeiro
alight *adv* em chamas
align *v* alinhar
alignment *n* alinhamento
alike *adj* similar, parecido
alive *adj* vivo
all *adj* todo
allegation *n* alegação
allege *v* alegar
allegedly *adv* supostamente
allegiance *n* fidelidade
allegory *n* alérgico
allergic *adj* alegoria
allergy *n* alergia
alleviate *v* aliviar
alley *n* beco
alliance *n* aliança
allied *adj* aliado
alligator *n* jacaré
allocate *v* partilhar
allot *v* lotear
allotment *n* lote
allow *v* permitir
allowance *n* mesada, auxílio
alloy *n* liga
allure *n* fascinação
alluring *adj* fascinante
allusion *n* alusão
ally *n* aliado

ally *v* aliar
almanac *n* almanaque
almighty *adj* onipotente
almond *n* amêndoa
almost *adv* quase
alms *n* donativo
alone *adj* sozinho
along *pre* adiante
alongside *pre* ao longo de
aloof *adj* indiferente
aloud *adv* alto, em voz alta
alphabet *n* alfabeto
already *adv* já
alright *adv* tudo bem
also *adv* também
altar *n* altar
alter *v* alterar
alteration *n* alteração
altercation *n* altercação
alternate *v* alternar
alternate *adj* alternado
alternative *n* alternativa
although *c* embora, contudo
altitude *n* altitude
altogether *adj* totalmente
aluminum *n* alumínio
always *adv* sempre
amass *v* aglomerar
amateur *adj* amador
amaze *v* pasmar
amazement *n* assombro
amazing *adj* assombroso

ambassador *n* embaixador
ambiguous *adj* ambíguo
ambition *n* ambição
ambitious *adj* ambicioso
ambivalent *adj* ambivalente
ambulance *n* ambulância
ambush *v* atacar de surpresa
amenable *adj* afável
amend *v* emendar
amendment *n* emendar
amenities *n* conforto
American *adj* americano
amiable *adj* amável
amicable *adj* amigável
amid *pre* entreaberto
ammonia *n* amônia
ammunition *n* munição
amnesia *n* amnésia
amnesty *n* anistia
among *pre* entre, no meio de
amoral *adj* sem moral
amorphous *adj* amorfo
amortize *v* amortizar
amount *n* quantia
amount to *v* equivaler a
amphibious *adj* anfíbio
amphitheater *n* anfiteatro
ample *adj* amplo
amplifier *n* amplificador
amplify *v* amplificar
amputate *v* amputar
amputation *n* amputação

amuse *v* divertir
amusement *n* diversão
amusing *adj* divertido
an *a* um
analogy *n* analogia
analysis *n* análise
analyze *v* analisar
anarchist *n* anarquista
anarchy *n* anarquia
anatomy *n* anatomia
ancestor *n* ancestral
ancestry *n* decendência
anchor *n* âncora
anchovy *n* anchova
ancient *adj* antigo
and *c* e
anecdote *n* anedota
anemia *n* anemia
anemic *adj* anêmico
anesthesia *n* anestesia
anew *adv* de novo
angel *n* anjo
angelic *adj* angelical
anger *v* enfurecer(se)
anger *n* raiva, fúria
angina *n* angina
angle *n* ângulo
Anglican *adj* Anglicano
angry *adj* furioso
anguish *n* agonia
animal *n* animal
animate *v* animar

animation *n* animação	**anticipate** *v* antecipar
animosity *n* animosidade	**anticipation** *n* antecipação
ankle *n* tornozelo	**antidote** *n* antídoto
annex *n* anexar	**antipathy** *n* antipatia
annexation *n* incorporação	**antiquated** *adj* antiquado
annihilate *v* aniquilar	**antiquity** *n* antiguidade
annihilation *n* aniquilação	**anvil** *n* bigorna
anniversary *n* aniversário	**anxiety** *n* ansiedade
annotate *v* anotar	**anxious** *adj* ansioso
annotation *n* anotação	**any** *adj* qualquer, algum
announce *v* anunciar	**anybody** *pro* qualquer pessoa
announcement *n* anúncio	**anyhow** *pro* de qualquer forma
announcer *n* anunciador	**anyone** *pro* qualquer um
annoy *v* irritar	**anything** *pro* qualquer coisa
annoying *adj* irritante	**apart** *adv* separadamente
annual *adj* anual	**apartment** *n* apartamento
annul *v* anular	**apathy** *n* apatia
annulment *n* anulação	**ape** *n* macaco
anoint *v* ungir	**aperitif** *n* aperitivo
anonymity *n* anonimidade	**apex** *n* ápice
anonymous *adj* anônimo	**aphrodisiac** *adj* afrodisíaco
another *adj* outro	**apiece** *adv* para cada
answer *v* responder	**apocalypse** *n* apocalipse
answer *n* resposta	**apologize** *v* pedir desculpa
ant *n* formiga	**apology** *n* apologia
antagonize *v* antagonizar	**apostle** *n* apóstolo
antecedent *n* antecedente	**apostolic** *adj* apostólico
antecedents *n* antecedentes	**apostrophe** *n* apóstrofe
antelope *n* antílope	**appall** *v* aterrorizar
antenna *n* antena	**appalling** *adj* apavorante
anthem *n* hino	**apparel** *n* vestuário
antibiotic *n* antibiótico	**apparent** *adj* aparente

apparently *adv* aparentemente
apparition *n* aparição
appeal *n* apelo
appeal *v* apelar
appealing *adj* atraente
appear *v* aparecer
appearance *n* aparecimento
appease *v* acalmar
appeasement *n* apaziguamento
appendicitis *n* apendicite
appendix *n* apêndice
appetite *n* apetite
appetizer *n* aperitivo
applaud *v* aplaudir
applause *n* aplauso
apple *n* maçã
appliance *n* dispositivo
applicable *adj* aplicável
applicant *n* aplicante
application *n* aplicação
apply *v* aplicar
apply for *v* registrar, pedir
appoint *v* designar, apontar
appointment *n* entrevista
appraisal *n* avaliação
appraise *v* avaliar
appreciate *v* apreciar
appreciation *n* apreciação
apprehend *v* apreender
apprehensive *adj* apreensivo
apprentice *n* aprendiz
approach *v* aproximar(se)

approach *n* abordagem
approachable *adj* acessível
approbation *n* aprovação
appropriate *adj* apropriado
approval *v* aprovação
approve *adj* aprovar
approximate *n* aproximado
apricot *n* damasco
April *n* Abril
apron *n* avental
aptitude *n* aptidão
aquarium *n* aquário
aquatic *adj* aquático
aqueduct *n* aqueduto
Arabic *adj* Árabe
arable *adj* cultivável
arbiter *n* árbitro
arbitrary *adj* arbitrário
arbitrate *v* arbitrar
arbitration *n* arbitragem
arc *n* arco
arch *n* arco
archaeology *n* Arqueologia
archaic *adj* arcaico
archbishop *n* arcebispo
architect *n* arquiteto
architecture *n* arquitetura
archive *n* arquivo
arctic *adj* artico
ardent *adj* ardente
ardor *n* ardor
arduous *adj* árduo

area *n* área

arena *n* arena

argue *v* discutir

argument *n* discussão

arid *adj* árido

arise *iv* surgir, levantar(se)

aristocracy *n* aristocracia

aristocrat *n* aristocrata

arithmetic *n* aritmética

ark *n* arcaico

arm *n* braço

arm *v* armar

armaments *n* armamentos

armchair *n* poltrona

armed *adj* armado

armistice *n* armistício

armor *n* armadura

armpit *n* axila

army *n* exército

aromatic *adj* aromático

around *pre* em torno

arouse *v* despertar

arrange *v* arranjar

arrangement *n* arranjo

arrest *v* prender

arrest *n* apreensão

arrival *n* chegada

arrive *v* chegar

arrogance *n* arrogância

arrogant *adj* arrogante

arrow *n* seta

arsenal *n* arsenal

arsenic *n* arsênico

arson *n* incêndio, arsão

arsonist *n* incendiário

art *n* arte

artery *n* artéria

arthritis *n* artrite

artichoke *n* alcachofra

article *n* artigo

articulate *v* articular

articulation *n* articulação

artificial *adj* artificial

artillery *n* artilharia

artisan *n* artesão

artist *n* artista

artistic *adj* artístico

artwork *n* ilustração

as *c* como, conforme

as *adv* tão, tanto quanto

ascend *v* ascender

ascendancy *n* ascensão

ascertain *v* apurar

ascetic *adj* ascético

ash *n* cinzas

ashamed *adj* envergonhado

ashore *adv* em terra firme

ashtray *n* cinzeiro

aside *adv* ao lado, longe

aside from *adv* com exceção de

ask *v* perguntar, pedir

asleep *adj* adormecido

asparagus *n* aspargo

aspect *n* aspecto

asphalt *n* asfalto

asphyxiate *v* asfixiar

asphyxiation *n* asfixiar

aspiration *n* aspiração

aspire *v* aspirar

aspirin *n* aspirina

assail *v* assaltar, atacar

assailant *n* assaltante

assassin *n* assassino

assassinate *v* assassinar

assassination *n* assassínio

assault *n* assalto

assault *v* assaltar, estuprar

assemble *v* ajuntar, montar

assembly *n* assembléia

assent *v* consentir

assert *v* afirmar

assertion *n* afirmação

assess *v* avaliar

assessment *n* avaliação

asset *n* posse

assets *n* posses

assign *v* apontar

assignment *n* atribuição, tarefa

assimilate *v* assimilar

assimilation *n* assimilação

assist *v* assistir, ajudar

assistance *n* assistência

associate *v* associar

association *n* associação

assorted *adj* sortido

assortment *n* sortimento

assume *v* aceitar, supor

assumption *n* suposição

assurance *n* certeza

assure *v* garantir

asterisk *n* asterisco

asteroid *n* asteróide

asthma *n* asma

asthmatic *adj* asmático

astonish *v* pasmar

astonishing *adj* extraordinário

astound *v* maravilhar

astounding *adj* maravilhoso

astray *v* perder, extraviar

astrologer *n* astrólogo

astrology *n* astrologia

astronaut *n* astronauta

astronomer *n* astrônomo

astronomic *adj* astronômico

astronomy *n* astronomia

astute *adj* astuto

asunder *adv* em partes

asylum *n* asilo

at *pre* in, on

atheism *n* ateísmo

atheist *n* ateu

athlete *n* atleta

athletic *adj* atlético

atmosphere *n* atmosfera

atmospheric *adj* atmosférico

atom *n* átomo

atomic *adj* atômico

atone *v* reconciliar

atonement *n* expiação

atrocious *adj* atroz

atrocity *n* atrocidade

atrophy *v* atrofia

attach *v* prender, juntar

attached *adj* agregado, preso

attachment *n* afeiçoado, anexo

attack *n* ataque

attack *v* atacar

attacker *n* atacante

attain *v* alcançar, obter

attainable *adj* alcançável

attainment *n* realização

attempt *v* tentar

attempt *n* tentativa

attend *v* atender, assistir

attendance *n* assistência

attendant *n* criado

attention *n* atenção

attentive *adj* atento

attenuate *v* atenuar

attenuating *adj* atenuado

attest *v* atestar

attic *n* sótão

attitude *n* atitude

attorney *n* advogado

attract *v* atrair

attraction *n* atração

attractive *adj* atraente

attribute *v* atribuir

auction *n* leilão

auction *v* leiloar

auctioneer *n* leiloeiro

audacious *adj* audacidade

audacity *n* audaz

audible *adj* audível

audience *n* audiência

audit *v* fazer auditoria

auditorium *n* auditório

augment *v* aumentar

August *n* Agosto

aunt *n* tia

auspicious *adj* auspicioso

austere *adj* austero

austerity *n* austeridade

authentic *adj* autêntico

authenticate *v* autenticar

authenticity *n* autenticidade

author *n* autor

authoritarian *adj* autoritário

authority *n* autoridade

authorization *n* autorização

authorize *v* autorizar

auto *n* automóvel

autograph *n* autógrafo

automatic *adj* automático

automobile *n* automóvel

autonomous *adj* autônomo

autonomy *n* autonomia

autopsy *n* autópsia

autumn *n* Outono

auxiliary *adj* auxiliar

avail *v* ajudar

availability *n* disponibilidade

available *adj* disponível
avalanche *n* avalanche
avarice *n* avareza
avaricious *adj* avaro
avenge *v* vingar
avenue *n* avenida
average *n* média
averse *adj* contrário
aversion *n* aversão
avert *v* evitar, desviar
aviation *n* aviação
aviator *n* aviador
avid *adj* ávido
avoid *v* evitar, esquivar
avoidable *adj* evitável
avoidance *n* evitação
avowed *adj* declarado
await *v* esperar
awake *iv* acordar
awake *adj* acordado
awakening *n* o despertar
award *v* premiar
award *n* prêmio
aware *adj* consciente
awareness *n* consciência
away *adv* embora
awe *n* temor; respeito
awesome *adj* impressionante
awful *adj* terrível
awkward *adj* embaraçoso
awning *n* toldo
ax *n* machado

axiom *n* axioma
axis *n* eixo
axle *n* eixo

B

babble *v* balbuciar
baby *n* bebê
babysitter *n* babá
bachelor *n* solteiro
back *n* costas
back *adv* atrás
back *v* suportar, ajudar
back down *v* desistir
back up *v* mover para trás
backbone *n* espinha, suporte
backdoor *n* porta dos fundos
background *n* fundo
backing *n* apoio
backlash *n* retrocesso
backlog *n* reserva
backpack *n* mochila
backup *n* ajuda
backward *adj* para trás
backwards *adv* de trás
bacon *n* toicinho
bacteria *n* bactéria
bad *adj* mau

badge *n* crachá, distintivo
badly *adv* mau
baffle *v* aturdir
bag *n* saco, bolsa
baggage *n* bagagem
baggy *adj* largo, folgado
baguette *n* jóia; pão
bail *n* fiança
bail out *v* libertar sob fiança
bailiff *n* xerife adjunto
bait *n* isca
bake *v* assar
baker *n* padeiro
bakery *n* padaria
balance *v* balançar
balance *n* balanço, equilibrio
balcony *n* balcão
bald *adj* careca
bale *n* fardo
ball *n* bola, baile
balloon *n* balão, bexiga
ballot *n* cédula de votação
ballroom *n* salão de baile
balm *n* bálsamo
balmy *adj* resinoso
bamboo *n* bambu
ban *n* proibição
ban *v* interditar
banality *n* banalidade
banana *n* banana
band *n* banda; fita; anel
bandage *n* bandagem

bandage *v* enfaixar
bandit *n* bandido
bang *v* golpear
banish *v* banir
banishment *n* expulsão
bank *n* banco; beira
bankrupt *v* falir
bankrupt *adj* falido
bankruptcy *n* falência
banner *n* faixa
banquet *n* banquete
baptism *n* batismo
baptize *v* batizar
bar *n* bar; barra
bar *v* barrar
barbarian *n* bárbaro
barbaric *adj* bárbaro
barbarism *n* barbarismo
barbecue *n* churrasco
barber *n* barbeiro
bare *adj* nu
barefoot *adj* descalço
barely *adv* dificilmente
bargain *n* barganha
bargain *v* negociar
bargaining *n* regateio
barge *n* barcaça
bark *v* latir
bark *n* casca; latido
barley *n* cevada
barmaid *n* garçonete
barman *n* garçom

B

barn *n* celeiro
barometer *n* barômetro
barracks *n* quartel
barrage *n* garragem
barrel *n* barril
barren *adj* estéril; árido
barricade *n* barricada
barrier *n* barreira
barring *pre* com exceção
barter *v* permutar
base *n* base
base *v* basear
baseball *n* sem base
baseless *adj* beisebol
basement *n* porão
bashful *adj* tímido
basic *adj* básico
basin *n* bacia, vasilha
basis *n* base
bask *v* lagartear
basket *n* cesta
basketball *n* basquetebol
bastard *n* bastardo
bat *n* bastão; morcego
batch *n* fornada, lote
bath *n* banheira
bathe *v* banhar
bathrobe *n* roupão de banho
bathroom *n* banheiro
bathtub *n* banheira
baton *n* cassetete
battalion *n* batalhão

batter *v* espancar
battery *n* bateria, pilha
battle *n* batalha
battle *v* batalhar
battleship *n* couraçado
bay *n* baía
bayonet *n* baioneta
bazaar *n* bazar
be *iv* ser, estar
be born *v* nascer
beach *n* praia
beacon *n* farol
beak *n* bico
beam *n* raio; viga
bean *n* feijão
bear *n* urso
bear *iv* suportar; dar à luz
bearable *adj* suportável
beard *n* barbarismo
bearded *adj* barbado
bearer *n* portador
beast *n* besta
beat *iv* bater
beat *n* golpe, latejo
beaten *adj* derrotado
beating *n* surra
beautiful *adj* bonito
beautify *v* embelezar
beauty *n* beleza
beaver *n* castor
because *c* porque
because of *pre* por causa de

beckon *v* acenar
become *iv* tornar-se
bed *n* cama
bedding *n* roupa de cama
bedroom *n* quarto
bedspread *n* colcha
bee *n* abelha
beef *n* carne de vaca
beef up *v* fortificar
beehive *n* colméia
beer *n* cerveja
beet *n* beterraba
beetle *n* besouro
before *adv* antes
before *pre* antes de
beforehand *adv* com antecedência
befriend *v* fazer amizade
beg *v* mendigar, implorar
beggar *n* mendigo
begin *iv* iniciar
beginner *n* iniciante
beginning *n* início
behalf (on) *adv* em favor de
behave *v* comportar-se
behavior *n* comportamento
behead *v* decapitar
behind *pre* atrás
behold *iv* ver
being *n* ser
belated *adj* atrasado
belch *v* arrotar, vomitar

belch *n* arroto
belfry *n* campanário
Belgian *adj* belga
Belgium *n* Bélgica
belief *n* crença
believable *adj* acreditável
believe *v* acreditar
believer *n* crente
belittle *v* depreciar
bell *n* sino, campainha
bell pepper *n* pimentão
belligerent *adj* briguento
belly *n* barriga
belly button *n* umbigo
belong *v* pertencer
belongings *n* pertences
beloved *adj* amado, adorado
below *adv* abaixo
belt *n* cinto
bench *n* banco
bend *iv* dobrar
bend down *v* abaixar-se
beneath *pre* sob
benediction *n* bênção
benefactor *n* benfeitor
beneficial *adj* benéfico
beneficiary *n* beneficiário
benefit *n* benefício
benefit *v* beneficiar
benevolence *n* benevolência
benevolent *adj* benevolente
benign *adj* benigno

bequeath *v* legar
bereaved *adj* enlutado
bereavement *n* perda
beret *n* boina
berserk *adv* furiosamente
berth *n* beliche, cabina
beseech *iv* implorar
beset *iv* assediar
beside *pre* ao lado
besides *pre* além de
besiege *iv* sitiar
best *adj* melhor
best man *n* padrinho
bestial *adj* bestial
bestiality *n* bestialidade
bestow *v* outorgar
bet *iv* apostar
bet *n* aposta
betray *v* trair
betrayal *n* traição
better *adj* melhor
between *pre* entre
beverage *n* bebida
beware *v* tomar cuidado
bewilder *v* transtornar
bewitch *v* enfeitiçar
beyond *adv* além de
bias *n* parcialidade
bible *n* Bíblia
biblical *adj* bíblico
bibliography *n* bibliografia
bicycle *n* bicicleta

bid *n* proposta
bid *iv* oferecer
big *adj* grande
bigamy *n* bigamia
bigot *adj* fanático
bigotry *n* fanatismo
bike *n* bicicleta
bile *n* bílis
bilingual *adj* bilíngue
bill *n* conta; nota
billiards *n* bilhar
billion *n* bilhão
billionaire *n* bilionário
bimonthly *adj* bimestral
bin *n* lata de lixo
bind *iv* atar, amarrar
binding *adj* encadernação
binoculars *n* binóculo
biography *n* biografia
biological *adj* biológico
biology *n* biologia
bird *n* pássaro
birth *n* nascimento
birthday *n* aniversário
biscuit *n* bolacha
bishop *n* bispo
bison *n* bisão
bit *n* pedaço, um pouco
bite *iv* morder
bite *n* mordida
bitter *adj* amargo
bitterly *adv* amargamente

bitterness *n* amargor
bizarre *adj* bizarro
black *adj* preto
blackberry *n* amora
blackboard *n* quadro-negro
blackmail *n* chantagem
blackmail *v* chantagear
blackness *n* escuridão
blackout *n* blecaute
blacksmith *n* ferreiro
bladder *n* bexiga
blade *n* lâmina
blame *n* culpa
blame *v* culpar
blameless *adj* sem culpa
bland *adj* insosso
blank *adj* em branco
blanket *n* cobertor
blaspheme *v* blasfemar
blasphemy *n* blasfêmia
blast *n* rajada
blaze *v* incêndio
bleach *v* alvejar, desbotar
bleach *n* alvejante
bleak *adj* ermo
bleed *iv* sangrar
bleeding *n* sangrento
blemish *n* mancha, cicatriz
blemish *v* estragar
blend *n* mistura
blend *v* misturar
blender *n* liquidificador

bless *v* abençoar
blessed *adj* abençoado
blessing *n* bênção
blind *v* cegar, enganar
blind *adj* cego
blindfold *n* venda
blindly *adv* cegamente
blindness *n* cegueira
blink *v* piscar
bliss *n* ventura, felicidade
blissful *adj* ditoso
blister *n* bolha
blizzard *n* neve com vento
bloat *v* defumar; inchar
bloated *adj* inchado
block *n* bloco
block *v* bloquear
blockade *v* bloquear
blockade *n* bloqueio
blockage *n* obstrução
blond *adj* loiro
blood *n* sangue
bloodthirsty *adj* sanguinário
bloody *adj* sangrento
bloom *v* florescer
blossom *v* florescer
blot *n* mancha
blot *v* manchar
blouse *n* blusa
blow *n* pancada, golpe
blow *iv* soprar; explodir
blow out *iv* apagar, soprar

blow up *iv* explodir
blowout *n* pneu furado
bludgeon *v* cacetear, amassar
blue *adj* azul
blueprint *n* projeto
bluff *v* blefar
blunder *n* tropeço
blunt *adj* cego
bluntness *n* rudeza
blur *v* enevoar
blurred *adj* embaçado
blush *v* ruborizar
blush *n* rubor
boar *n* javali
board *n* prancha; painel
board *v* embarcar
boast *v* vangloriar-se
boat *n* bote, barco
bodily *adj* corporalmente
body *n* corpo
bog *n* pântano
bog down *v* atolar
boil *v* ferver
boiler *n* caldeira
boisterous *adj* ruidoso
bold *adj* ousado
boldness *n* ousadia
bolster *v* apoiar
bolt *n* tranca, parafuso
bolt *v* trancar
bomb *n* bomba
bomb *v* bombardear

bombing *n* bombardeio
bombshell *n* bomba
bond *n* vínculo; fiador
bondage *n* cativeiro
bone *n* osso
bone marrow *n* tutano
bonfire *n* fogueira
bonus *n* bônus
book *n* livro
bookcase *n* estante para livros
bookkeeper *n* contador
bookkeeping *n* contadoria
booklet *n* livrete
bookseller *n* livreiro
bookstore *n* livraria
boom *n* estrondo; crescimento
boom *v* ribombar
boost *v* inchar, melhorar
boost *n* impulso
boot *n* bota
booth *n* barraca
booty *n* butim
booze *n* bebida alcoólica
border *n* fronteira, canteiro
border on *v* fazer fronteira
borderline *adj* limítrofe
bore *v* perfurar
bored *adj* entediado
boredom *n* tédio
boring *adj* maçante
born *adj* nascido
borough *n* município

borrow v tomar emprestado
bosom n seio
boss n chefe
boss around v mandar
bossy adj autoritário
botany n botânica
botch v estragar
both adj ambos
bother v incomodar
bothersome adj incômodo
bottle n garrafa
bottle v engarrafar
bottleneck n engarrafamento
bottom n fundo; nádegas
bottomless adj sem fundo
bough n ramo
boulder n penedo
boulevard n bulevar
bounce v saltar
bounce n pulo, ímpeto
bound adj direcionado
bound for adj direcionado a
boundary n fronteira, limite
boundless adj ilimitado
bounty n generosidade
bourgeois adj burguês
bow n arco; reverência
bow v curvar-se
bow out v bater em retirada
bowels n intestino
bowl n tigela
box n caixa

box office n bilheteria
boxer n boxeador
boxing n boxe
boy n menino
boycott v boicotar
boyfriend n namorado
boyhood n infância
bra n sutiã
brace for v preparar-se para
bracelet n bracelete
bracket n parêntese
brag v gabar-se
braid n trança
brain n cérebro
brainwash n lavagem cerebral
brake n freio
brake v brecar
branch n galho
branch office n filial, ramal
branch out v ramificar
brand n marca
brand-new adj novo em folha
brandy n conhaque
brat adj fedelho, pirralho
brave adj bravo, corajoso
bravely adv corajosamente
bravery n bravura
brawl n briga
breach n ruptura; infração
bread n pão
breadth n largura
break n pausa; ruptura

B

break *iv* quebrar
break away *v* fugir, escapar
break down *v* arrombar
break free *v* libertar-se
break in *v* arrombar
break off *v* cessar
break open *v* abrir à força
break out *v* desabafar-se
break up *v* separar-se
breakable *adj* frágil, quebrável
breakdown *n* colapso
breakfast *n* café da manhã
breakthrough *n* avanço
breast *n* peito, seio
breath *n* hálito
breathe *v* respirar
breathing *n* respiração
breathtaking *adj* de tirar o fôlego
breed *iv* reproduzir
breed *n* raça
breeze *n* brisa
brethren *n* irmãos
brevity *n* brevidade
brewery *n* cervejaria
bribe *v* subornar
bribe *n* suborno
bribery *n* suborno
brick *n* tijolo
bricklayer *n* pedreiro
bridal *adj* nupcial
bride *n* noiva
bridegroom *n* noivo

bridesmaid *n* dama de honra
bridge *n* ponte
bridle *n* rédea
brief *adj* breve
brief *v* informar
briefly *adv* brefemente
briefs *n* calcinha, cueca
brigade *n* brigada
bright *adj* brilhante
brighten *v* clarear, alegrar
brightness *n* brilho
brilliant *adj* brilhante
brim *n* borda, aba
bring *iv* trazer
bring back *v* devolver
bring down *v* derrubar
bring up *v* educar
brink *n* beira
brisk *adj* ativo
Britain *n* Britanha
British *adj* britânico
brittle *adj* quebradiço
broad *adj* largo
broadcast *v* transmitir
broadcast *n* emissão
broadcaster *n* locutor
broaden *v* alargar
broadly *adv* de maneira geral
broadminded *adj* tolerante
brochure *n* folheto
broil *v* grelhar
broiler *n* grelhar

broke *adj* falido
broken *adj* quebrado
bronchitis *n* bronquite
bronze *n* bronze
broom *n* vassoura
broth *n* caldo, sopa
brothel *n* bordel
brother *n* irmãos
brotherhood *n* cunhado
brother-in-law *n* fraternal
brotherly *adj* irmandade
brow *n* sobrancelha
brown *adj* marrom
browse *v* folhear; pastar
browser *n* navegador
bruise *n* contusão
bruise *v* contundir
brunette *adj* morena
brush *n* escova, atrito
brush *v* escovar, varrer
brush aside *v* ignorar
brush up *v* recordar
brusque *adj* brusco
brutal *adj* brutal
brutality *n* brutalidade
brutalize *v* brutalizar
brute *adj* bruto
bubble *n* bolha
bubble gum *n* chiclete
buck *n* macho
bucket *n* balde
buckle *n* fivela

buckle up *v* afivelar
bud *n* broto
buddy *n* companheiro
budge *v* mexer
budget *n* orçamento
buffalo *n* búfalo
bug *n* inseto
build *iv* construir
builder *n* construtor
building *n* prédio
buildup *n* crescimento
built-in *adj* embutido
bulb *n* bulbo, lâmpada
bulge *n* protuberância
bulk *n* a granel, massa
bulky *adj* volumoso
bull *n* touro
bull fight *n* tourada
bull fighter *n* toureiro
bulldoze *v* bulldozer
bullet *n* bala
bulletin *n* boletim
bully *adj* valentão
bulwark *n* amurada
bum *n* vagabundo
bump *n* baque; solavanco
bump into *v* topar com
bumper *n* pára-choque
bun *n* pão
bunch *n* cacho, feixe, maço
bundle *n* trouxa
bundle *v* entrouxar

bunk bed *n* beliche
buoy *n* bóia
burden *n* fardo
burden *v* sobrecarregar
burdensome *adj* opressivo
bureau *n* escrivaninha
bureaucracy *n* burocracia
bureaucrat *n* burocrata
burger *n* hamburger
burglar *n* ladrão
burglarize *v* arrombar
burglary *n* roubo, assalto
burial *n* enterro
burly *adj* robusto
burn *iv* queimar
burn *n* queimadura
burp *v* arrotar
burp *n* arroto
burrow *n* toca
burst *iv* rebentar
burst into *v* irromper
bury *v* enterrar
bus *n* ônibus
bush *n* arbusto
busily *adv* ativamente
business *n* negócio
bust *n* busto
bustling *adj* agitado
busy *adj* ocupado
but *c* mas, exceto
butcher *n* açougueiro
butchery *n* abatedouro

butler *n* mordomo
butt *n* alvo; toco; bunda
butter *n* manteiga
butterfly *n* borboleta
button *n* botão
buttonhole *n* casa de botão
buy *iv* comprar
buy off *v* subornar
buyer *n* comprador
buzz *n* zumbido
buzz *v* zumbir
buzzard *n* búteo
buzzer *n* campainha
by *pre* perto de
bye *e* tchau
bypass *n* atalho, desvio
bypass *v* desviar
by-product *n* subproduto
bystander *n* espectador

C

cab *n* taxi
cabbage *n* repolho
cabin *n* cabana, camarote
cabinet *n* armário
cable *n* cabo
cafeteria *n* restaurante

caffeine *n* cafeína
cage *n* gaiola
cake *n* bolo
calamity *n* calamidade
calculate *v* calcular
calculation *n* cálculo
calculator *n* calculadora
calendar *n* calendário
calf *n* bezerro; panturrilha
caliber *n* alibre
calibrate *v* calibrar
call *n* chamada
call *v* chamar, telefonar
call off *v* cancelar
call on *v* visitar
call out *v* gritar por ajuda
calling *n* profissão
callous *adj* duro
calm *adj* calmo
calm *n* calmaria
calm down *v* acalmar
calorie *n* caloria
calumny *n* calúnia
camel *n* camelo
camera *n* câmera
camouflage *v* camuflar
camouflage *n* camuflagem
camp *n* acampamento
camp *v* acampar
campaign *v* fazer campanha
campaign *n* campanha
campfire *n* fogueira

can *iv* poder, conseguir
can *v* enlatar
can *n* lata
can opener *n* abridor de lata
canal *n* canal
canary *n* canário
cancel *v* cancelar
cancellation *n* cancelamento
cancer *n* câncer
cancerous *adj* canceroso
candid *adj* cândido
candidacy *n* candidatura
candidate *n* candidato
candle *n* vela
candlestick *n* castiçal
candor *n* sinceridade
cane *n* cana; bengala
canister *n* lata
canned *adj* enlatado
cannibal *n* canibal
cannon *n* canhão
canoe *n* canoa
canonize *v* canonizar
cantaloupe *n* melão
canteen *n* cantina
canvas *n* lona; tela
canvas *v* angariar votos
canyon *n* desfiladeiro
cap *n* chapéu; tampa
capability *n* capacidade
capable *adj* capaz
capacity *n* capacidade

cape *n* capa, cabo
capital *n* capital maiúscula
capital letter *n* letra maiúscula
capitalism *n* capitalismo
capitalize *v* capitalize
capitulate *v* capitular
capsize *v* virar, capotar
capsule *n* cápsula
captain *n* capitão
captivate *v* cativar
captive *n* cativo
captivity *n* catividade
capture *v* capturar
capture *n* captura
car *n* carro
carat *n* quilate
caravan *n* reboque, trailer
carburetor *n* carburador
carcass *n* carcaça
card *n* cartão
cardboard *n* papelão
cardiac *adj* cardíaco
cardiac arrest *n* ataque de coração
cardiology *n* cardiologia
care *n* cuidado
care *v* cuidar
care about *v* gostar de
care for *v* cuidar de
career *n* carreira
carefree *adj* displicente
careful *adj* cuidadoso

careless *adj* descuidado
carelessness *n* descuido
caress *n* carícia
caress *v* acariciar
caretaker *n* guarda, zelador
cargo *n* carga
caricature *n* caricatura
caring *adj* afetivo, atencioso
carnage *n* carnificina
carnal *adj* carnal
carnation *n* cravo
carol *n* hino
carpenter *n* carpinteiro
carpentry *n* carpintaria
carpet *n* carpete
carriage *n* carruagem
carrot *n* cenoura
carry *v* carregar
carry on *v* prosseguir
carry out *v* realizar
cart *n* carroça
cart *v* carregar
cartoon *n* desenho animado
cartridge *n* cartucho
carve *v* entalhar; cortar
cascade *n* cascata
case *n* caso; estojo
cash *n* dinheiro vivo
cashier *n* caixa
casino *n* cassino
casket *n* estojo; ataúde
casserole *n* caçarola

cassock *n* sotaina
cast *iv* jogar; expelir
castaway *n* náufrago
caste *n* casta
castle *n* castelo
casual *adj* casual, informal
casualty *n* baixa
cat *n* gato
cataclysm *n* cataclismo
catacomb *n* catacumba
catalog *n* catálogo
catalog *v* catalogar
cataract *n* catarata
catastrophe *n* catástrofe
catch *iv* apanhar
catch up *v* alcançar
catching *adj* contagioso
catchword *n* slogan
catechism *n* catecismo
category *n* categoria
cater to *v* abastecer
caterpillar *n* lagarta
cathedral *n* catedral
catholic *adj* católico
Catholicism *n* Catolicismo
cattle *n* gado
cauliflower *n* couve-flor
cause *n* causa
cause *v* causar
caution *n* cuidado
cautious *adj* cuidadoso
cavalry *n* cavalaria

cave *n* gruta
cave in *v* desmoronar
cavern *n* caverna
cavity *n* cavidade, cárie
cease *v* cessar
cease-fire *n* cessar-fogo
ceaselessly *adv* continuamente
ceiling *n* teto
celebrate *v* celebrar
celebration *n* celebração
celebrity *n* celebridade
celery *n* aipo
celestial *adj* celestial
celibacy *n* celibato
celibate *adj* celibatário
cell phone *n* telefone celular
cellar *n* porão, adega
cement *n* cimento
cemetery *n* cemitério
censorship *n* censura
censure *v* censurar
census *n* censo
cent *n* centavo
centenary *n* centenário
center *n* centímetro
center *v* centro
centimeter *n* centrar
central *adj* central
centralize *v* centralizar
century *n* século
ceramic *n* cerâmica
cereal *n* cereal

cerebral *adj* cerebral
ceremony *n* cerimônia
certain *adj* certo, seguro
certainty *n* certeza
certificate *n* certificado
certify *v* certificar
chagrin *n* desgosto
chain *n* corrente
chain *v* acorrentar
chainsaw *n* motosserra
chair *n* cadeira
chair *v* presidir
chairman *n* presidente
chalet *n* chalé
chalice *n* cálice
chalk *n* giz
chalkboard *n* quadro
challenge *v* desafiar
challenge *n* desafio
challenging *adj* desafiador
chamber *n* quarto
champ *n* campeão
champion *n* campeão
champion *v* defender
chance *n* chance
chancellor *n* chanceler
chandelier *n* candelabro
change *v* mudar, trocar
change *n* mudança
channel *n* canal
chant *n* cântico
chaos *n* caos

chaotic *adj* caótico
chapel *n* capela
chaplain *n* capelão
chapter *n* capítulo
char *v* carbonizar
character *n* caráter
characteristic *adj* característico
charade *n* charada
charbroil *adj* assado à carvão
charcoal *n* carvão vegetal
charge *v* cobrar; incriminar
charge *n* encargo; carga
charisma *n* carisma
charismatic *adj* carismático
charitable *adj* caridoso
charity *n* caridade
charm *v* encantar
charm *n* charme
charming *adj* encantador
chart *n* mapa; gráfico
charter *n* contrato
charter *v* fretar
chase *n* perseguição
chase *v* perseguir
chase away *v* enxotar
chasm *n* abismo
chaste *adj* casto
chastise *v* castigar
chastisement *n* castigo
chastity *n* castidade
chat *v* bater papo
chauffeur *n* chofer

cheap *adj* barato
cheat *v* trapacear, trair
cheater *n* trapaceiro
check *n* cheque
check *v* checar, verificar
check in *v* check-in
check up *n* exame geral
checkbook *n* talão de cheques
cheek *n* bochecha
cheekbone *n* zigoma
cheeky *adj* atrevido
cheer *v* viva
cheer up *v* animar
cheerful *adj* animado, alegre
cheers *n* à saúde
cheese *n* queijo
chef *n* chefe de cozinha
chemical *adj* químico
chemist *n* químico
chemistry *n* química
cherish *v* acarinhar
cherry *n* cereja
chess *n* xadrez
chest *n* peito; baú; cofre
chestnut *n* castanha
chew *v* mastigar, mascar
chick *n* filhote de ave
chicken *n* frango, galinha
chicken out *v* catapora
chicken pox *n* tirar o corpo fora
chide *v* repreender
chief *n* chefe

chiefly *adv* principalmente
child *n* criança
childhood *n* infância
childish *adj* pueril, infantil
childless *adj* sem filhos
children *n* crianças
chill *n* friagem
chill *v* arrefecer, esfriar
chilly *adj* frio
chimney *n* chaminé
chimpanzee *n* chimpanzé
chin *n* queixo
chip *n* lasca, fatia; ficha
chisel *n* cinzel, talhadeira
chocolate *n* chocolate
choice *n* escolha, opção
choir *n* coro
choke *v* sufocar, asfixiar
cholera *n* cólera
cholesterol *n* colesterol
choose *iv* escolher
choosy *adj* exigente
chop *v* picar
chop *n* mandíbula
chopper *n* cutelo
chore *n* tarefa doméstica
chorus *n* coro, refrão
christen *v* batizar
christening *n* batizado
Christian *adj* cristão
Christianity *n* Cristianismo
Christmas *n* Natal

C

chronic *adj* crônico
chronicle *n* crônica
chronology *n* cronologia
chubby *adj* rechonchudo
chuckle *v* dar risinhos
chunk *n* naco, pedaço
church *n* igreja
chute *n* conduto
cider *n* sidra
cigar *n* charuto
cigarette *n* cigarro
cinder *n* borralho
cinema *n* cinema
cinnamon *n* canela
circle *n* círculo
circle *v* cercar, rodear
circuit *n* circuito
circular *adj* circular
circulate *v* circular
circulation *n* circulação
circumcise *v* circuncisar
circumcision *n* circuncisão
circumstance *n* circunstância
circumstantial *adj* circunstancial
circus *n* circo
cistern *n* cisterna
citizen *n* cidadão
citizenship *n* cidadania
city *n* cidade
city hall *n* prefeitura
civic *adj* cívico
civil *adj* civil

civilization *n* civilização
civilize *v* civilizar
claim *v* afirmar; reclamar
claim *n* reclamação
clam *n* amêijoa
clamor *v* clamar; vociferar
clamp *n* torniquete
clan *n* clã; raça
clandestine *adj* clandestino
clap *v* aplaudir; trancafiar
clarification *n* esclarecimento
clarify *v* esclarecer
clarinet *n* clarinete
clarity *n* limpidez, clareza
clash *v* colidir
clash *n* colisão
class *n* classe; categoria
classic *adj* clássico
classify *v* classificar
classmate *n* colega de classe
classroom *n* sala de aula
classy *adj* elegante, bacana
clause *n* oração; cláusula
claw *n* garra, presa
claw *v* arranhar
clay *n* argila
clean *adj* limpo
clean *v* limpar
cleaner *n* limpador
cleanliness *n* limpeza
cleanse *v* purificar
cleanser *n* removedor

clear *adj* claro; certo
clear *v* desimpedir, inocentar
clearance *n* promoção
clear-cut *adj* nítido
clearly *adv* claramente
clearness *n* clareza
cleft *n* fissura
clemency *n* clemência
clench *v* cerrar
clergy *n* clero
clergyman *n* clérigo
clerical *adj* clerical
clerk *n* balconista
clever *adj* esperto
click *v* clicar
client *n* cliente
clientele *n* clientela
cliff *n* penhasco
climate *n* clima
climatic *adj* climático
climax *n* clímax
climb *v* escalar
climbing *n* alpinismo
clinch *v* concluir
cling *iv* agarrar
clinic *n* clínica
clip *v* cortar, segurar
clipping *n* recorte de jornal
cloak *n* capa
clock *n* relógio
clog *v* entupir
cloister *n* claustro

clone *v* clonar
cloning *n* clonagem
close *v* fechar
close *adj* íntimo
close to *pre* perto de
closed *adj* fechado
closely *adv* de perto
closet *n* armário
closure *n* fechamento
clot *n* coágulo
cloth *n* pano
clothe *v* vestir
clothes *n* roupas
clothing *n* roupas
cloud *n* nuvem
cloudless *adj* sem nuvens
cloudy *adj* nublado
clown *n* palhaço
club *n* clube; danceteria
club *v* espancar
clue *n* pista
clumsiness *n* falta de jeito
clumsy *adj* atrapalhado
cluster *n* aglomerado, feixe
cluster *v* enfeixar
clutch *n* domínio
coach *v* treinar
coach *n* treinador; vagão
coaching *n* instrução
coagulate *v* coagular
coagulation *n* coagulação
coal *n* carvão

C

coalition *n* coalisão
coarse *adj* áspero; rude
coast *n* costa
coastal *adj* costeiro
coastline *n* litoral
coat *n* casaco; camada
coax *v* persuadir
cobweb *n* teira de aranha
cocaine *n* cocaína
cock *n* galo; pica
cockpit *n* cabina do piloto
cockroach *n* barata
cocktail *n* coquetel
cocky *adj* convencido
cocoa *n* cacau
coconut *n* coco
cod *n* bacalhau
code *n* código; cifra
codify *v* codificar
coefficient *n* coeficiente
coerce *v* coagir
coercion *n* coação
coexist *v* coexistir
coffee *n* café
coffin *n* caixão
cohabit *v* coabitar
coherent *adj* coerente
cohesion *n* coesão
coin *n* moeda
coincide *v* coincidir
coincidence *n* coincidência
coincidental *adj* coincidente

cold *adj* frio
coldness *n* frieza
colic *n* cólica
collaborate *v* colaborar
collaboration *n* colaboração
collaborator *n* colaborador
collapse *v* desmoronar
collapse *n* colapso
collar *n* gola, coleira
collarbone *n* clavícula
collateral *adj* colateral
colleague *n* colega
collect *v* coletar
collection *n* coleção
collector *n* coletor
college *n* faculdade
collide *v* colidir
collision *n* colisão
cologne *n* colônia
colon *n* cólon; dois-pontos (:)
colonel *n* coronel
colonial *adj* colonial
colonization *n* colonização
colonize *v* colonizar
colony *n* colônia
color *n* cor
color *v* colorir
colorful *adj* colorido
colossal *adj* colossal
colt *n* potro
column *n* coluna
coma *n* coma

comb *n* pente
comb *v* pentear
combat *n* combate
combat *v* combater
combatant *n* combatente
combination *n* combinação
combine *v* combinar
combustible *n* combustível
combustion *n* combustão
come *iv* vir
come about *v* acontecer
come across *v* deparar com
come apart *v* quebrar
come back *v* voltar
come down *v* descer, desmoronar
come forward *v* apresentar-se
come from *v* vir de
come in *v* entrar
come out *v* revelar
come over *v* visitar
come up *v* surgir
comeback *n* voltar
comedian *n* comediante
comedy *n* comédia
comet *n* cometa
comfort *n* conforto
comfortable *adj* confortável
comforter *n* edredon
comical *adj* cômico
coming *n* vinda; chegada
coming *adj* próximo

comma *n* vírgula
command *v* comardar
commander *n* comandante
commandment *n* comando
commemorate *v* comemorar
commence *v* começar
commend *v* elogiar
commendation *n* elogio
comment *v* comentar
comment *n* comentário
commerce *n* comércio
commercial *adj* comercial
commission *n* comissão
commit *v* cometer
commitment *n* compromisso
committed *adj* comprometido
committee *n* comitê
common *adj* comum
commotion *n* comoção
communicate *v* comunicar
communication *n* comunicação
communion *n* comunhão
communism *n* comunismo
communist *adj* comunista
community *n* comunidade
commute *v* comutar
compact *adj* compacto
compact *v* compactar
companion *n* companheiro
companionship *n* companhia
company *n* companhia
comparable *adj* comparável

C

C

comparative adj relativo
compare v comparar
comparison n comparação
compartment n compartimento
compass n compasso
compassion n compaixão
compassionate adj compassivo
compatibility n compatibilidade
compatible adj compatível
compatriot n compatriota
compel v obrigar
compelling adj atrativo
compendium n compêndio
compensate v compensar
compensation n compensação
compete v competir
competence n competência
competent adj competente
competition n competição
competitive adj competitivo
competitor n competidor
compile v compilar
complain v reclamar
complaint n queixa
complement n complemento
complete adj completo
complete v completar
completely adv completamente
completion n término
complex adj complexo
complexion n complexão
complexity n complexidade

compliance n obediência
compliant adj obediente
complicate v complicar
complication n complicação
complicity n cumplicidade
compliment n elogio
complimentary adj lisonjeiro, gratuito
comply v obedecer, acatar
component n componente
compose v compor; conter-se
composed adj composto; calmo
composer n compositor
composition n composição
compost n composto
composure n compostura
compound n composto; recinto
compound v compor, misturar
comprehend v compreender
comprehensive adj amplo
compress v comprimir
compression n compressão
comprise v compreender
compromise n conciliação
compromise v fazer acordo
compulsion n compulsão
compulsive adj compulsivo
compulsory adj compulsório
compute v computar
computer n computador
comrade n camarada
con man n vigarista

conceal *v* dissimular
concede *v* conceder, admitir
conceited *adj* presunçoso
conceive *v* conceber
concentrate *v* concentrar
concentration *n* concentração
concentric *adj* concêntrico
concept *n* conceito
conception *n* concepção
concern *v* preocupar-se
concern *n* preocupação
concerning *pre* a respeito de
concert *n* concerto
concession *n* concessão
conciliate *v* conciliar
conciliatory *adj* conciliatório
concise *adj* conciso
conclude *v* concluir
conclusion *n* conclusão
conclusive *adj* conclusivo
concoct *v* preparar; inventar
concoction *n* preparado
concrete *n* concreto
concrete *adj* concreto
concur *v* concordar
concurrent *adj* coincidente
concussion *n* concussão
condemn *v* condenar
condemnation *n* condenação
condensation *n* condensação
condense *v* condensar
condescend *v* condescender

condiment *n* condimento
condition *n* condição
conditional *adj* condicional
conditioner *n* condicionador
condo *n* apartamento
condolences *n* condolências
condone *v* perdoar
conducive *adj* conducente, útil
conduct *n* conduta; gestão
conduct *v* conduzir
conductor *n* condutor
cone *n* cone
confer *v* conferenciar
conference *n* conferência
confess *v* confessar
confession *n* confissão
confessional *n* confissional
confessor *n* confessor
confidant *n* confidente
confide *v* confiar
confidence *n* confiança
confident *adj* confiante
confidential *adj* confidencial
confine *v* confinar
confinement *n* confinamento
confirm *v* confirmar
confirmation *n* confirmação
confiscate *v* confiscar
confiscation *n* confisco
conflict *n* conflito
conflict *v* conflitar
conflicting *adj* conflitante

C

C

conform *v* conformar
conformist *adj* conformista
conformity *n* conformidade
confound *v* confundir
confront *v* confrontar
confrontation *n* confrontação
confuse *v* confundir
confusing *adj* confuso
confusion *n* confusão
congenial *adj* agradável
congested *adj* congestionado
congestion *n* congestão
congratulate *v* cumprimentar
congratulations *n* cumprimentos
congregate *v* congregar
congregation *n* congregação
congress *n* congresso
conjecture *n* conjectura
conjugal *adj* conjugal
conjugate *v* conjugar
conjunction *n* conjunção
conjure up *v* invocar
connect *v* conectar
connection *n* conexão
connote *v* conotar, implicar
conquer *v* conquistar
conqueror *n* conquistador
conquest *n* conquista
conscience *n* conciência
conscious *adj* consciente
consciousness *n* consciência
conscript *n* conscrito, recruta

consecrate *v* consagrar
consecration *n* consagração
consecutive *adj* consecutivo
consensus *n* consenso
consent *v* consentir
consent *n* consentimento
consequence *n* consequência
consequent *adj* consequente
conservation *n* conservação
conservative *adj* conservador
conserve *v* conservar
conserve *n* conserva
consider *v* considerar
considerable *adj* considerável
considerate *adj* atencioso
consideration *n* consideração
consignment *n* remessa
consist *v* consistir
consistency *n* consistência
consistent *adj* consistente
consolation *n* consolação
console *v* consolar
consolidate *v* consolidar
consonant *n* consoante
conspicuous *adj* evidente
conspiracy *n* conspiração
conspirator *n* conspirador
conspire *v* conspirar
constancy *n* constância
constant *adj* constante
constellation *n* constelação
consternation *n* consternação

constipate _v_ constipar
constipated _adj_ constipado
constipation _n_ constipação
constitute _v_ constituir
constitution _n_ constituição
constrain _v_ constranger
constraint _n_ constrangimento
construct _v_ construir
construction _n_ construção
constructive _adj_ construtivo
consul _n_ cônsul
consulate _n_ consulado
consult _v_ consultar
consultation _n_ consulta
consume _v_ consumir
consumer _n_ consumidor
consumption _n_ consumo
contact _v_ contactar
contact _n_ contato
contagious _adj_ contagioso
contain _v_ conter
container _n_ recipiente
contaminate _v_ contaminar
contamination _n_ contaminação
contemplate _v_ contemplar
contemporary _adj_ contemporâneo
contempt _n_ desprezo
contend _v_ contender
contender _n_ contendor
content _adj_ contente
content _v_ contentar
contentious _adj_ briguento

contents _n_ conteúdo
contest _n_ disputar
contestant _n_ disputante
context _n_ contexto
continent _n_ continente
continental _adj_ continental
contingency _n_ contingência
contingent _adj_ contingente
continuation _n_ continuação
continue _v_ continuar
continuity _n_ continuidade
continuous _adj_ contínuo
contour _n_ contorno
contraband _n_ contrabando
contract _v_ contratar
contract _n_ contrato
contraction _n_ contração
contradict _v_ contradizer
contradiction _n_ contradição
contrary _adj_ contrário
contrast _v_ contrastar
contrast _n_ contraste
contribute _v_ contribuir
contribution _n_ contribuição
contributor _n_ contribuinte
contrition _n_ contrição
control _n_ controle
control _v_ controlar
controversial _adj_ controverso
controversy _n_ controvérsia
convalescent _adj_ convalescente
convene _v_ convocar

convenience *n* conveniência
convenient *adj* conveniente
convent *n* convento
convention *n* convenção
conventional *adj* convencional
converge *v* convergir
conversation *n* conversação
converse *v* conversar
conversely *adv* inversamente
conversion *n* conversão
convert *v* converter
convert *n* converso
convey *v* transportar
convict *v* condenar
conviction *n* convicção
convince *v* convencer
convincing *adj* convincente
convoluted *adj* enrolado
convoy *n* comboio
convulse *v* sacudir
convulsion *n* convulsão
cook *v* cozinhar
cook *n* cozinheiro
cookie *n* biscoito
cooking *n* cozinha
cool *adj* fresco; calmo
cool *v* esfriar
cool down *v* esfriar; acalmar
cooling *adj* refrescante
coolness *n* frescor, friagem
cooperate *v* cooperar
cooperation *n* cooperação

cooperative *adj* cooperativo
coordinate *v* coordenar
coordination *n* coordenação
coordinator *n* coordenador
cop *n* guarda, polícia
cope *v* enfrentar
copier *n* copiadora
copper *n* cobre; trocado
copy *v* copiar
copy *n* cópia
copyright *n* direitos autorais
cord *n* cordão, corda
cordial *adj* cordial
cordless *adj* sem fio
cordon off *v* isolar
core *n* núcleo; caroço
cork *n* rolha, cortiça
corn *n* milho, grão
corner *n* esquina, ângulo
cornerstone *n* pedra angular
cornet *n* corneta
corollary *n* corolário
coronary *adj* coronário
coronation *n* coroação
corporal *adj* corporal
corporal *n* cabo
corporation *n* corporação
corpse *n* corpo, cadáver
corpulent *adj* corpulento
corpuscle *n* corpúsculo
correct *v* corrigir
correct *adj* correto

correction *n* correção
correlate *v* correlacionar
correspond *v* corresponder
correspondent *n* correspondente
corresponding *adj* correspondente
corridor *n* corredor
corroborate *v* corroborar
corrode *v* corroer
corrupt *v* corromper
corrupt *adj* corrupto
corruption *n* corrupção
cosmetic *n* cosmético
cosmic *adj* cósmico
cosmonaut *n* cosmonauta
cost *iv* custar, avaliar
cost *n* custo, preço
costly *adj* caro
costume *n* traje, disfarce
cottage *n* casa de campo
cotton *n* algodão
couch *n* sofá, divã
cough *n* tosse
cough *v* tossir
council *n* conselho, câmara
counsel *v* aconselhar
counsel *n* advogado
counselor *n* conselheiro
count *v* contar; importar
count *n* conde; contagem
countenance *n* rosto
counter *n* balcão
counter *v* contrariar

counteract *v* neutralizar
counterfeit *v* falsificar
counterfeit *adj* falsificado
counterpart *n* contrapartida
countess *n* condessa
countless *adj* incontável
country *n* país
countryman *n* compatriota
countryside *n* zona rural
county *n* condado
coup *n* golpe
couple *n* casal; par
coupon *n* cupom
courage *n* coragem
courageous *adj* corajoso
courier *n* guia, mensagem
course *n* curso; prato
court *n* viela; tribunal
court *v* cortejar, namorar
courteous *adj* cortês, gentil
courtesy *n* cortesia
courthouse *n* tribunal
courtship *n* galanteio
courtyard *n* pátio
cousin *n* primo
cove *n* enseada
covenant *n* pacto, convênio
cover *n* cobertura
cover *v* cobrir
cover up *v* encobrir, ocultar
coverage *n* cobertura
covert *adj* secreto

cover-up *n* cobertura
covet *v* cobiçar
cow *n* vaca
coward *n* covard
cowardice *n* covardia
cowardly *adv* covardemente
cowboy *n* caubói
cozy *adj* aconchegante
crab *n* caranguejo
crack *n* rachadura
crack *v* rachar, quebrar
cradle *n* berço
craft *n* arte, astúcia
craftsman *n* artífice
cram *v* abarrotar; socar
cramp *n* cãibra
crane *n* guindaste; grou
crank *n* excêntrico
cranky *adj* mal-humorado
crap *n* bosta; besteira
crappy *adj* cagado
crash *n* estrondo, craque
crash *v* colidir; falir
crass *adj* crasso
crater *n* cratera
crave *v* ansiar
craving *n* desejo
crawl *v* engatinhar, rastejar
crayon *n* giz de cera
craziness *n* loucura
crazy *adj* louco
creak *v* ranger, chiar

creak *n* rangido, chiado
cream *n* creme, nata
creamy *adj* cremoso
crease *n* ruga, vinco
crease *v* amassar
create *v* criar
creation *n* criação
creative *adj* criativo
creativity *n* criatividade
creator *n* criador
creature *n* criatura
credibility *n* credibilidade
credible *adj* crível
credit *n* crédito, saldo
creditor *n* credor
creed *n* credo
creek *n* riacho, enseada
creep *v* insinuar-se
creepy *adj* horripilante
cremate *v* cremar
crematorium *n* crematório
crest *n* crista, penacho
crevice *n* fenda
crew *n* tripulação, bando
crib *n* berço, burro
cricket *n* críquete; grilo
crime *n* crime
criminal *adj* criminal
cripple *adj* aleijado
cripple *v* aleijar
crisis *n* crise
crisp *adj* quebradiço

crispy *adj* crocante
criss-cross *v* xadrez
criterion *n* critério
critical *adj* crítico
criticism *n* crítica
criticize *v* criticar
critique *n* crítica
crockery *n* louça
crocodile *n* crocodilo
crony *n* companheiro
crook *n* cajado; ladrão
crooked *adj* torto, desonesto
crop *n* colheira; chicote
cross *n* cruz
cross *adj* zangado, irritado
cross *v* cruzar, contrariar
cross out *v* riscar
crossfire *n* fogo cruzado
crossing *n* travessia
crossroads *n* encruzilhada
crossword *n* palavras cruzadas
crouch *v* agachar-se
crow *n* corvo
crow *v* cantar (galo)
crowbar *n* pé-de-cabra
crowd *n* multidão, turma
crowd *v* aglomerar-se
crowded *adj* abarrotado
crown *n* coroa
crown *v* coroar
crucial *adj* crucial
crucifix *n* crucifixo

crucifixion *n* crucificação
crucify *v* crucificar
crude *adj* cru, rude
cruel *adj* cruel
cruelty *n* crueldade
cruise *v* navegar
crumb *n* migalha
crumble *v* desintegrar-se
crunchy *adj* crocante
crusade *n* cruzada
crusader *n* cruzado
crush *v* esmagar
crushing *adj* esmagador
crust *n* crosta; ousadia
crusty *adj* crostoso
crutch *n* muleta
cry *n* croro, grito
cry *v* chorar, gritar
cry out *v* gritar
crying *n* choro, pranto
crystal *n* cristal
cub *n* filhote
cube *n* cubo
cubic *adj* cúbico
cubicle *n* cabine
cucumber *n* pepino
cuddle *v* aconchegar
cuff *n* punho, algema
cuisine *n* cozinha
culminate *v* culminar
culpability *n* culpa
culprit *n* culpado

C

cult *n* culto

cultivate *v* cultivar

cultivation *n* cultura

cultural *adj* cultural

culture *n* cultura

cumbersome *adj* incômodo

cunning *adj* velhaco

cup *n* copo, taça, copa

cupboard *n* armário

curable *adj* curável

curator *n* curador

curb *v* restringir

curb *n* meio-fio, freio

curdle *v* coalhar

cure *v* curar

cure *n* cura

curfew *n* toque de recolher

curiosity *n* curiosidade

curious *adj* curioso

curl *v* encaracolar

curl *n* cacho de cabelo

curly *adj* encaracolado

currency *n* moeda

current *adj* corrente

currently *adv* atualmente

curse *v* maldizer

curtail *v* encurtar

curtain *n* cortina

curve *n* curva

curve *v* curvar

cushion *n* almofada

cushion *v* amortecer

cuss *v* amaldiçoar

custard *n* creme, molho

custodian *n* guardião

custody *n* custódia

custom *n* costume

customary *adj* habitual

customer *n* cliente, freguês

custom-made *adj* sob medida

customs *n* alfândega

cut *n* corte, redução

cut *iv* cortar, aparar

cut back *v* cortar, aparar

cut down *v* abater

cut off *v* cortar for a

cut out *v* recortar

cute *adj* engraçadinho

cutlery *n* faqueiro, cutelaria

cutter *n* cortador

cyanide *n* cianeto

cycle *n* ciclo

cyclist *n* ciclista

cyclone *n* ciclone

cylinder *n* cilindro

cynic *adj* cínico

cynicism *n* cinismo

cypress *n* cipreste

cyst *n* cisto, quisto

czar *n* czar

D

dad *n* papai
dagger *n* punhal, adaga
daily *adv* diariamente
daisy *n* margarida
dam *n* represa, dique
damage *n* dano
damage *v* danificar
damaging *adj* prejudicial
damn *v* condenar
damnation *n* danação
damp *adj* úmido
dampen *v* umedecer
dance *n* dança; baile
dance *v* dançar
dancing *n* dança
dandruff *n* caspa
danger *n* perigo
dangerous *adj* perigoso
dangle *v* balançar, pender
dare *v* ousar, desafiar
dare *n* risco, desafio
daring *adj* atrevido, audaz
dark *adj* escuro
darken *v* escurecer
darkness *n* escuridão
darling *adj* querido, preferido
darn *v* remendar, consertar
dart *n* dardo
dash *v* destruir

dashing *adj* vistoso, elegante
data *n* informação, dados
database *n* banco de dados
date *n* encontro; data
date *v* datar; sair juntos
daughter *n* filha; raça, cidade
daughter-in-law *n* nora
daunt *v* assustar, intimidar
daunting *adj* assustador
dawn *n* alvorada
day *n* dia
daydream *v* sonhar acordado
daze *v* ofuscar
dazed *adj* estupefato
dazzle *v* deslumbrar
dazzling *adj* deslumbrante
deacon *n* diácono
dead *adj* morto
dead end *n* sem saída
deaden *v* enfraquecer
deadline *n* prazo final
deadlock *adj* congelado
deadly *adj* mortal
deaf *adj* surdo
deafen *v* ensurdecer
deafening *adj* ensurdecedor
deafness *n* surdez
deal *iv* negociar, tratar de
deal *n* acordo; parte
dealer *n* negociante
dealings *n* relacionamento
dean *n* deão; decano

D

dear *adj* favorito, caro
dearly *adv* caro
death *n* morte
death toll *n* número de mortos
death trap *n* cilada de morte
deathbed *n* leito de morte
debase *v* humilhar, degradar
debatable *adj* discutível
debate *v* debater, discutir
debate *n* debate
debit *n* débito, dívida
debrief *v* interrogar
debris *n* escombros
debt *n* dívida, obrigação
debtor *n* devedor
debunk *v* desmascarar
debut *n* estréia
decade *n* década
decadence *n* decadência
decaf *adj* descafeinado
decapitate *v* decapitar
decay *v* decair, cariar
decay *n* decomposição
deceased *adj* morto, falecido
deceit *n* engano, fraude
deceitful *adj* enganoso
deceive *v* enganar
December *n* Dezembro
decency *n* decência
decent *adj* decente
deception *n* decepção
deceptive *adj* enganador

decide *v* decidir
deciding *adj* decisivo
decimal *adj* decimal
decimate *v* destruir
decipher *v* decifrar
decision *n* decisão
decisive *adj* decisivo
deck *n* convés; terraço
declaration *n* declaração
declare *v* declarar
declension *n* declinação
decline *v* declinar, recusar
decline *n* declínio, declive
decompose *v* decompor
décor *n* decoração
decorate *v* decorar
decorative *adj* ornamental
decorum *n* decoro
decrease *v* decrescer
decrease *n* decréscimo
decree *n* decreto
decree *v* decretar
decrepit *adj* decrépito
dedicate *v* dedicar
dedication *n* dedicação
deduce *v* deduzir, inferir
deduct *v* deduzir, subtrair
deductible *adj* deduzível
deduction *n* dedução
deed *n* ação, fato
deem *v* avaliar
deep *adj* fundo

deepen *v* aprofundar
deer *n* cervídeo: veado
deface *v* desfigurar
defame *v* difamar
defeat *v* derrotar
defeat *n* derrotar
defect *n* defeito
defect *v* desertar
defection *n* deserção
defective *adj* defeituoso
defend *v* defender
defendant *n* réu, acusado
defender *n* defensor
defense *n* defesa
defenseless *adj* indefeso
defer *v* adiar, submeter-se
defiance *n* desafio, rebeldia
defiant *adj* desafiante
deficiency *n* deficiência
deficient *adj* deficiente
deficit *n* deficit, shortage
defile *v* macular
define *v* definir
definite *adj* definido
definition *n* definição
definitive *adj* definitivo
deflate *v* desinflar
deform *v* deformar
deformity *n* deformidade
defraud *v* defraudar
defray *v* pagar
defrost *v* descongelar

deft *adj* esperto, destro
defuse *v* acalmar
defy *v* desafiar
degenerate *v* degenerar
degenerate *adj* degenerado
degeneration *n* degeneração
degradation *n* degradação
degrade *v* degradar
degrading *adj* degradante
degree *n* degrau, título
dehydrate *v* desidratar
deign *v* condescender
deity *n* divindade
dejected *adj* abatido
delay *v* atrasar
delay *n* atraso
delegate *v* delegar
delegate *n* delegado
delegation *n* delegação
delete *v* apagar, deletar
deliberate *v* deliberar
deliberate *adj* deliberado
delicacy *n* delicadeza
delicate *adj* delicado
delicious *adj* delicioso
delight *n* deleite, prazer
delight *v* deleitar
delightful *adj* deleitoso
delinquency *n* delinquência
delinquent *n* delinquente
deliver *v* entregar
delivery *n* entregar

delude _v_ iludir; enganar

deluge _n_ dilúvio

delusion _n_ ilusão, desilusão

deluxe _adj_ de luxo

demand _v_ demandar, exigir

demand _n_ demanda

demanding _adj_ exigente

demean _v_ rebaixar, humilhar

demeaning _adj_ humilhante

demeanor _n_ comportamento

demented _adj_ demente, louco

demise _n_ fim, legado

democracy _n_ democracia

democratic _adj_ democrático

demolish _v_ demolir

demolition _n_ demolição

demon _n_ demônio

demonstrate _v_ demonstrar

demonstrative _adj_ demonstrativo

demoralize _v_ desmoralizar

demote _v_ degradar

den _n_ toca; recanto

denial _n_ negativa, rejeição

denigrate _v_ denegrir

Denmark _n_ Dinamarca

denominator _n_ denominador

denote _v_ denotar

denounce _v_ denunciar

dense _adj_ denso

density _n_ densidade

dent _n_ entalhe; dente

dental _adj_ dental

dentist _n_ dentista

dentures _n_ dentadura

deny _v_ negar

deodorant _n_ desodorante

depart _v_ partir

department _n_ departamento

departure _n_ partida

depend _v_ depender

dependable _adj_ confiável

dependence _n_ dependência

dependent _adj_ dependente

depict _v_ descrever

deplete _v_ esgotar

deplorable _adj_ deplorável

deplore _v_ deplorar

deploy _v_ posicionar

deployment _n_ posicionamento

deport _v_ deportar

deportation _n_ deportação

depose _v_ depor

deposit _n_ depósito

depot _n_ armazém

deprave _v_ perverter

depravity _n_ depravação

depreciate _v_ depreciar

depreciation _n_ depreciação

depress _v_ deprimir

depressing _adj_ deprimente

depression _n_ depressão

deprivation _n_ privação, perda

deprive _v_ privar, despojar

deprived _adj_ desprovido

depth *n* profundidade
derail *v* descarrilhar
derailment *n* descarrilhamento
deranged *adj* louco
derelict *adj* abandonado
deride *v* escarnecer
derivative *adj* derivado
derive *v* derivar
derogatory *adj* depreciativo
descend *v* descender
descendant *n* descendente
descent *n* decida, caída
describe *v* descrever
description *n* descrição
descriptive *adj* descritivo
desecrate *v* profanar, violar
desegregate *v* desagregar
desert *n* deserto
desert *v* desertar
deserted *adj* solitário
deserter *n* desertor
deserve *v* merecer
deserving *adj* merecedor
design *n* projeto, modelo
designate *v* designar
desirable *adj* desejável
desire *n* desejo
desire *v* desejar
desist *v* desistir
desk *n* escrivaninha
desolate *adj* desolado
desolation *n* desolação

despair *n* desespero
desperate *adj* desesperado
despicable *adj* desprezível
despise *v* desprezar
despite *c* apesar de
despondent *adj* deprimido
despot *n* déspota, tirano
despotic *adj* despótico
dessert *n* sobremesa
destination *n* destino
destiny *n* destino
destitute *adj* desamparado
destroy *v* destruir
destroyer *n* destruidor
destruction *n* destruição
destructive *adj* destrutivo
detach *v* separar, desunir
detachable *adj* separável
detail *n* detalhe
detail *v* detalhar
detain *v* deter
detect *v* detectar
detective *n* detetive
detector *n* detector
detention *n* detenção
deter *v* deter
detergent *n* detergente
deteriorate *v* deteriorar
deterioration *n* deterioração
determination *n* determinação
determine *v* determinar
deterrence *n* retrocesso

D

detest v detestar
detestable adj detestável
detonate v detonar
detonation n detonação
detonator n detonador
detour n desvio
detriment n detrimento
detrimental adj prejudicial
devaluation n desvalorização
devalue v desvalorizar
devastate v devastar
devastating adj devastador
devastation n devastação
develop v desenvolver
development n desenvolvimento
deviation n desvio
device n aparelho
devil n diabo
devious adj desnesto
devise v planejar
devoid adj destituído, livre
devote v devotar
devotion n devoção
devour v devorar
devout adj devoto
dew n orvalho; suor
diabetes n diabete
diabetic adj diabético
diabolical adj diabólico
diagnose v diagnosticar
diagnosis n diagnóstico
diagonal adj diagonal

diagram n diagrama
dial v discar
dialect n dialeto
dialogue n diálogo
diameter n diâmetro
diamond n diamante
diaper n fralda
diarrhea n diarréia
diary n diário, agenda
dice n dado
dictate v ditar
dictator n ditador
dictatorial adj ditatorial
dictatorship n ditadura
dictionary n dicionário
die v morrer
die out v extinguir-se
diet n dieta
differ v diferir
difference n diferença
different adj diferente
difficult adj difícil
difficulty n dificuldade
diffuse v difundir
dig iv cavar
digest v digerir
digestion n digestão
digestive adj digestivo
digit n dígito
dignify v dignificar
dignitary n dignatário
dignity n dignidade

digress v desviar, divagar
dike n dique, represa
dilapidated adj dilapidado
dilemma n dilema
diligence n diligência
diligent adj diligente
dilute v diluir
dim adj escuro, sombrio
dim v ofuscar, escurecer
dime n dez centavos
dimension n dimensão
diminish v diminuir
dine v jantar
dining room n sala de jantar
dinner n jantar
dinosaur n dinossauro
diocese n diocese
diphthong n ditongo
diploma n diploma
diplomacy n diplomacia
diplomat n diplomata
diplomatic adj diplomático
dire adj perigoso
direct adj direto
direct v dirigir, orientar
direction n direção
director n diretor
directory n diretório
dirt n sujeira
dirty adj sujo
disability n invalidez
disabled adj inválido

disadvantage n desvantagem
disagree v discordar
disagreeable adj desagradável
disagreement n discordância
disappear v desaparecer
disappearance n desaparição
disappoint v desapontar
disappointing adj decepcionante
disappointment n decepção
disapproval n desaprovação
disapprove v desaprovar
disarm v desarmar
disarmament n desarmamento
disaster n desastre
disastrous adj desastroso
disband v debandar
disbelief n descrença
disburse v desembolsar
discard v descartar
discern v discernir
discharge v descarregar
discharge n descarga
disciple n discípulo
discipline n disciplina
disclaim v renegar
disclose v revelar
discomfort n desconforto
disconnect v desconectar
discontent adj descontente
discontinue v descontinuar
discord n discórdia
discordant adj dissonante

D

discount n desconto
discount v descontar
discourage v desencorajar
discouragement n desânimo
discouraging adj desanimador
discourtesy n indelicadeza
discover v descobrir
discovery n descoberta
discredit v descrédito
discreet adj discreto
discrepancy n discrepância
discretion n discrição
discriminate v discriminar
discrimination n discriminação
discuss v discutir
discussion n discussão
disdain n desdém
disease n doença
disembark v desembarque
disenchanted adj desencantado
disentangle v desenredar
disfigure v desfigurar
disgrace n desgraça
disgrace v desgraçar
disgraceful adj vergonhoso
disgruntled adj insatisfeito
disguise v disfarçar
disguise n disfarce
disgust n desgosto, nojo
disgusting adj repugnante
dish n prato
dishearten v desanimar

dishonest adj desonesto
dishonesty n desonestidade
dishonor n desonra
dishonorable adj desonroso
dishwasher n lavalouças
disillusion n desilusão
disinfect v desinfetar
disinfectant v desinfetante
disinherit v deserdar
disintegrate v desintegrar
disintegration n desintegração
disinterested adj desinteressado
disk n disco
dislike v desgostar
dislike n desgosto
dislocate v deslocar
dislodge v desalojar
disloyal adj deslear
disloyalty n deslealdade
dismal adj sombrio
dismantle v desmantelar
dismay n consternação
dismay v consternar
dismiss v despedir
dismissal n demissão
dismount v apear
disobedience n desobediência
disobedient adj desobediente
disobey v desobedecer
disorder n desordem
disorganized adj desorganizado
disoriented adj desorientado

disown *v* renegar
disparity *n* disparidade
dispatch *v* despachar
dispel *v* dissipar
dispensation *n* dispensação
dispense *v* dispensar, aviar
dispersal *n* dispersão
disperse *v* dispersar
displace *v* deslocar
display *n* exposição
display *v* expor, mostrar
displease *v* desagradar
displeasing *adj* desagradável
displeasure *n* desprazer
disposable *adj* descartável
disposal *n* descarte
dispose *v* dispor, ordenar
disprove *v* refutar, desmentir
dispute *n* disputa
dispute *v* disputar
disqualify *v* desqualificar
disregard *v* desprezar
disrepair *n* mau estado
disrespect *n* desrespeito
disrespectful *adj* desrespeitoso
disrupt *v* perturbar
disruption *n* perturbação
dissatisfied *adj* insatisfação
disseminate *v* disseminar
dissent *v* divergir
dissident *adj* dissidente
dissimilar *adj* diferente

dissipate *v* dissipar
dissolute *adj* dissoluto
dissolution *n* dissolução
dissolve *v* dissolver
dissonant *adj* dissonante
dissuade *v* dissuadir
distance *n* distância
distant *adj* distante
distaste *n* desgosto
distasteful *adj* disagradável
distill *v* destilar
distinct *adj* distinto
distinction *n* distinção
distinctive *adj* distintivo
distinguish *v* distinguir
distort *v* deformar, distorcer
distortion *n* distorção
distract *v* distrair
distraction *n* distração
distraught *adj* transtornado
distress *n* aflição
distress *v* afligir
distressing *adj* aflitivo
distribute *v* distribuir
distribution *n* distribuição
district *n* distrito
distrust *n* desconfiança
distrust *v* desconfiar
distrustful *adj* desconfiado
disturb *v* perturbar, agitar
disturbance *n* distúrbio
disturbing *adj* perturbador

D

disunity *n* desunidade
disuse *n* disuso
ditch *n* vala
dive *v* mergulhar
diver *n* mergulhador
diverse *adj* diverso
diversify *v* diversificar
diversion *n* diversão
diversity *n* diversidade
divert *v* desviar
divide *v* dividir
dividend *n* dividendo
divine *adj* divino
diving *n* mergulho
divinity *n* divindade
divisible *adj* divisível
division *n* divisão
divorce *n* divórcio
divorce *v* divorciar
divorcee *n* divorciado
divulge *v* divulgar
dizziness *n* tonteira
dizzy *adj* tonto
do *iv* fazer, realizar
docile *adj* dócil
docility *n* docilidade
dock *n* labaça; dique
dock *v* cortar a cauda
doctor *n* doutor
doctrine *n* doutrina
document *n* documento
documentary *n* documentário

documentation *n* documentação
dodge *v* esquivar, evitar
dog *n* cachorro
dogmatic *adj* dogmático
dole out *v* distribuir, repartir
doll *n* boneca
dollar *n* dólar
dolphin *n* golfinho
dome *n* cúpula
domestic *adj* doméstico
domesticate *v* domesticar
dominate *v* dominar
domination *n* dominação
domineering *adj* dominante
dominion *n* domínio
donate *v* donar
donation *n* doação
donkey *n* burro, jumento
donor *n* doador
doom *n* sorte, condenação
doomed *adj* condenado
door *n* porta
doorbell *n* campainha de porta
doorstep *n* degrau da porta
doorway *n* entrada
dope *n* narcótico
dope *v* dopar
dormitory *n* dormitório
dosage *n* dosagem, dose
dossier *n* dossiê
dot *n* ponto
double *adj* duplo, dobro

double *v* duplicar, desdobrar
double-check *v* rechecar
double-cross *v* passar pra trás
doubt *n* dúvida
doubt *v* duvidar
doubtful *adj* duvidoso, incerto
dough *n* masca
dove *n* pomba, rola
down *adv* para baixo
down payment *n* entrada
downcast *adj* abatido
downfall *n* ruína
downhill *adv* em declive
downpour *n* aguaceiro
downsize *v* reduzir, contrair
downstairs *adv* no andar de baixo
downtown *n* centro
downtrodden *adj* oprimido
downturn *n* declínio
dowry *n* dote
doze *n* cochilo
doze *v* cochilar
dozen *n* dúzia
draft *n* rascunho; saque
draft *v* rascunhar; alistar
draftsman *n* desenhista
drag *v* puxar, arrastar
dragon *n* dragão
drain *v* drenar, esgotar
drainage *n* drenagem, esgoto
dramatic *adj* dramático
dramatize *v* dramatizar

drape *n* cortina
drastic *adj* drástico
draw *n* empate; extração
draw *iv* desenhar; extrair
drawback *n* inconveniente
drawer *n* gaveta
drawing *n* desenho
dread *v* temer
dreaded *adj* temido
dreadful *adj* pavoroso
dream *iv* sonhar
dream *n* sonho
dress *n* vestido
dress *v* vestir
dresser *n* comoda
dressing *n* tempero; curativo
dried *adj* seco
drift *v* ser levado
drift apart *v* apartar-se
drifter *n* barco de pesca
drill *v* furar; exercitar
drill *n* broca, exercício
drink *iv* beber
drink *n* bebida
drinkable *adj* potável
drinker *n* bebedor
drip *v* pingar, gotejar
drip *n* gota, gotímetro
drive *n* passeio de carro
drive *iv* dirigir, levar de carro
drive at *v* pretender dizer
drive away *v* expulsar

driver *n* motorista
driveway *n* entrada para carro
drizzle *v* chuviscar
drizzle *n* chuvisco
drop *n* gota, queda
drop *v* deixar cair, cair
drop in *v* dar um pulo
drop off *v* cair, deixar
drop out *v* desistir
drought *n* seca
drown *v* afogar
drowsy *adj* sonolento
drug *n* droga, remédio
drug *v* drogar
drugstore *n* farmácia
drum *n* bateria; tambor
drunk *adj* bêbado
drunkenness *n* embriaguez
dry *v* secar
dry *adj* seco
dry-clean *v* lavar a seco
dryer *n* secador
dual *adj* duplo, dobro
dubious *adj* incerto
duchess *n* duquesa
duck *n* pato
duck *v* esquivar-se
duct *n* tubo, conduto
due *adj* devido, esperado
duel *n* duelo
dues *n* dívida, tributo
duke *n* duque

dull *adj* obtuso; tedioso
duly *adv* devidamente
dumb *adj* mudo, idiota
dummy *n* imitação
dummy *adj* idiota, estúpido
dump *v* largar, despejar
dump *n* despejo
dung *n* esterco
dungeon *n* calabouço
dupe *v* ludibriar
duplicate *v* duplicar, copiar
duplication *n* cópia
durable *adj* durável
duration *n* duração
during *pre* durante
dusk *n* penumbra
dust *n* pó, poeira
dusty *adj* empoeirado
Dutch *adj* holandês
duty *n* dever, taxa
dwarf *n* anão, duende
dwell *iv* morar
dwelling *n* moradia
dwindle *v* minguar
dye *v* tingir
dye *n* tintura, corante
dying *adj* agonizante
dynamic *adj* dinâmico
dynamite *n* dinamite
dynasty *n* dinastia

E

each *adj* cada
each other *adj* mutuamente
eager *adj* ávido
eagerness *n* avidez
eagle *n* águia
ear *n* orelha, ouvido
earache *n* dor de ouvido
eardrum *n* tímpano
early *adv* cedo, no início
earmark *v* designar
earn *v* ganhar, merecer
earnestly *adv* seriamente
earnings *n* salario
earphones *n* fone de ouvido
earring *n* brinco
earth *n* Terra, terra
earthquake *n* terremoto
earwax *n* cera do ouvido
ease *v* aliviar, abrandar
ease *n* alivio, facilidade
easily *adv* facilmente
east *n* Leste
eastbound *adj* para leste
Easter *n* Páscoa
eastern *adj* oriental
easterner *n* oriental
eastward *adv* para leste
easy *adj* fácil
eat *iv* comer

eat away *v* corroer, destruir
eavesdrop *v* espreitar, espiar
ebb *v* refluir
eccentric *adj* excêntrico
echo *n* eco
eclipse *n* eclipse
ecology *n* ecologia
economical *adj* econômico
economize *v* economizar
economy *n* economia
ecstasy *n* êxtase
ecstatic *adj* extático
edge *n* beira, gume, orla
edgy *adj* irritadiço
edible *adj* comestível
edifice *n* edifício
edit *v* editar
edition *n* edição
educate *v* educar, instruir
educational *adj* educacional
eerie *adj* lúgubre
effect *n* efeito
effective *adj* eficaz
effectiveness *n* efetividade
efficiency *n* eficiência
efficient *adj* eficiente
effigy *n* efígie
effort *n* esforço, façanha
effusive *adj* efusivo
egg *n* ovo, óvulo
egg white *n* clara
egoism *n* egoísmo

E

egoist *n* egoísta
eight *adj* oito
eighteen *adj* dezoito
eighth *adj* oitavo
eighty *adj* oitenta
either *adj* um ou outro
either *adv* também não
eject *v* expulsar, ejetar
elapse *v* transcorrer
elastic *adj* elástico
elated *adj* exultante
elbow *n* cotovelo
elder *n* mais velho
elderly *adj* idoso, velho
elect *v* eleger
election *n* eleição
electric *adj* elétrico
electrician *n* eletricista
electricity *n* eletricidade
electrify *v* eletrificar
electrocute *v* eletrocutar
electronic *adj* eletrônico
elegance *n* elegância
elegant *adj* elegante
element *n* elemento
elementary *adj* elementar
elephant *n* elefante
elevate *v* elevar, exaltar
elevation *n* elevação
elevator *n* elevador; silo
eleven *adj* onze
eleventh *adj* undécimo

eligible *adj* qualificado
eliminate *v* eliminar
elm *n* olmo
eloquence *n* eloqüência
else *adv* mais, outro
elsewhere *adv* em outro lugar
elude *v* esquivar, escapar
elusive *adj* esquivo
emaciated *adj* emaciado
emanate *v* emanar
emancipate *v* emancipado
embalm *v* embalsamar
embark *v* embarcar
embarrass *v* embaraçar
embassy *n* embaixada
embellish *v* embelezar
embers *n* brasa
embezzle *v* desfalcar
embitter *v* amargurar
emblem *n* emblema
embody *v* personificar
emboss *v* modelar
embrace *v* abraçar
embrace *n* abraço
embroider *v* bordar
embroidery *n* bordado
embroil *v* envolver
embryo *n* embrião
emerald *n* esmeralda
emerge *v* emergir, surgir
emergency *n* emergência
emigrant *n* emigrante

emigrate *v* emigrar
emission *n* emissão, emanação
emit *v* emitir, emanar
emotion *n* emoção
emotional *adj* emocional
emperor *n* imperador
emphasis *n* ênfase
emphasize *v* enfatizar
empire *n* império
employ *v* empregar
employee *n* empregado
employer *n* empregador
employment *n* emprego
empress *n* imperatriz
emptiness *n* vazio
empty *adj* vazio
empty *v* esvaziar
enable *v* possibilitar
enchant *v* encantar
enchanting *adj* encantador
encircle *v* cercar
enclave *n* enclave
enclose *v* incluir; cercar
enclosure *n* encerramento
encompass *v* cercar; incluir
encounter *v* deparar com
encounter *n* encontro, conflito
encourage *v* encorajar, animar
encroach *v* usurpar, invadir
encyclopedia *n* enciclopédia
end *n* fim, finalidade
end *v* terminar

E

end up *v* acabar, terminar
endanger *v* pôr em perigo
endeavor *v* tentar
endeavor *n* tentativa
ending *n* fim, conclusão
endless *adj* interminável
endorse *v* endossar
endorsement *n* endosso
endure *v* agüentar, tolerar
enemy *n* inimigo
energetic *adj* enérgico
energy *n* energia
enforce *v* executar
engage *v* contratar, prender
engaged *adj* comprometido
engagement *n* compromisso
engine *n* motor, locomotiva
engineer *n* engenheiro
England *n* Inglaterra
English *adj* inglês
engrave *v* gravar
engraving *n* estampa, gravura
engrossed *adj* absorto
engulf *v* tragar
enhance *v* realçar
enjoy *v* gostar de, apreciar
enjoyable *adj* agradável
enjoyment *n* prazer, gozo
enlarge *v* ampliar, aumentar
enlargement *n* ampliação
enlighten *v* esclarecer
enlist *v* alistar-se

enormous *adj* enorme
enough *adv* suficiente
enrage *v* enfurecer
enrich *v* enriquecer
enroll *v* inscrever
enrollment *n* inscrição
ensure *v* assegurar
entail *v* acarretar
entangle *v* emaranhar
enter *v* entrar
enterprise *n* empreendimento
entertain *v* receber, entreter
entertaining *adj* divertido
entertainment *n* divertimento
enthrall *v* cativar, fascinar
enthralling *adj* cativante
enthuse *v* entusiarmar(-se)
enthusiasm *n* entusiasmo
entice *v* tentar
enticement *n* tentação
enticing *adj* tentador
entire *adj* inteiro
entirely *adv* inteiramente
entrance *n* entrada
entreat *v* suplicar
entree *n* entrada
entrenched *adj* entrincheirado
entrepreneur *n* empreendedor
entrust *v* confiar
entry *n* entrada
enumerate *v* enumerar
envelop *v* embrulhar

envelope *n* envelope
envious *adj* invejoso
environment *n* ambiente
envisage *v* encarar
envoy *n* enviado
envy *n* inveja
envy *v* invejar
epidemic *n* epidemia
epilepsy *n* epilepsia
episode *n* episódio
epistle *n* epístola
epitaph *n* epitáfio
epitomize *v* resumir
epoch *n* época
equal *adj* igual
equality *n* igualdade
equate *v* equiparar
equation *n* equação
equator *n* equador
equilibrium *n* equilíbrio
equip *v* equipar, preparar
equipment *n* equipamento
equivalent *adj* equivalente
era *n* era
eradicate *v* erradicar
erase *v* apagar
eraser *n* apagador, borracha
erect *v* eregir, erguer
erect *adj* ereto
err *v* errar
errand *n* recado; missão
erroneous *adj* rerrôneo

error *n* erro
erupt *v* explodir
eruption *n* explosão; erupção
escalate *v* escalar, subir
escalator *n* escada rolante
escapade *n* escapada
escape *v* escapar, fugir
escort *n* escolta
esophagus *n* esôfago
especially *adv* especialmente
espionage *n* espionagem
essay *n* ensaio, redação
essence *n* essência
essential *adj* essencial
establish *v* estabelecer
esteem *v* estima
estimate *v* estimar; avaliar
estimation *n* opinião
estranged *adj* afastado, alienado
estuary *n* estuário
eternity *n* eternidade
ethical *adj* ético
ethics *n* ética
etiquette *n* etiqueta
euphoria *n* euforia
Europe *n* Europa
European *adj* europeu
evacuate *v* evacuar
evade *v* evadir
evaluate *v* avaliar
evaporate *v* evaporar
evasion *n* evasão

evasive *adj* evasivo
eve *n* véspera
even *adj* uniforme; par; liso
even if *c* mesmo que
even more *c* ainda mais
evening *n* noite
event *n* evento
eventuality *n* eventualidade
eventually *adv* eventualmente
ever *adv* sempre
everlasting *adj* perpétuo
every *adj* todo, todos, cada
everybody *pro* todo o mundo
everyday *adj* todo dia
everyone *pro* todo o mundo
everything *pro* tudo
evict *v* despejar
evidence *n* evidência, prova
evil *n* mau
evil *adj* mau
evoke *v* evocar
evolution *n* evolução
evolve *v* evoluir
exact *adj* exato
exaggerate *v* exagerar
exalt *v* exaltar
examination *n* exame
examine *v* examinar
example *n* exemplo
exasperate *v* exasperar
excavate *v* escavar
exceed *v* exceder

E

exceedingly *adv* extremamente

excel *v* sobressair

excellence *n* excelência

excellent *adj* excelente

except *pre* exceto

exception *n* exceção

exceptional *adj* excepcional

excerpt *n* excerto

excess *n* excesso

excessive *adj* excessivo

exchange *v* trocar

excite *v* excitar

excitement *n* excitação

exciting *adj* excitante

exclaim *v* exclamar

exclude *v* excluir, eliminar

excruciating *adj* lancinante

excursion *n* excursão

excuse *v* desculpar, escusar

excuse *n* desculpa, escusa

execute *v* executar

executive *n* executivo

exemplary *adj* exemplar

exemplify *v* exemplificar

exempt *adj* isentar

exemption *n* isenção

exercise *n* exercício

exercise *v* exercitar

exert *v* exercer; esforçar-se

exertion *n* exercício; esforço

exhaust *v* exaurir, esgotar

exhausting *adj* exaustivo, cansativo

exhaustion *n* exaustão

exhibit *v* exibir, expor

exhibition *n* exibição

exhilarating *adj* hilariante

exhort *v* exortar

exile *v* exilar

exile *n* exílio

exist *v* existir

existence *n* existência

exit *n* saída

exodus *n* êxodo

exonerate *v* exonerar

exorbitant *adj* exorbitante

exorcist *n* exorcista

exotic *adj* exótico

expand *v* expandir

expansion *n* expansão

expect *v* esperar, contar com

expectancy *n* expectativa

expectation *n* expectativa

expediency *n* conveniência

expedient *adj* conveniente

expedition *n* expedição

expel *v* expelir, expulsar

expenditure *n* despesa, gasto

expense *n* despesa, custo

expensive *adj* caro

experience *n* experiência

experiment *n* experimento

expert *adj* especializado

expiate *v* expiar
expiation *n* expiação
expiration *n* expiração
expire *v* expirar
explain *v* explicar
explicit *adj* explícito
explode *v* explodir
exploit *v* explorar
exploit *n* façanha
exploitation *n* exploração
explore *v* explorar
explorer *n* explorador
explosion *n* explosão
explosive *adj* explosivo
export *v* exportar
expose *v* exportar
exposed *adj* exposto
express *n* expresso
expression *n* expressão
expressly *adv* expressamente
expropriate *v* expropriar
expulsion *n* expulsão
exquisite *adj* primoroso
extend *v* extender
extension *n* extensão
extent *n* extensão
extenuating *adj* atenuante
exterior *adj* exterior
exterminate *v* exterminar
external *adj* externo
extinct *adj* extinto
extinguish *v* extinguir

extort *v* extorquir
extortion *n* extorsão
extra *adv* extra
extract *v* extrair
extradite *v* extraditar
extradition *n* extradição
extraneous *adj* estranho
extravagance *n* extravagância
extravagant *adj* extravagante
extreme *adj* extremo
extremist *adj* extremista
extremities *n* extremidades
extricate *v* desenredar
extroverted *adj* extrovertido
exude *v* transpirar
exult *v* exultar
eye *n* olho
eyebrow *n* sobrancelha
eye-catching *adj* chamativo
eyeglasses *n* óculos, lentes
eyelash *n* cílio
eyelid *n* pálpebra
eyesight *n* visão
eyewitness *n* testemunha ocular

fable *n* fábula
fabric *n* tecido
fabricate *v* manufaturar
fabulous *adj* fabuloso
face *n* face, rosto
face up to *v* enfrentar
facet *n* faceta
facilitate *v* facilitar
facing *pre* em frente a
fact *n* fato
factor *n* fator
factory *n* fábrica
factual *adj* factual
faculty *n* faculdade
fade *v* enfraquecer
faded *adj* desbotado
fail *v* falhar, fracassar
failure *n* falta, fracasso
faint *v* desmaiar
faint *n* desmaio
faint *adj* fraco, tênue
fair *n* feira, bazar
fair *adj* loiro, claro; justo
fairness *n* beleza, justiça
fairy *n* fada
faith *n* fé, confiança
faithful *adj* fiel
fake *v* falsificar, fingir
fake *adj* falso, fingido

fall *n* Outono, queda
fall *iv* cair, caber
fall back *v* recuar
fall behind *v* ficar para trás
fall through *v* fracassar
fallacy *n* falácia, sofisma
falsehood *n* mentira
falsify *v* falsificar
falter *v* vacilar
fame *n* fama
familiar *adj* familiar
family *n* família
famine *n* fome, escassez
famous *adj* famoso
fan *n* fã; ventilador
fanatic *adj* fanático
fancy *adj* chique, luxuoso
fang *n* presa, canino
fantastic *adj* fantástico
fantasy *n* fantasia
far *adv* longe, distante
faraway *adj* distante, longínquo
farce *n* farsa; palhaçada
fare *n* passagem
farewell *n* despedida
farm *n* fazenda
farmer *n* fazendeiro
farming *n* agricultura
farmyard *n* terreiro
farther *adv* mais longe
fascinate *v* fascinar
fashion *n* moda, modo

fashionable *adj* da moda

fast *adj* rápido, adiantado

fasten *v* firmar, apertar

fat *n* gordura, banha

fat *adj* gordo

fatal *adj* fatal

fate *n* destino, sorte

fateful *adj* decisivo

father *n* pai; padre

fatherhood *n* paternidade

father-in-law *n* sogro

fatherly *adj* paternalmente

fathom out *v* entender; decifrar

fatigue *n* fatiga

fatten *v* engordar

fatty *adj* gorduroso

faucet *n* torneira

fault *n* falta, culpa, falha

faulty *adj* defeituoso

favor *n* agrado, favor

favorable *adj* favorável

favorite *adj* favorito

fear *n* medo, receio

fearful *adj* medroso

feasible *adj* viável

feast *n* banquete, festa

feat *n* feito, proeza

feather *n* pena

feature *n* característica, traço

February *n* Fevereiro

fed up *adj* farto

federal *adj* federal

fee *n* honorários

feeble *adj* fraco, tênue

feed *iv* alimentar

feedback *n* retroalimentação

feel *iv* sentir, apalpar

feeling *n* sentimento

feelings *n* sentimentos

feet *n* pé

feign *v* fingir

fellow *n* sujeito, colega

fellowship *n* camaradagem

felon *n* delinqüente

felony *n* delito grave

female *n* fêmea

feminine *adj* feminino

fence *n* cerca

fencing *n* cerca

fend *v* cuidar-se

fend off *v* defender-se

fender *n* proteção, defesa

ferment *v* fermentar

ferment *n* fermento

ferocious *adj* feroz

ferocity *n* ferocidade

ferry *n* balsa

fertile *adj* fértil

fertility *n* fertilidade

fertilize *v* fertilizar

fervent *adj* fervoroso

fester *v* infeccionar

festive *adj* festivo

festivity *n* festividade

fetid *adj* fétido

fetus *n* feto

feud *n* feudo; rixa

fever *n* febre

feverish *adj* febril

few *adj* poucos

fewer *adj* menos

fiancé *n* noivo

fiber *n* fibra

fickle *adj* instável

fiction *n* ficção

fictitious *adj* fictício

fiddle *n* violino; burla

fidelity *n* fidelidade

field *n* campo

fierce *adj* feroz, ferrenho

fiery *adj* belicoso

fifteen *adj* quinze

fifth *adj* quinto

fifty *adj* cinqüenta

fifty-fifty *adv* meio a meio

fig *n* figo

fight *iv* lutar, combater

fight *n* luta, briga

fighter *n* lutador

figure *n* figura; dígito

figure out *v* entender

file *v* arquivo; limar

file *n* arquivo, fila; lima

fill *v* encher, preencher

filling *n* recheio; obturação

film *n* filme, película

filter *n* filtro

filter *v* filtrar

filth *n* sujeira

filthy *adj* obsceno, sujo

fin *n* nadadeira

final *adj* final, último

finalize *v* finalizar

finance *v* finança

financial *adj* financeiro

find *iv* encontrar

find out *v* descobrir

fine *n* multa

fine *v* multar

fine *adv* muito bem

fine *adj* bem, ótimo, lindo

finger *n* dedo

fingernail *n* unha

fingerprint *n* impressão digital

fingertip *n* ponta do dedo

finish *v* terminar, acabar

Finland *n* Finlândia

Finnish *adj* finlandês

fire *v* queimar; demitir

fire *n* fogo, lume, ardor

firearm *n* arma de fogo

firecracker *n* rojão

firefighter *n* bombeiro

fireman *n* bombeiro

fireplace *n* lareira

firewood *n* lenha

fireworks *n* fogos de artifício

firm *adj* firme

firm n firmar, apertar
firmness n firmeza
first adj primeiro
fish n peixe
fisherman n pescador
fishy adj suspeito
fist n punho
fit n corte, ajuste
fit v adequar(-se)
fitness n boa forma
fitting adj adequado
five adj cinco
fix v fixar, consertar
fjord n fiorde
flag n bandeira
flagpole n mastro
flamboyant adj vistoso
flame n flama, chama
flammable adj inflamável
flank n flanco
flare n luz; ostentação
flare-up v acender-se
flashlight n lanterna
flashy adj espalhafatoso
flat n apartamento
flat adj plano, raso
flatten v aplanar
flatter v adular; gabar-se
flattery n lisonja, adulação
flaunt v exibir, ostentar
flavor n sabor, tempero
flaw n defeito, falha

flawless adj impecável
flea n pulga
flee iv fugir
fleece n velo
fleet n frota
fleeting adj transitório
flesh n carne, polpa
flex v flectir, dobrar
flexible adj flexível
flicker v tremular
flier n aviador; folheto
flight n vôo; fuga
flimsy adj leve, frágil
flirt v flertar
float v flutuar
flock n bando, rebanho
flog v açoitar, chicotear
flood v inundar; iluminar
floodgate n comporta, gate
flooding n inundação
floodlight n holofote
floor n piso, assoalho
flour n farinha
flourish v florescer
flow v subir
flow n fluxo
flower n flor
flowerpot n vaso
flu n influenza, gripe
fluctuate v flutuar, oscilar
fluently adv fluentement
fluid n fluido

F

F

flunk *v* levar bomba
flush *v* dar descarga; corar
flute *n* flauta
flutter *v* adejar, esvoaçar
fly *iv* voar; fugir de
fly *n* mosca
foam *n* espuma
focus *n* foco
focus on *v* concentrar
foe *n* adversário
fog *n* neblina, névoa
foggy *adj* enevoado
foil *v* frustrar
fold *v* dobrar
folder *n* dobrador
folks *n* parentes
folksy *adj* simples, popular
follow *v* seguir, acompanhar
follower *n* seguidor
folly *n* desatino
fond *adj* querido, mais caro
fondle *v* afagar
fondness *n* afeição
food *n* comida, alimento
fool *v* enganar
fool *n* tolo, idiota
foolproof *adj* garantido
foot *n* pé
football *n* futebol americano
footnote *n* nota de rodapé
footprint *n* pegada
footstep *n* passo

footwear *n* calçado
for *pre* para, por
forbid *iv* proibir
force *n* força
force *v* forçar, obrigar
forceful *adj* vigoroso
forcibly *adv* forçadamente
forecast *iv* prever
forefront *n* vanguarda
foreground *n* primeiro plano
forehead *n* testa
foreign *adj* estranho
foreigner *n* estrangeiro
foreman *n* presidente
foremost *adj* primeiro
foresee *iv* prever
foreshadow *v* pressagiar
foresight *n* previdência
forest *n* floresta
foretaste *n* prenúncio
foretell *v* predizer
forever *adv* eternamente
forewarn *v* prevenir, precaver
foreword *n* prefácio
forfeit *v* perder
forge *v* falsificar; avançar
forgery *n* falsificação
forget *v* esquecer
forgivable *adj* perdoável
forgive *v* perdoar
forgiveness *n* perdão
fork *n* garfo, forcado

form *n* forma, formulário
formal *adj* formal
formality *n* formalidade
formalize *v* formalizar
formally *adv* formalmente
format *n* formato
formation *n* formação
former *adj* passado
formerly *adv* antigamente
formidable *adj* tremendo
formula *n* fórmula
forsake *iv* abandonar
fort *n* fort
forthcoming *adj* futuro
forthright *adj* correto
fortify *v* fortificar
fortitude *n* força
fortress *n* fortalezà
fortunate *adj* afortunado
fortune *n* fortuna
forty *adj* quarenta
forward *adv* adiante
fossil *n* fóssil
foster *v* cuidar; encorajar
foul *adj* nojento, sujo; falta
foundation *n* fundação
founder *n* fundador
foundry *n* fundição
fountain *n* fonte
four *adj* quatro
fourteen *adj* catorze
fourth *adj* quarto

fox *n* raposa
foxy *adj* astutu
fraction *n* fração
fracture *n* fratura
fragile *adj* frágil
fragment *n* fragmento
fragrance *n* fragrância
fragrant *adj* perfumado
frail *adj* frágil
frailty *n* fragilidade
frame *n* armação, moldura
frame *v* emoldurar; tramar
framework *n* estrutura
France *n* França
franchise *n* direito de voto
frank *adj* franco
frankly *adv* francamente
frankness *n* franqueza
frantic *adj* frenético
fraternal *adj* fraternal
fraternity *n* fraternidade
fraud *n* fraude
fraudulent *adj* fraudulento
freckle *n* sarda
freckled *adj* sardento
free *v* libertar, livrar-se
free *adj* livre; gratuito
freedom *n* liberdade
freeway *n* auto-estrada
freeze *iv* congelar, paralizar
freezer *n* congelador
freezing *adj* gelado

F

freight *n* carga, frete
French *adj* francês
frenetic *adj* frenético, louco
frenzied *adj* frenético
frenzy *n* frenesi
frequency *n* frequência
frequent *adj* frequente
frequent *v* frequentar
fresh *adj* fresco, novo
freshen *v* refrescar
freshness *n* frescura, frescor
friar *n* frade, monge
friction *n* fricção, atrito
Friday *n* Sexta-feira
fried *adj* frito
friend *n* amigo
friendship *n* amizade
fries *n* batata frita
frigate *n* frigata
fright *n* pavor, susto
frighten *v* assustar
frightening *adj* assustador
frigid *adj* frio, frígido
fringe *n* franja, orla
frivolous *adj* frívolo
frog *n* rã
from *pre* de
front *n* frente; fachada
front *adj* frontal, dianteira
frontage *n* fachada
frontier *n* fronteira
frost *n* geada

frostbitten *adj* rachado pelo frio
frosty *adj* coberto de geada
frown *v* franzir a testa
frozen *adj* congelado
frugal *adj* frugal, econômico
frugality *n* frugalidade
fruit *n* fruta
fruitful *adj* frutífero
fruity *adj* de fruta, como fruta
frustrate *v* frustrar
frustration *n* frustração
fry *v* fritar
frying pan *n* frigideira
fuel *n* combustível
fuel *v* estimular
fugitive *n* fugitivo
fulfill *v* cumprir, preencher
fulfillment *n* cumprimento
full *adj* cheio, completo
fully *adv* plenamente
fumes *n* fumaça
fumigate *v* fumigar; defumar
fun *n* diversão
function *n* função
fund *n* fundo, repertório
fund *v* financiar, fundar
fundamental *adj* fundamental
funds *n* fundos
funeral *n* funeral
fungus *n* fungo
funny *adj* engraçado
fur *n* pelo, pele**

furious *adj* furioso
furiously *adv* furiosamente
furnace *n* fornalha
furnish *v* mobiliar, prover
furnishings *n* mobilia, acessórios
furniture *n* móveis
furor *n* furor, escândalo
furrow *n* sulgo, rego, ruga
furry *adj* peludo
further *adv* mais longe
furthermore *adv* além disso
fury *n* fúria
fuse *n* fusível
fusion *n* fusão
fuss *n* alvoroço
fussy *adj* delicado, nervoso
futile *adj* fútil
futility *n* futilidade
future *n* futuro
fuzzy *adj* frisado; vago

G

gadget *n* aparelho
gag *n* mordaça; piada
gag *v* amordaçar
gage *v* penhorar
gain *v* ganhar

gain *n* ganho, benefício
gal *n* girl
galaxy *n* galáxia
gale *n* vendaval
gall bladder *n* vesícula biliar
gallant *adj* galante, valente
gallery *n* galeria
gallon *n* galão
gallop *v* galopar
gallows *n* forca, patíbulo
galvanize *v* galvanizar
gamble *v* apostar
game *n* jogo; caça
gang *n* gangue
gangrene *n* gangrena
gangster *n* gângster
gap *n* intervalo, brecha
garage *n* garagem
garbage *n* lixo; besteira
garden *n* jardim, horta
gardener *n* jardineiro
gargle *v* gargarejar
garland *n* grinalda
garlic *n* alho
garment *n* vestimenta
garnish *v* guarnecer
garnish *n* guarnição, enfeite
garrison *n* guarnição militar
garrulous *adj* gárrulo, falador
garter *n* liga
gas *n* gás, gasolina
gash *n* corte profundo, talho

F
G

gasoline *n* gasolina
gasp *v* ofegar, arfar
gastric *adj* gástrico
gate *n* portão, entrada
gather *v* juntar, recolher
gathering *n* reunião; pregas
gauge *v* medir, calibrar
gauze *n* gaze
gaze *v* olhar fixamente
gear *n* engrenagem
geese *n* gansos
gem *n* gema, jóia
gender *n* gênero
gene *n* gene, gen
general *n* geral, general
generalize *v* generalizar
generate *v* gerar
generation *n* geração
generator *n* gerador
generic *adj* genérico
generosity *n* generosidade
genetic *adj* genético
genial *adj* genial, cordial
genius *n* gênio
genocide *n* genocídio
genteel *adj* fino, refinado
gentle *adj* gentil, terno
gentleman *n* cavalheiro
gentleness *n* gentileza, ternura
genuflect *v* fazer genuflexão
genuine *adj* genuíno
geography *n* geografia

geology *n* geologia
geometry *n* geometria
germ *n* germe, micróbio
German *adj* alemão
Germany *n* Alemanha
germinate *v* germinar
gerund *n* gerúndio
gestation *n* gestação
gesticulate *v* gesticular
gesture *n* gesto
get *iv* obter; entender
get along *v* relacionar-se
get away *v* ir embora, sair
get back *v* voltar, recuperar
get by *v* sobreviver, se virar
get down *v* deprimir; baixar
get down to *v* começar a fazer
get in *v* entrar; chegar
get off *v* sair; descer
get out *v* sair, tirar, descer
get over *v* recuperar-se
get together *v* juntar-se
get up *v* levantar-se
geyser *n* gêiser
ghastly *adj* horrível, espantoso
ghost *n* fantasma
giant *n* gigante
gift *n* presente, dom
gifted *adj* dotado, talentoso
gigantic *adj* gigantesco
giggle *v* dar risadinhas
gimmick *n* truque publicitário**

ginger *n* gengibre
gingerly *adv* cuidadosamente
giraffe *n* girafa
girl *n* moça, menina
girlfriend *n* amiga, namorada
give *iv* dar; dedicar, prestar
give away *v* dar; revelar
give back *v* devolver, regressar
give in *v* render-se
give out *v* repartir, distribuir
give up *v* abandonar; desistir
glacier *n* geleira
glad *adj* alegre, contente
gladiator *n* gladiador
glamorous *adj* glamouroso
glance *v* olhar de relance
glance *n* olhadela
gland *n* glândula
glare *n* brilhoo
glass *n* vidro, copo
glasses *n* óculos
glassware *n* objeto de cristal
gleam *n* vislumbre, lampejo
gleam *v* reluzir, raiar, cintilar
glide *v* deslizar, planar
glimmer *n* luz tênue; raio
glimpse *n* vislumbre
glimpse *v* vislumbrar, entrever
glitter *v* reluzir, brilhar
globe *n* globo
globule *n* glóbulo
gloom *n* pessimismo

gloomy *adj* escuro; pessimista
glorify *v* glorificar
glorious *adj* glorioso
glory *n* glória
gloss *n* lustre, brilho
glossary *n* glossário
glossy *adj* brilhoso, lustroso
glove *n* luva
glow *v* brilhar
glucose *n* glicose
glue *n* cola
glue *v* colar, grudar
glut *n* excesso, abundância
glutton *n* glutão
gnaw *v* roer
go *iv* ir, seguir
go ahead *v* avançar, progredir
go away *v* partir, ir embora
go back *v* voltar
go down *v* afundar, decair
go in *v* entrar
go on *v* continuar
go out *v* apagar-se; sair
go over *v* examinar, repetir
go through *v* passar por
go under *v* sucumbir, fracassar
go up *v* subir
goad *v* incitar
goal *n* gol; objetivo, meta
goalkeeper *n* goleiro
goat *n* bode, cabra
gobble *v* engolir; grugulejar

G

God *n* Deus
goddess *n* deusa
godless *adj* ateu, herege, infiel
gold *n* ouro
golden *adj* dourado
good *adj* bom, bem, apto
good-looking *adj* bonito
goodness *n* bondade
goods *n* mercadoria
goodwill *n* benevolencia
goof *n* estupidez
goose *n* ganso
gorge *n* desfiladeiro
gorgeous *adj* lindíssimo
gorilla *n* gorila
gory *adj* sangrento
gospel *n* evangelho
gossip *v* fofoca, bate-papo
gossip *n* fofocar, bater-papo
gout *n* gota
govern *v* governar
government *n* governo
governor *n* governador
gown *n* toga
grab *v* agarrar
grace *n* graça, decoro
graceful *adj* gracioso, elegante
gracious *adj* cortês
grade *n* categoria; declive
gradual *adj* gradual
graduate *v* grarduar-se
graduation *n* graduação

graft *v* enxertar
graft *n* enxerto
grain *n* grão, cereal
gram *n* grama
grammar *n* gramática
grand *adj* grandioso
grandchild *n* neto
granddad *n* vovô
grandfather *n* avô, vô
grandmother *n* avó, vó
grandparents *n* avós
grandson *n* neto
grandstand *n* tribuna principal
granite *n* granito
grant *v* conceder, admitir
grant *n* subvenção
grape *n* uva
grapefruit *n* toronja, grapefruit
grapevine *n* vinha
graphic *adj* gráfico; vívido
grasp *n* aperto; alcance
grasp *v* apertar; alcançar
grass *n* grama, capim
grateful *adj* grato
gratify *v* gratificar
gratifying *adj* gratificante
gratitude *n* gratidão
gratuity *n* gratuidade
grave *adj* grave
grave *n* túmulo
gravel *n* pedregulho
gravely *adv* gravemente

gravestone *n* lápide
graveyard *n* cemitério
gravitate *v* gravitar
gravity *n* gravidade
gravy *n* molho de carne
gray *adj* cinza, grisalho
grayish *adj* cinzento
graze *v* roçar; pastar
graze *n* esfoladura; pasto
grease *v* lubrificar, untar
grease *n* gordura, graxa
greasy *adj* gorduroso
great *adj* grande, ótimo
greatness *n* grandeza
Greece *n* Grécia
greed *n* ganância, gula
greedy *adj* ganancioso
Greek *adj* grego
green *adj* verde; imaturo
green bean *n* vagem
Greenland *n* Groenlândia
greet *v* saudar
greetings *n* saudações
gregarious *adj* gregário, sociável
grenade *n* granada
greyhound *n* galgo
grief *n* pesar
grievance *n* queixa
grieve *v* afligir
grill *v* grelhar; interrogar
grill *n* grelhar
grim *adj* sinistro

grimace *n* careta
grime *n* encardimento
grind *iv* moer, triturar
grip *v* agarrar
grip *n* aperto; dominio
gripe *n* queixa
grisly *adj* pavoroso
groan *v* gemer
groan *n* gemido
groceries *n* mantimentos
groin *n* virilha
groom *n* noivo; cavalariço
groove *n* ranhura
gross *adj* grosseiro; grosso
grossly *adv* grosseiramente
grotesque *adj* grotesco
grotto *n* gruta, caverna
grouch *v* resmungar
grouchy *adj* rabugento
ground *n* solo, terreno
ground floor *n* andar térreo
groundless *adj* infundado
groundwork *n* esboço
group *n* grupo, conjunto
grow *iv* crescer, tornar-se
grow up *v* crescer
growl *v* rosnar
grown-up *n* adulto
growth *n* crescimento
grudge *n* rancor
grudgingly *adv* de má vontade
grueling *adj* exaustivo

G

gruesome *adj* horrível

grumble *v* murmurar; grunhir

grumpy *adj* amuado

guarantee *v* garantir

guarantee *n* garantia

guarantor *n* avalista, fiador

guard *n* guarda, vigia

guardian *n* guardião, tutor

guerrilla *n* guerrilheiro

guess *v* adivinhar, achar

guess *n* adivinhação

guest *n* hóspede

guidance *n* orientação

guide *v* guiar

guide *n* guiar

guidebook *n* guiar

guidelines *n* diretrizes

guild *n* associação

guile *n* malícia

guillotine *n* guilhotina

guilt *n* culpa

guilty *adj* culpado

guise *n* falsa, aparência

guitar *n* violão

gulf *n* golfo

gull *n* gaivota

gullible *adj* crédulo

gulp *v* engolir

gum *n* chiclete; gengiva

gun *n* arma de fogo

gun down *v* ferir com tiro

gunfire *n* tiroteio

gunman *n* pistoleiro

gunpowder *n* pólvora

gunshot *n* tiro

gust *n* rajada

gusto *n* entusiasmo

gusty *adj* tempestuoso

gut *n* intestino, tripa

guts *n* coragem; vísceras

gutter *n* sarjeta, canaleta

guy *n* sujeito

gymnasium *n* ginásio

gynecology *n* ginecologista

gypsy *n* cigano

habit *n* hábito

habitable *adj* habitável

habitual *adj* habitual

hack *v* picar, talhar

haggle *v* regatear

hail *n* saraiva, granizo

hail *v* chover granizo

hair *n* cabelo, pelo

hairbrush *n* escova de cabelo

haircut *n* corte de cabelo

hairdo *n* penteado

hairdresser *n* cabeleireiro**

hairy *adj* cabeludo, peludo

half *n* metade, meio

half *adj* meio

hall *n* salão; corredor

hallucinate *v* ter alucinação

hallway *n* vestíbulo

halt *v* parar

halve *v* cortar no meio

ham *n* presunto

hamburger *n* hambúrguer

hamlet *n* vila, aldeia

hammer *n* martelo

hammock *n* rede (de deitar)

hand *n* mão; ponteiro

hand in *v* entregar

hand out *v* distribuir, repartir

hand over *v* ceder, transferir

handbag *n* bolsa de mão

handbook *n* manual

handcuff *v* algemar

handcuffs *n* algemar

handful *n* punhado

handgun *n* arma de mão

handicap *n* deficiência física

handkerchief *n* lenço

handle *v* lidar com, tratar

handle *n* cabo, maçaneta

handmade *adj* feito à mão

handout *n* folheto

handrail *n* corrimão

handshake *n* aperto de mão

handsome *adj* bonito, elegante

handwriting *n* letra, caligrafia

handy *adj* prático, acessível

hang *iv* pendurar, enforcar

hang around *v* vadiar

hang on *v* esperar; agarrar

hang up *v* pendurar

hanger *n* cabide, cruzeta

hang-up *n* inibição, fixação

happen *v* acontecer; dar com

happening *n* acontecimento

happiness *n* felicidade

happy *adj* feliz, contente

harass *v* importunar

harassment *n* assédio

harbor *n* porto

hard *adj* difícil, duro, severo

harden *v* endurecer

hardly *adv* dificilmente

hardness *n* valentia

hardship *n* dureza

hardware *n* ferragens

hardwood *n* madeira dura

hardy *adj* forte, resistente

hare *n* lebre

harm *v* prejudicar

harm *n* mal, dano

harmful *adj* prejudicial

harmless *adj* inofensivo

harmonize *v* harmonizar

harmony *n* harmonia

harp *n* harpa

harpoon *n* arpão

H

harrowing *adj* doloroso

harsh *adj* severo; áspero

harshly *adv* severamente

harshness *n* severidade

harvest *n* colheita, ceifa

harvest *v* colher, ceifar

hashish *n* haxixe

hassle *v* aborrecer, disputar

hassle *n* problema, dispulta

haste *n* pressa

hasten *v* apressar

hastily *adv* apressadamente

hasty *adj* apressado

hat *n* chapéu

hatchet *n* machadinha

hate *v* odiar, detestar

hateful *adj* odioso

hatred *n* ódio

haughty *adj* altivo

haul *v* carrear, puxar

haunt *v* perseguir

have *iv* ter; haver

have to *v* ter de, ter que

haven *n* porto, refúgio

havoc *n* devastação

hawk *n* falcão

hay *n* feno

haystack *n* palheiro

hazard *n* risco

hazardous *adj* arriscado

haze *n* neblina, névoa

hazelnut *n* avelã

hazy *adj* enevoado

he *pro* ele, aquele

head *n* cabeça, chefe

head for *v* ir para; dirigir-se a

headache *n* dor de cabeça

heading *n* cabeçalho, título

head-on *adv* de frente

headphones *n* fones de ouvido

headquarters *n* quartel-general

headway *n* progresso

heal *v* curar

healer *n* curandeiro

health *n* saúde

healthy *adj* saudável

heap *n* monte

heap *v* amontoar

hear *iv* ouvir, escutar

hearing *n* ouvido; audiência

hearsay *n* boato

hearse *n* carro fúnebre

heart *n* coração, âmago

heartbeat *n* batimento cardíaco

heartburn *n* azia

hearten *v* animar

heartfelt *adj* sincero

hearth *n* lareira

heartless *adj* impiedoso

hearty *adj* cordial

heat *v* esquentar, aquecer

heat *n* calor, quentura

heat wave *n* onda de calor

heater *n* aquecedor

heathen *n* pagão
heating *n* aquecimento
heatstroke *n* insolação
heaven *n* céu, paraíso
heavenly *adj* divino
heaviness *n* peso
heavy *adj* pesado
heckle *v* importunar
hectic *adj* agitado
heed *v* prestar atenção
heel *n* calcanhar, salto
height *n* altura; auge
heighten *v* elevar, intensificar
heinous *adj* atroz
heir *n* herdeiro
heiress *n* herdeira
heist *n* roubo, assalto
helicopter *n* helicóptero
hell *n* inferno
hello *e* olá, ei
helm *n* leme, timão
helmet *n* capacete
help *v* ajudar, socorrer
help *n* ajuda, socorro
helper *n* auxiliar
helpful *adj* útil
helpless *adj* desamparado
hem *n* bainha
hemisphere *n* hemisfério
hemorrhage *n* hemorragia
hen *n* galinha
hence *adv* portanto, daqui a

henchman *n* capanga
her *adj* ela, seu, sua
herald *v* anunciar
herald *n* arauto
herb *n* erva
here *adv* aqui, aí
hereafter *adv* a partir de agora
hereby *adv* pela presente
hereditary *adj* hereditário
heresy *n* heresia
heretic *adj* herege
heritage *n* herança
hermetic *adj* hermético
hermit *n* ermitão
hernia *n* hérnia
hero *n* herói
heroic *adj* heróico
heroin *n* heroína
heroism *n* heroísmo
hers *pro* dela, seu (s), sua (s)
herself *pro* ela mesma, se
hesitant *adj* hesitante
hesitate *v* hesitar
hesitation *n* hesitação
heyday *n* auge
hiccup *n* soluço
hidden *adj* escondido
hide *iv* esconder
hideaway *n* refúgio
hideous *adj* horroroso
hierarchy *n* hierarquia
high *adj* alto, elevado

highlight *n* ponto culminante

highly *adv* altamente

Highness *n* Alteza

highway *n* rodovia, estrada

hijack *v* seqüestrar

hijack *n* seqüestro

hijacker *n* seqüestrador

hike *v* caminhar

hike *n* caminhada

hilarious *adj* hilariante

hill *n* colina, ladeira

hillside *n* encosta

hilltop *n* cume, topo

hilly *adj* montanhoso

hilt *n* punho

hinder *v* estorvar

hindrance *n* estorvo

hindsight *n* percepção tardia

hinge *v* dobrar, girar

hinge *n* dobradiça, gonzo

hint *n* pista, insinuação

hint *v* insinuar, sugerir

hip *n* quadril

hire *v* contratar; alugar

his *adj* dele, seu(s), sua(s)

his *pro* dele, seu(s), sua(s)

Hispanic *adj* hispânico

hiss *v* sibilar

historian *n* historiador

history *n* história

hit *n* golpe; sucesso

hit *iv* bater, acertar

hit back *v* revidar

hitch up *v* puxar

hitchhike *n* pedir carona

hitherto *adv* até agora

hive *n* colméia, enxame

hoard *v* armazenar

hoarse *adj* rouco

hoax *n* brincadeira

hobby *n* passatempo

hog *n* porco

hoist *v* levantar, içar

hold *iv* conter; guardar

hold back *v* esconder

hold on to *v* segurar

hold out *v* resistir, durar

hold up *v* deter; assaltar

holdup *n* assalto

hole *n* buraco, furo

holiday *n* feriado

holiness *n* santidade

Holland *n* Holanda

hollow *adj* oco, vazio

holocaust *n* holocausto

holy *adj* santo

homage *n* homenagem

home *n* lar, casa

homeland *n* terra natal

homeless *adj* sem-teto

homely *adj* caseiro

homemade *adj* feito em casa

homesick *adj* nostálgico

hometown *n* cidade natal

homework *n* tarefa
homicide *n* homicídio
homily *n* homília, sermão
honest *adj* honesto
honesty *n* honestidade
honey *n* mel; querido
honeymoon *n* lua-de-mel
honk *v* buzinar
honor *n* honra
hood *n* capuz, capota
hoodlum *n* arruaceiro
hoof *n* casco
hook *n* anzol, gancho
hooligan *n* rufião, vândalo
hop *v* saltar, saltitar
hope *n* esperança
hopeful *adj* esperançoso
hopeless *adj* inútil, sofrível
horizon *n* horizonte
horizontal *adj* horizontal
hormone *n* hormônio
horn *n* buzina; corneta
horrendous *adj* horrendo
horrible *adj* horrível
horrify *v* horrorizar
horror *n* horror
horse *n* cavalo
hose *n* mangueira; meia
hospital *n* hospital
hospitality *n* hospitalidade
hospitalize *v* hospitalizar
host *n* anfitrião

hostage *n* refém
hostess *n* anfitriã
hostile *adj* hostil
hostility *n* hostilidade
hot *adj* quente, picante
hotel *n* hotel
hound *n* cão de caça
hour *n* hora
hourly *adv* de hora em hora
house *n* casa
household *n* grupo domiciliar
housekeeper *n* governanta
housewife *n* dona de casa
housework *n* serviço doméstico
how *adv* como, quantto
however *c* no entanto
howl *v* uivar
howl *n* uivo
hub *n* eixo
hug *v* abraçar
hug *n* abraço
huge *adj* enorme
hull *n* casco
human *adj* humano
human being *n* ser humano
humanities *n* humanidades
humankind *n* humanidade
humble *adj* humilde
humbly *adv* humildemente
humid *adj* úmido
humidity *n* umidade
humiliate *v* humilhar

H

humility *n* humildade
humor *n* humor, cômico
humorous *adj* humorístico
hump *n* corcova, lombada
hunch *n* palpite
hunchback *n* corcunda
hunched *adj* encurvado
hundred *adj* cem, centena
hundredth *adj* centésimo
hunger *n* fome
hungry *adj* faminto, esfomeado
hunt *v* caçar
hunter *n* caçador
hunting *n* caça
hurdle *n* obstáculo
hurl *v* lançar
hurricane *n* furacão
hurriedly *adv* apressadamente
hurry *v* apressar
hurry up *v* apressar-se
hurt *iv* ferir, prejudicar
hurt *adj* ferido, magoado
hurtful *adj* lesivo, ofensivo
husband *n* marido, esposo
hush *n* silêncio
hush up *v* silenciar
husky *adj* rouco
hustle *n* atropelo
hut *n* cabana
hydraulic *adj* hidráulico
hydrogen *n* hidrogênio
hyena *n* hiena

hygiene *n* higiene
hymn *n* hino
hyphen *n* hífen
hypnosis *n* hipnose
hypnotize *v* hipnotizar
hypocrisy *n* hipocrisia
hypocrite *adj* hipócrita
hypothesis *n* hipótese
hysteria *n* histeria
hysterical *adj* histérico

I *pro* eu
ice *n* gelo
ice cream *n* sorvete
ice cube *n* cubo de gelo
ice skate *v* patinar no gelo
iceberg *n* iceberg
icebox *n* geladeira
ice-cold *adj* gelado
icon *n* ícone
icy *adj* gelado
idea *n* idéia, impressão
ideal *adj* ideal
identical *adj* idêntico
identify *v* identificar
identity *n* identidade

ideology *n* ideologia

idiot *n* idiota

idiotic *adj* idiota

idle *adj* inativo, ocioso, vão

idol *n* ídolo

idolatry *n* idolatria

if *c* se

ignite *v* inflamar

ignorance *n* ignorância

ignorant *adj* ignorante

ignore *v* ignorar

ill *adj* doente, mau, mal

illegal *adj* ilegal

illegible *adj* ilegível

illegitimate *adj* ilegítimo

illicit *adj* ilícito

illiterate *adj* analfabeto

illness *n* doença

illogical *adj* ilógico

illuminate *v* iluminar

illusion *n* ilusão

illustrate *v* ilustrar

illustration *n* ilustração

illustrious *adj* ilustre

image *n* imagem, retrato

imagination *n* imaginação

imagine *v* imaginar

imbalance *n* desequilíbrio

imitate *v* imitar

imitation *n* imitação

immaculate *adj* imaculado

immature *adj* imaturo, verde

immaturity *n* imaturidade

immediately *adv* imediatamente

immense *adj* imenso

immensity *n* imensidade

immerse *v* imergir

immersion *n* imersão

immigrant *n* imigrante

immigrate *v* imigrar

immigration *n* imigração

imminent *adj* iminente

immobile *adj* imóvel

immobilize *v* imobilizar

immoral *adj* imoral

immorality *n* imoralidade

immortal *adj* imortal

immortality *n* imortalidade

immune *adj* imune

immunity *n* imunidade

immunize *v* imunizar

immutable *adj* imutável

impact *n* impacto

impact *v* impactar

impair *v* prejudicar

impartial *adj* imparcial

impatience *n* impaciência

impatient *adj* impaciente

impeccable *adj* impecável

impediment *n* impedimento

impending *adj* impendente

imperfection *n* imperfeição

imperial *adj* imperial

imperialism *n* imperialismo

I

impersonal *adj* impessoal
impertinence *n* impertinência
impertinent *adj* impertinente
impetuous *adj* impetuoso
implacable *adj* implacável
implant *v* implantar
implement *v* implementar
implicate *v* implicar
implication *n* implicação
implicit *adj* implícito
implore *v* implorar
imply *v* insinuar
impolite *adj* impolido, rude
import *v* importar
importance *n* importância
importation *n* importação
impose *v* impor
imposing *adj* imponente
imposition *n* imposição
impossibility *n* impossibilidade
impossible *adj* impossível
impotent *adj* impotente
impound *v* apreender
impoverished *adj* empobrecido
impractical *adj* não prático
imprecise *adj* impreciso
impress *v* impressionar
impressive *adj* impressionante
imprison *v* aprisionar
improbable *adj* improvável
impromptu *adv* de improviso
improper *adj* impróprio

improve *v* melhorar
improvement *n* melhoria
improvise *v* improvisar
impulse *n* impulso
impulsive *adj* impulsivo
impunity *n* impunidade
impure *adj* impuro
in *pre* em; dentro
in depth *adv* a fundo
inability *n* inabilidade
inaccessible *adj* inacessível
inaccurate *adj* incorreto
inadequate *adj* inadequado
inadmissible *adj* inadmissível
inappropriate *adj* inapropriado
inasmuch as *c* visto que
inaugurate *v* inaugurar
inauguration *n* inauguração
incalculable *adj* incalculável
incapable *adj* incapaz
incapacitate *v* incapacitar
incarcerate *v* encarcerar
incense *n* incenso
incentive *n* incentivo
inception *n* princípio, começo
incessant *adj* incessante
inch *n* polegada
incident *n* incidente
incidentally *adv* aliás
incision *n* incisão
incite *v* incitar
incitement *n* incitação

inclination *n* inclinação

incline *v* inclinar

include *v* incluir

inclusive *adv* inclusive

incoherent *adj* incoerente

income *n* rendimento

incoming *adj* entrante

incompatible *adj* imcompatível

incompetence *n* incompetência

incompetent *adj* incompetente

incomplete *adj* incompleto

inconsistent *adj* inconsistente

incontinence *n* incontinência

inconvenient *adj* inconveniente

incorporate *v* incorporar

incorrect *adj* incorreto

incorrigible *adj* incorrigível

increase *v* aumentar

increase *n* aumento

increasing *adj* crescente

incredible *adj* incrível

increment *n* incremento

incriminate *v* incriminar

incur *v* incorrer, contrair

incurable *adj* incurável

indecency *n* indecência

indecision *n* indecisão

indecisive *adj* indeciso

indeed *adv* de fato, mesmo

indefinite *adj* indefinido

indemnify *v* indenizar

indemnity *n* indenização

independence *n* independência

independent *adj* independente

index *n* índice

indicate *v* indicar

indication *n* indicação

indict *v* acusar, processar

indifference *n* indiferença

indifferent *adj* indiferente

indigent *adj* indigente

indigestion *n* indigestão

indirect *adj* indireto

indiscreet *adj* indiscreto

indiscretion *n* indiscreção

indispensable *adj* indispensável

indisposed *adj* indisposto

indisputable *adj* indiscutível

indivisible *adj* indivisível

indoctrinate *v* doutrinar

indoor *adv* interno

induce *v* induzir

indulge *v* mimar

indulgent *adj* indulgente

industrious *adj* industrioso

industry *n* indústria

ineffective *adj* ineficaz

inefficient *adj* ineficiente

inept *adj* inepto

inequality *n* desigualdade

inevitable *adj* inevitável

inexcusable *adj* imperdoável

inexpensive *adj* barato

inexperienced *adj* inexperiente

I

inexplicable *adj* inexplicável
infallible *adj* infalível
infamous *adj* infame, vil
infancy *n* infância
infant *n* bebê, criança
infantry *n* infantaria
infect *v* infeccionar
infection *n* infecção
infectious *adj* infeccioso
infer *v* inferir
inferior *adj* inferior
infertile *adj* infértil
infested *adj* infestado
infidelity *n* infidelidade
infiltrate *v* infiltrar
infiltration *n* infiltração
infinite *adj* infinito
infirmary *n* enfermaria
inflammation *n* inflamação
inflate *v* inflar, encher
inflation *n* inflação
inflexible *adj* inflexível
inflict *v* infligir
influence *n* influência
influential *adj* influente
influenza *n* gripe
influx *n* afluência
inform *v* informar
informal *adj* informal
informality *n* informalidade
informant *n* informante
information *n* informação

informer *n* informante
infraction *n* infração
infrequent *adj* infreqüente
infuriate *v* enfurecer
infusion *n* infusão
ingenuity *n* ingenuidade
ingest *v* ingerir
ingot *n* lingote
ingrained *adj* enraizado
ingratiate *v* agradar
ingratitude *n* ingratidão
ingredient *n* ingrediente
inhabit *v* habitar
inhabitable *adj* habitável
inhabitant *n* habitante
inhale *v* inalar
inherit *v* herdar
inheritance *n* herança
inhibit *v* inibir, impedir
inhuman *adj* inumano
initial *adj* inicial
initially *adv* inicialmente
initials *n* iniciais, rúbrica
initiate *v* iniciar
initiative *n* iniciativa
inject *v* injetar
injection *n* injeção
injure *v* ferir, magoar
injurious *adj* prejudicial
injury *n* lesão, ferimento
injustice *n* injustiça
ink *n* tinta

inkling *n* alusão
inlaid *adj* incrustado
inland *adv* no interior
inland *adj* interior
inmate *n* interno
inn *n* albergue
innate *adj* inato
inner *adj* interior, interno
innocence *n* inocência
innocent *adj* inocente
innovation *n* inovação
innuendo *n* insinuação, indireta
innumerable *adj* inumerável
input *n* input, insumo
inquest *n* inquérito
inquire *v* indagar, perguntar
inquiry *n* interrogatório
inquisition *n* inquisição
insane *adj* insano, louco
insanity *n* insanidade
insatiable *adj* insaciável
inscription *n* inscrição
insect *n* inseto
insecurity *n* insegurança
insensitive *adj* insensível
inseparable *adj* inseparável
insert *v* inserir
insertion *n* inserção
inside *adj* interno
inside *pre* dentro de
inside out *adv* pelo avesso
insignificant *adj* insignificante

insincere *adj* insincero
insincerity *n* insinceridade
insinuate *v* insinuar
insinuation *n* insunuação
insipid *adj* insípido
insist *v* insistir
insistence *n* insistência
insolent *adj* insolente
insoluble *adj* insolúvel
insomnia *n* insônia
inspect *v* inpecionar
inspection *n* inspeção
inspector *n* inspetor
inspiration *n* inspiração
inspire *v* inspirar
instability *n* instabilidade
install *v* instalar
installation *n* instalação
installment *n* prestação
instance *n* exemplo
instant *n* instante
instantly *adv* instantaneamente
instead *adv* em substituição
instigate *v* instigar
instill *v* instilar, incutir
instinct *n* instinto
institute *v* instituir
institution *n* instituição
instruct *v* instruir
instructor *n* instrutor
insufficient *adj* insuficiente
insulate *v* isolar

insulation *n* isolamento
insult *v* insultar
insult *n* insulto
insurance *n* seguro
insure *v* segurar
insurgency *n* insurgência
insurrection *n* inssurreição
intact *adj* intacto
intake *n* admissão; sucção
integrate *v* integrar
integration *n* integração
integrity *n* integridade
intelligent *adj* inteligente
intend *v* pretender, tencionar
intense *adj* intenso
intensify *v* intensificar
intensity *n* intensidade
intensive *adj* intensivo
intention *n* intenção
intercede *v* interceder
intercept *v* interceptar
intercession *n* intercessão
interchange *v* trocar, permutar
interchange *n* troca, intercâmbio
interest *n* interesse
interested *adj* interessado
interesting *adj* interessante
interfere *v* interferir
interference *n* interferência
interior *adj* interior
interlude *n* interlúdio
intermediary *n* intermediário

intern *v* confinar, internar
interpret *v* interpretar
interpretation *n* interpretação
interpreter *n* intérpreter
interrogate *v* interrogar
interrupt *v* interromper
interruption *n* interrupção
intersect *v* interceptar, cruzar
intertwine *v* entrelaçarer
interval *n* intervalo
intervene *v* enterferir, intervir
intervention *n* intervenção
interview *n* entrevista
intestine *n* intestino
intimacy *n* intimidade
intimate *adj* íntimo
intimidate *v* intimidar
intolerable *adj* intolerável
intolerance *n* intolerância
intoxicated *adj* intoxicado
intravenous *adj* intravenoso
intrepid *adj* intrépido
intricate *adj* intricado
intrigue *n* intriga
intriguing *adj* intrigante
intrinsic *adj* intrínseco
introduce *v* introduzir
introduction *n* introdução
introvert *adj* introvertido
intrude *v* intrometer
intruder *n* intruso
intrusion *n* intrusão

intuition *n* intuição
inundate *v* inundar
invade *v* invadir
invader *n* invasor
invalid *n* inválido
invalidate *v* invalidar
invaluable *adj* inestimável
invasion *n* invasão
invent *v* inventar
invention *n* invenção
inventory *n* inventório
invest *v* investir
investigate *v* investigar
investigation *n* investigação
investment *n* investimento
investor *n* investidor
invincible *adj* invencível
invisible *adj* invisível
invitation *n* convite
invite *v* convidar
invoice *n* fatura
invoke *v* invocar
involve *v* envolver
involved *adj* envolvido
involvement *n* envolvimento
inward *adj* íntimo
inwards *adv* para dentro
iodine *n* iodo
irate *adj* irado
Ireland *n* Irlanda
Irish *adj* irlandês
iron *n* ferro

iron *v* passar a ferro
ironic *adj* irônico
irony *n* ironia
irrational *adj* irracional
irrefutable *adj* irrefutável
irregular *adj* irregular
irrelevant *adj* irrelevante
irreparable *adj* irreparável
irresistible *adj* irresistível
irreversible *adj* irreversível
irrevocable *adj* irrevogável
irrigate *v* irrigar
irrigation *n* irrigação
irritate *v* irritar
irritating *adj* irritante
Islamic *adj* islâmico
island *n* ilha
isle *n* ilha, ilhota
isolate *v* isolar
isolation *n* isolamento
issue *n* assunto; número
Italian *adj* italiano
italics *adj* itálico
Italy *n* Itália
itch *v* coçar; ansiar
itchiness *n* coceira
item *n* item, artigo
itemize *v* detalhar
itinerary *n* itinerário
ivory *n* marfim

I

J

jackal *n* chacal

jacket *n* jaqueta

jackpot *n* bolo de apostas

jail *n* cadeia

jail *v* prender

jailer *n* carcereiro

jam *n* geléia

janitor *n* porteiro, zelador

January *n* Janeiro

Japan *n* Japão

Japanese *adj* japonês

jar *n* pote

jasmine *n* jasmim

jaw *n* mandíbula

jealous *adj* invejoso

jealousy *n* ciúme, inveja

jeans *n* jeans

jeopardize *v* pôr em risco

jerk *n* empurrão, puxão

jerk *adj* idiota

jersey *n* camisa de malha

Jew *n* judeu

jewel *n* jóia

jeweler *n* joalheiro

jewelry store *n* joalheria

Jewish *adj* judeu

job *n* trabalho, tarefa

jobless *adj* desempregado

join *v* ligar, unir, juntar-se

joint *n* junta, articulação

jointly *adv* conjuntamente

joke *n* piada, brincadeira

joke *v* brincar, caçoar

jokingly *adv* por brincadeira

jolly *adj* jovial; muito

jolt *v* sacolejar

jolt *n* tranco

journal *n* revista, jornal

journalist *n* jornalista

journey *n* viagem

jovial *adj* jovial

joy *n* alegria

joyful *adj* alegre

joyfully *adv* alegremente

jubilant *adj* jubilante

Judaism *n* judaísmo

judge *n* juiz

judgment *n* julgamento

judicious *adj* judicioso

jug *n* cântaro, caneco

juggler *n* malabarista

juice *n* suco

juicy *adj* suculento

July *n* julho

jump *v* pular, saltar

jump *n* pulo, salto

jumpy *adj* sobressaltado

junction *n* entroncamento

June *n* junho

jungle *n* selva

junk *n* refugo, traste

jury *n* júri
just *adj* justo
justice *n* justiça
justify *v* justificar
justly *adv* justamente
juvenile *n* juvenil
juvenile *adj* juvenil; imaturo

kangaroo *n* cangaru
karate *n* caratê
keep *iv* guardar, manter
keep on *v* continuar
keep up *v* manter
keg *n* barril
kettle *n* chaleira
key *n* chave; código
key ring *n* chaveiro
keyboard *n* teclado
kick *v* chutar, escoicear
kickback *n* suborno
kickoff *n* dar o pontapé inicial
kid *n* criança; cabrito
kidnap *v* raptar, seqüestrar
kidnapper *n* sequestrador
kidnapping *n* sequestro
kidney *n* rim

kidney bean *n* feijão-roxo
kill *v* matar, exterminar
killer *n* matador, assassino
killing *n* matança, assassinato
kilogram *n* quilograma, quilo
kilometer *n* quilômetro
kilowatt *n* quilowatt
kind *adj* gentil
kindle *v* acender
kindly *adv* bondoso
kindness *n* gentileza
king *n* rei
kingdom *n* reino
kinship *n* parentesco
kiosk *n* quiosque
kiss *v* beijar
kiss *n* beijo
kitchen *n* cozinha
kite *n* pipa
kitten *n* gatinho
knee *n* joelho
kneecap *n* rótula
kneel *iv* ajoalhar
knife *n* faca
knight *n* cavaleiro
knit *v* tricotar; ligar
knob *n* calombo
knock *n* batida, golpe
knock *v* derrubar, golpear
knot *n* nó; grupo
know *iv* saber, conhecer
knowledge *n* conhecimento

J
K

L

lab *n* laboratory

label *n* rótulo, etiqueta

labor *n* mão-de-obra

laborer *n* trabalhador

labyrinth *n* labirinto

lace *n* cordão, renda

lack *v* ter falta de, faltar

lack *n* falta

lad *n* menino

ladder *n* escada portátil

laden *adj* carregado

lady *n* senhora, mulher

ladylike *adj* refinado

lagoon *n* laguna

lake *n* lago

lamb *n* cordeiro, carneiro

lame *adj* manco

lament *v* lamentar

lament *n* lamento

lamp *n* abajur, lampião

lamppost *n* poste de iluminação

lampshade *n* abajur

land *n* terra, terras

land *v* aterrissar, ancorar

landing *n* aterrissagem

landlocked *adj* cercado de terra

landlord *n* senhorio

landscape *n* paisagem

lane *n* caminho, rua

language *n* linguagem, língua

languish *v* definhar

lantern *n* lanterna

lap *n* colo; volta

lapse *n* lapso, intervalo

lapse *v* caducar, cair

larceny *n* furto, roubo

lard *n* toucinho, lardo

large *adj* grande

larynx *n* laringe

laser *n* laser

lash *n* cílio; chicote

lash *v* surrar; chicotear

lash out *v* atacar

last *v* durar

last *adj* último

last name *n* sobrenome

last night *adv* noite passada

lasting *adj* duradouro,

lastly *adv* enfim

latch *n* ferrolho, trinco

late *adv* atrasado, tarde

lately *adv* ultimamente

later *adv* mais tarde

later *adj* posterior

lateral *adj* lateral

latest *adj* último

lather *n* espuma

latitude *n* latitude

latter *adj* último

laugh *v* rir

laugh *n* risada, riso**

laughable *adj* risível
laughing stock *n* alvo de riso
laughter *n* risada
launch *n* lançamento
launch *v* lançar
laundry *n* lavanderia
lavatory *n* sanitário
lavish *adj* pródigo
lavish *v* esbanjar
law *n* lei
law-abiding *adj* cumpridor das leis
lawful *adj* legal, lícito
lawmaker *n* legislador
lawn *n* gramado
lawsuit *n* processo
lawyer *n* advogado
lax *adj* descuidado
laxative *adj* laxante
lay *n* situação; leigo
lay *iv* deitar; enterrar
lay off *v* despedir
layer *n* camada
layman *n* leigo
lay-out *n* desenho, formato
laziness *n* preguiça
lazy *adj* preguiçoso
lead *iv* conduzir, levar
lead *n* vanguarda
leaded *adj* chumbado
leader *n* chefe, líder
leadership *n* liderança

leading *adj* principal, primeiro
leaf *n* folha, aba
leaflet *n* folheto
league *n* liga; légua
leak *v* vazar
leak *n* vazamento
leakage *n* vazamento
lean *adj* magro, escasso
lean *iv* inclinar-se
lean on *v* apoiar-se
leaning *n* inclinação
leap *iv* saltar, pular
leap *n* pulo, salto
leap year *n* ano bissexto
learn *iv* aprender
learned *adj* erudito
learner *n* aprendiz
learning *n* erudição
lease *v* arrendar, alugar
lease *n* arrendamento
leash *n* coleira
least *adj* mínimo, menos
leather *n* couro
leave *iv* deixar, partir, sair
leave out *v* omitir
lectern *n* atril
lecture *n* conferência
ledger *n* livro-razão
leech *n* sanguessuga
leftovers *n* sobra, resto
leg *n* perna; etapa
legacy *n* legado

L

legal *adj* legal, jurídico
legality *n* legalidade
legalize *v* legalizar
legend *n* lenda
legible *adj* legível
legion *n* legião
legislate *v* legislar
legislation *n* legislação
legislature *n* legislatura
legitimate *adj* legítimo
leisure *n* lazer
lemon *n* limão
lemonade *n* limonada
lend *iv* emprestar
length *n* duração, extensão
lengthen *v* encompridar
lengthy *adj* comprido
leniency *n* indulgência
lenient *adj* leniente, brando
lens *n* lente; cristalino
Lent *n* Quaresma
lentil *n* lentilha
leopard *n* leopardo
leper *n* leproso
leprosy *n* lepra
less *adj* menos, menor
lessee *n* arrendatário
lessen *v* diminuir
lesser *adj* menor
lesson *n* lição
lessor *n* arrendador
let *iv* deixar

let down *v* baixar, descer
let go *v* largar
let in *v* fazer entrar
let out *v* fazer sair
lethal *adj* letal
letter *n* carta; letra
lettuce *n* alface
leukemia *n* leucemia
level *v* nivelar, igualar
level *n* nível
lever *n* alavanca
leverage *n* força de alavanca
levy *v* impor
lewd *adj* lascivo
liability *n* sujeição a
liable *adj* suscetível
liaison *n* ligação, contato
liar *adj* mentiroso
libel *n* difamação
liberate *v* liberar
liberation *n* liberação
liberty *n* liberdade
librarian *n* bibliotecário
library *n* biblioteca
lice *n* piolho
license *n* licença
license *v* autirizar
lick *v* lamber
lid *n* tampa
lie *iv* mentir
lie *v* deitar; situar-se
lie *n* mentira

lieu *n* lugar, em vez de
lieutenant *n* tenente
life *n* vida
lifeguard *n* salva-vidas
lifeless *adj* inanimado, morto
lifestyle *n* estilo de vida
lifetime *adj* vida
lift *v* levantar, carregar
lift off *v* decolar
lift-off *n* decolagem
ligament *n* ligamento
light *iv* iluminar, acender
light *adj* leve, claro
light *n* luz, fogo
lighter *n* isqueiro
lighthouse *n* farol
lighting *n* iluminação
lightly *adv* ligeiramente
lightning *n* raio, relâmpago
lightweight *n* leve
likable *adj* amável
like *pre* como
like *v* gostar de
likelihood *n* probabilidade
likely *adv* provável
likeness *n* semelhança
likewise *adv* igualmente
liking *n* gosto
limb *n* membro; ramo
lime *n* cal; lima, limão
limestone *n* calcário
limit *n* limite, limitação

limit *v* limitar
limitation *n* limitação
limp *v* mancar
limp *n* manco, mole
line *n* linha, ruga; fila
line up *v* fazer fila, alinhar
linen *n* linho
linger *v* subsistir
lingerie *n* roupa de baixo
lingering *adj* demorado
lining *n* forro
link *v* ligar
link *n* elo, vínculo
lion *n* leão
lioness *n* leoa
lip *n* lábio, borda
liqueur *n* licor
liquid *n* líquido
liquidate *v* liquidar
liquidation *n* liquidação
liquor *n* bebida alcoólica
list *v* listar; adernar
list *n* lista; adernagem
listen *v* escutar
listener *n* ouvinte
litany *n* litania
liter *n* litro
literal *adj* literal
literally *adv* literalmente
literate *adj* alfabetizado
literature *n* literatura
litigate *v* litigar

L

litigation *n* litígio

litter *n* palha; maca

little *adj* pequeno, pouco

little bit *n* pouquinho

little by little *adv* pouco a pouco

liturgy *n* liturgia

live *adj* vivo, ao vivo

live *v* viver

live off *v* viver à custa de

live up *v* viver à altura de

livelihood *n* sustento

lively *adj* vivaz

liver *n* fígado

livestock *n* rebanho

livid *adj* lívido

living room *n* sala de estar

lizard *n* lagarto, lagartixa

load *v* carregar

load *n* carga

loaded *adj* carregado

loaf *n* pão

loan *v* emprestar

loan *n* empréstimo

loathe *v* abominar

loathing *n* abominação

lobby *n* vestíbulo

lobby *v* fazer pressão

lobster *n* lagosta

local *adj* local

localize *v* localizar

locate *v* localizar

located *adj* localizado

location *n* localização

lock *v* trancar

lock *n* tranca, fechadura

lock up *v* encerrar

locker room *n* vestiário

locksmith *n* serralheiro

locust *n* locusta

lodge *v* alojar

lodging *n* alojamento

lofty *adj* alto

log *n* tora, lenha

log in *v* entrar

log off *v* cessar

logic *n* lógica

logical *adj* lógico

loin *n* lombo

loiter *v* flanar

loneliness *n* solidão

lonely *adv* solitário, isolado

loner *n* solitário

lonesome *adj* solitário

long *adj* longo

long for *v* sentir saudade

longing *n* desejo

longitude *n* longitude

long-standing *adj* antiquado

long-term *adj* longo prazo

look *n* olhada, aspecto

look *v* olhar; parecer

look after *v* cuidar de

look at *v* olhar para

look down *v* menosprezar

look for *v* procurar
look forward *v* esperar
look into *v* examinar
look out *v* observar
look over *v* examinar
look through *v* passar os olhos
looking glass *n* espelho
looks *n* beleza
loom *n* tear
loom *v* assomar
loophole *n* buraco, fenda
loose *v* afrouxar, soltar
loose *adj* solto, frouxo
loosen *v* desatar, afrouxar
loot *v* saquear
loot *n* saquear
lord *n* senhor, lorde
lordship *n* senhoria
lose *iv* perder
loser *n* perdedor
loss *n* perda
lot *n* sort, destino
lotion *n* loção
lots *adj* muito
lottery *n* loteria
loud *adj* alto, berrante
loudly *adv* ruidosamente
loudspeaker *n* alto-falante
lounge *n* sala de estar
louse *n* piolho
lousy *adj* piolhento
lovable *adj* adorável

love *v* amar
love *n* amor
lovely *adj* encantador
lover *n* amante
loving *adj* amoroso
low *adj* baixo, inferior
low key *adj* reservado
lower *adj* mais baixo
lowly *adj* humildemente
loyal *adj* leal
loyalty *n* lealdade
lubricate *v* lubrificar
lubrication *n* lubrificação
lucid *adj* lúcido
luck *n* sorte, acaso
lucky *adj* sortudo
lucrative *adj* lucrativo
ludicrous *adj* ridículo
luggage *n* bagagem
lukewarm *adj* tépido, morno
lull *n* calmaria
lumber *n* traste; madeira
luminous *adj* luminoso
lump *n* inchaço
lump sum *n* quantia total
lump together *v* amontoar
lunacy *n* loucura
lunatic *adj* lunático
lunch *n* almoço
lung *n* pulmão
lure *v* atrair
lurid *adj* chamativo

L

lurk *v* esconder-se
lush *adj* viçoso
lust *v* desejar
lust *n* lascívia
lustful *adj* lascivo, desejoso
luxurious *adj* luxuoso
luxury *n* luxo
lynch *v* linchar
lynx *n* lince
lyrics *n* letra de música

machine *n* máquina
machine gun *n* metralhadora
mad *adj* louco
madam *n* madame, senhora
madden *v* enlouquecer
madly *adv* loucamente
madman *n* louco
madness *n* loucura
magazine *n* revista
magic *n* mágica, magia
magical *adj* mágico
magician *n* mágico
magistrate *n* magistrado
magnet *n* ímã
magnetic *adj* magnético

magnetism *n* magnetismo
magnificent *adj* magnificente
magnify *v* ampliar, exaltar
magnitude *n* magnitude
maiden *n* donzela, moça
mail *v* enviar por correio
mail *n* correio
mailbox *n* caixa de correio
mailman *n* carteiro
maim *v* aleijar
main *adj* principal
mainland *n* continente
mainly *adv* principalmente
maintain *v* manter
maintenance *n* manutenção
majestic *adj* majestoso
majesty *n* majestade
major *n* maioria, major
major *adj* principal
majority *n* maioridade
make *n* marca
make *iv* fazer, tornar, ser
make up *v* inventar
make up for *v* compensar
maker *n* fabricante
makeup *n* maquiagem
malaria *n* malária
male *n* macho
malevolent *adj* malevolente
malice *n* malícia
malign *v* falar mal de
malignancy *n* malignidade

malignant *adj* maligno
malnutrition *n* desnutrição
malpractice *v* negligenciar
mammal *n* mamífero
mammoth *n* mamute
man *n* homem
manage *v* administrar
manageable *adj* controlável
management *n* administração
manager *n* diretor, dirigente
mandate *n* mandato, ordem
mandatory *adj* mandatório
maneuver *n* manobra
manger *n* manjedoura
mangle *v* estraçalhar
manhandle *v* maltratar
manhunt *n* perseguição
maniac *adj* maníaco
manifest *v* manifestar
manipulate *v* manipular
mankind *n* humanidade
manliness *n* virilidade
manly *adj* viril
manner *n* maneira, estilo
mannerism *n* maneirismo
manners *n* educação
mansion *n* mansão
manslaughter *n* homicídio
manual *n* manual
manual *adj* manual
manufacture *v* fabricar
manure *n* esterco

manuscript *n* manuscrito
many *adj* muitos
map *n* mapa
marble *n* mármore
march *v* marchar
march *n* marcha
March *n* Março
mare *n* égua
margin *n* margem
marginal *adj* marginal
marinate *v* marinar
marine *adj* marinho
marital *adj* marital
mark *n* marca, sinal
mark *v* marcar, assinalar
mark down *v* baixar preço
marker *n* marcador
market *n* mercado, feira
marksman *n* atirador
marmalade *n* geléia
marriage *n* casamento
married *adj* casado
marrow *n* tutano, medula
marry *v* casar
Mars *n* Marte
marshal *n* marechal
martyr *n* mártir
martyrdom *n* martírio
marvel *n* maravilha
marvelous *adj* maravilhoso
Marxist *adj* marxista
masculine *adj* masculino

M

mash *v* esmagar

mask *n* máscara

masochism *n* masoquismo

mason *n* pedreiro, maçom

masquerade *v* disfarçar-se

mass *n* massa; montes

massacre *n* massacre

massage *n* massagem

massage *v* massagear

masseur *n* massagista

masseuse *n* massagista

massive *adj* maciço

mast *n* mastro

master *n* patrão; amo

master *v* dominar

mastermind *n* mentor, cabeça

mastermind *v* planejar

masterpiece *n* obra-prima

mastery *n* mestria, perícia

mat *n* capacho, tapete

match *n* fósforo; partida

match *v* igualar, emparelhar

mate *n* cônjuge, mate

material *n* material

materialism *n* materialismo

maternal *adj* maternal

maternity *n* maternidade

math *n* matemática

matriculate *v* matricular

matrimony *n* matrimônio

matter *n* assunto; pus

mattress *n* colchão

mature *adj* maduro

maturity *n* maturidade

maul *v* lacerar; espancar

maxim *n* máxima

maximum *adj* máximo

May *n* Maio

may *iv* ser possível

may-be *adv* talvez

mayor *n* prefeito

maze *n* labirinto

meadow *n* prado, campina

meager *adj* insuficiente

meal *n* refeição; farinha

mean *iv* significar

mean *adj* mesquinho

meaning *n* sentido, significado

meaningful *adj* significativo

meaningless *adj* sem sentido

meanness *n* mesquinharia

means *n* meios

meantime *adv* nesse ínterim

measles *n* sarampo

measure *v* medir, avaliar

measurement *n* medida

meat *n* carne

meatball *n* almôndega

mechanic *n* mecânico

mechanism *n* mecanismo

mechanize *v* mecanizar

medal *n* medalha

medallion *n* medalhão

meddle *v* interferir

mediate *v* mediar
mediator *n* mediador
medication *n* medicação
medicinal *adj* medicinal
medicine *n* medicina
medieval *adj* medieva
mediocre *adj* medíocre
mediocrity *n* mediocridade
meditate *v* meditar
meditation *n* meditação
medium *adj* médio
meek *adj* dócil
meekness *n* docilidade
meet *iv* encontrar
meeting *n* encontro, reunião
melancholy *n* melancolia
mellow *adj* meigo; suave
mellow *v* amadurecer
melodic *adj* melódico
melody *n* melodia
melon *n* melão
melt *v* derreter
member *n* membro
membrane *n* membrana
memento *n* recordação
memo *n* memorando
memoirs *n* memórias
memorable *adj* memorável
memorize *v* memorizar
memory *n* memórias
men *n* homens
menace *n* ameaça

mend *v* remendar
meningitis *n* meningite
menopause *n* menopausa
menstruation *n* menstruação
mental *adj* mental
mentality *n* mentalidade
mentally *adv* mentalmente
mention *v* mencionar
mention *n* menção
menu *n* menu
merchandise *n* mercadoria
merchant *n* comerciante
merciful *adj* misericordioso
merciless *adj* impiedoso
mercury *n* mercúrio
mercy *n* misericórdia
merely *adv* meramente
merge *v* fundir-se
merger *n* fusão
merit *n* mérito
merit *v* merecer
mermaid *n* sereia
merry *adj* alegre, jovial
mesh *n* malha
mesmerize *v* hipnotizar
mess *n* bagunça
mess up *v* bagunçar
message *n* mensagem
messenger *n* mensageiro
Messiah *n* Messias
messy *adj* bagunçado
metal *n* metal

M

metallic *adj* metálico

metaphor *n* metáfora

meteor *n* meteoro

meter *n* metro; contador

method *n* método

methodical *adj* metódico

meticulous *adj* meticuloso

metric *adj* métrico

metropolis *n* metrópole

Mexican *adj* mexicano

mice *n* ratos

microbe *n* micróbio

microphone *n* microfone

microscope *n* microscópio

microwave *n* microondas

midday *n* meio-dia

middle *n* meio

middleman *n* intermediário

midget *n* anão

midnight *n* meia-noite

midsummer *n* pleno verão

midwife *n* parteira

mighty *adj* poderoso

migraine *n* enxaqueca

migrant *n* migrante

migrate *v* migrar

mild *adj* brando, meigo

mildew *n* mofo, bolor

mile *n* milha

mileage *n* milhagem

milestone *n* marco

militant *adj* militante

milk *n* leite

milky *adj* leitoso

mill *n* moinho

millennium *n* milênio

milligram *n* miligrama

millimeter *n* milímetro

million *n* milhão

millionaire *adj* milionário

mime *v* mimicar

mince *v* picar fininho

mincemeat *n* picadinho

mind *v* tomar conta

mind *n* mente, espírito

mind-boggling *adj* surpreendente

mindful *adj* atento, cuidadoso

mindless *adj* insensato

mine *n* mina

mine *v* extrair, minar

mine *pro* meu, minha

minefield *n* campo minado

miner *n* meneiro

mineral *n* mineral

mingle *v* misturar-se

miniature *n* miniatura

minimize *v* minimizar

minimum *n* mínimo

miniskirt *n* minissaia

minister *n* ministro, pastor

minister *v* atender, ministrar

ministry *n* ministério

minor *adj* menor

minority *n* minoria**

M

mint *n* menta
mint *v* cunhar moeda
minus *adj* negativo
minute *n* minuto; ata
miracle *n* milagre
miraculous *adj* milagroso
mirage *n* miragem
mirror *n* espelho
misbehave *v* comportar-se mal
miscalculate *v* calcular mal
miscarriage *n* aborto, malogro
miscarry *v* abortar; falhar
mischief *n* travessura; dano
mischievous *adj* travesso; danoso
misconduct *n* má conduta
misconstrue *v* interpretar mal
misdemeanor *n* delito leve
miser *n* avarento
miserable *adj* miserável
misery *n* miséria
misfit *adj* desajustado
misfortune *n* infortúnio
misgiving *n* apreensão
misguided *adj* desencaminhado
misinterpret *v* interpretar mal
misjudge *v* julgar mal
mislead *v* enganar
misleading *adj* enganoso
mismanage *v* administrar mal
misplace *v* extraviar
misprint *n* erro de impressão
miss *v* errar; perder; falhar

miss *n* senhorita
missile *n* míssil, projétil
missing *adj* desaparecido
mission *n* mission
missionary *n* missionário
mist *n* névoa
mistake *iv* confundir
mistake *n* erro
mistaken *adj* errado
mister *n* senhor
mistreat *v* maltratar
mistreatment *n* maltrato
mistress *n* amante, patroa
mistrust *n* desconfiança
mistrust *v* desconfiar
misty *adj* nebuloso
misunderstand *v* entender mal
misuse *n* mau uso
mitigate *v* mitigar
mix *v* misturar
mixed-up *adj* confuso
mixer *n* misturador
mixture *n* mistura
mix-up *n* confusão
moan *v* lamentar, gemer
moan *n* gemido, lamento
mob *v* rodear
mob *n* multidão
mobile *adj* móvel, portátil
mobilize *v* mobilizar
mobster *n* brigão, agressor
mock *v* zombar

M

mockery *n* zombaria
mode *n* modo, meio
model *n* modelo, manequin
moderate *adj* moderado, médio
moderation *n* moderação
modern *adj* moderno
modernize *v* modernizar
modest *adj* modesto
modesty *n* modéstia
modify *v* modificar
module *n* módulo
moisten *v* umedecer
moisture *n* umidade
molar *n* molar
mold *v* moldar
moldy *adj* mofado
mole *n* verruga; toupeira
molecule *n* molécula
molest *v* molestar
mom *n* mãe
moment *n* momento
momentous *adj* importante
monarch *n* monarca
monarchy *n* monarquia
monastery *n* monastério
monastic *adj* monástico
Monday *n* Segunda-feira
money *n* dinheiro
money order *n* vale postal
monitor *v* monitorar
monk *n* monge
monkey *n* macaco

monogamy *n* monogamia
monologue *n* monólogo
monopolize *v* monopolizar
monopoly *n* monopólio
monotonous *adj* monótono
monotony *n* monotonia
monster *n* monstro
monstrous *adj* monstruoso
month *n* mês
monthly *adv* mensal
monument *n* monumento
monumental *adj* monumental
mood *n* humor
moody *adj* mal-humorado
moon *n* lua
moor *v* amarrar
mop *v* esfregar, limpar
moral *adj* virtuoso
moral *n* moral
morality *n* moralidade
more *adj* mais
moreover *adv* mais
morning *n* manhã
moron *adj* bobão
morphine *n* morfina
morsel *n* bocado
mortal *adj* mortal
mortality *n* mortalidade
mortar *n* morteiro
mortgage *n* hipoteca
mortification *n* mortificação
mortify *v* mortificar

mortuary _n_ necrotério
mosaic _n_ mosaico
mosque _n_ mesquita
mosquito _n_ mosquito
moss _n_ musgo
most _adj_ mais; a maioria
mostly _adv_ principalmente
motel _n_ motel
moth _n_ mariposa, traça
mother _n_ mãe
motherhood _n_ maternidade
mother-in-law _n_ sogra
motion _n_ movimento, gesto
motionless _adj_ imóvel
motivate _v_ motivar
motive _n_ motivo
motor _n_ motor
motorcycle _n_ motocicleta
motto _n_ lema, mote
mount _n_ monte; montaria
mount _v_ montar, instalar
mountain _n_ montanha
mountainous _adj_ montanhoso
mourn _v_ estar de luto
mourning _n_ luto
mouse _n_ rato, mouse
mouth _n_ boca, embocadura
move _n_ lance; mudança
move _v_ mover, mudar
move back _v_ voltar, regressar
move forward _v_ avançar
move out _v_ mudar-se

move up _v_ promover
movement _n_ movimento
movie _n_ filme
mow _v_ cortar grama
much _adv_ muito
mucus _n_ muco, catarro
mud _n_ lama
muddle _n_ desordem
muddy _adj_ enlameado
muffle _v_ abafar
muffler _n_ cachecol
mug _n_ caneca; cara
mug _v_ assaltar
mugging _n_ assalto, roubo
mule _n_ mula
multiple _adj_ múltiplo
multiplication _n_ multiplicação
multiply _v_ multiplicar
multitude _n_ multidão
mumble _v_ resmungar
mummy _n_ múmia
mumps _n_ caxumba
munch _v_ mastigar
munitions _n_ munições
murder _n_ assassinato
murderer _n_ assassino
murky _adj_ escuro
murmur _v_ murmurar
murmur _n_ murmúrio
muscle _n_ músculo
museum _n_ museu
mushroom _n_ cogumelo

M

music *n* música
musician *n* músico
Muslim *adj* muçulmano
must *iv* dever
mustache *n* bigode
mustard *n* mostarda
muster *v* reunir, juntar
mutate *v* mudar, transformar
mute *adj* mudo
mutilate *v* mutilar
mutiny *n* motim
mutually *adv* mutualmente
muzzle *v* pôr focinheira
muzzle *n* focinheira, focinho
my *adj* meu, minha
myopic *adj* míope
myself *pro* me, eu mesmo
mysterious *adj* misterioso
mystery *n* mistério
mystic *adj* místico
mystify *v* mistificar, iludir
myth *n* mito, lenda

N

nag *v* incomodar
nagging *adj* irritante
nail *n* unha; prego
naive *adj* ingênuo, singelo
naked *adj* nu
name *n* nome; fama
namely *adv* isto é
nanny *n* babá, ama
nap *n* soneca, cochilo
napkin *n* guardanapo
narcotic *n* narcótico
narrate *v* narrar
narrow *adj* estreito
narrowly *adv* por um triz
nasty *adj* sórdido
nation *n* nação
national *adj* nacional
nationality *n* nacionalidade
nationalize *v* nacionalizar
native *adj* nativo, natal
natural *adj* natural
naturally *adv* naturalmente
nature *n* natureza
naughty *adj* malcriado
nausea *n* náusea
nave *n* nave
navel *n* umbigo
navigate *v* navegar, pilotar
navigation *n* navegação

navy *n* marinha
navy blue *adj* azul marinho
near *pre* perto de
nearby *adj* perto de
nearly *adv* quase
nearsighted *adj* míope
neat *adj* arrumado, correto
neatly *adv* caprichosamente
necessary *adj* necessário
necessitate *v* necessitar
necessity *n* necessidade
neck *n* percoço, gola
necklace *n* colar
necktie *n* gravata
need *v* necessitar
need *n* necessidade
needle *n* agulha
needless *adj* supérfluo
needy *adj* necessitado
negative *adj* negativo
neglect *v* negligenciar
neglect *n* negligência
negligence *n* negligência
negligent *adj* negligente
negotiate *v* negociar
negotiation *n* negociação
neighbor *n* vizinho
neighborhood *n* bairro
neither *adj* nenhum dos dois
neither *adv* tampouco
nephew *n* sobrinho
nerve *n* nervo; coragem

nervous *adj* nervoso
nest *n* ninho
net *n* rede
Netherlands *n* Holanda
network *n* rede
neurotic *adj* neurótico
neutral *adj* neutro
neutralize *v* neutralizar
never *adv* nunca
nevertheless *adv* apesar de tudo
new *adj* novo
newborn *n* recém-nascido
newcomer *n* recém-chegado
newly *adv* recentemente
newlywed *adj* recém-casado
news *n* notícias, novidades
newscast *n* noticiário
newsletter *n* circular
newspaper *n* jornal
newsstand *n* banca de jornal
next *adj* próximo, seguinte
next door *adj* vizinho
nibble *v* mordiscar
nice *adj* bonito, bom
nickel *n* níquel
nickname *n* apelido
nicotine *n* nicotina
niece *n* sobrinha
night *n* noite
nightfall *n* crepúsculo
nightgown *n* camisola
nightingale *n* rouxinol

N

nightmare *n* pesadelo
nine *adj* nove
nineteen *adj* dezenove
ninety *adj* noventa
ninth *adj* nono
nip *n* pinçada, mordida
nip *v* morder, pinçar
nipple *n* mamilo; chupeta
nitpicking *adj* minucioso
nitrogen *n* nitrogênio
no one *pro* ninguém
nobility *n* nobreza
noble *adj* nobre
nobleman *n* nobre
nobody *pro* ninguém
nocturnal *adj* noturno
nod *v* cabecear
noise *n* barulho, ruído
noisily *adv* ruidosamente
noisy *adj* ruidoso
nominate *v* nomear
none *pre* nenhum
nonetheless *c* apesar disso
nonsense *n* disparate
nonsmoker *n* não-fumante
nonstop *adv* direto
noon *n* meio-dia
noose *n* nó corredio
nor *c* nem
norm *n* norma
normal *adj* normal
normalize *v* normalizar

normally *adv* normalmente
north *n* norte
northeast *n* nordeste
northern *adj* do norte
northerner *adj* nortista
Norway *n* Noruega
Norwegian *adj* norueguês
nose *n* nariz, offato
nostalgia *n* nostalgia
nostril *n* narina
nosy *adj* intrometido
not *adv* não, que não
notable *adj* notável
notably *adv* particularmente
notary *n* notário, tabelião
notation *n* notação, anotação
note *v* anotar, notar
notebook *n* caderno
noteworthy *adj* notável
nothing *n* nada, zero
notice *v* notar
notice *n* aviso, anúncio
noticeable *adj* visível
notification *n* notificação
notify *v* notificar
notion *n* noção
notorious *adj* notório
noun *n* nome, substantivo
nourish *v* nutrir
nourishment *n* alimento
novel *n* novela
novelist *n* romancista**

novelty *n* novidade
November *n* Novembro
novice *n* noviço
now *adv* agora
nowadays *adv* atualmente
nowhere *adv* em nenhum lugar
noxious *adj* nóxio, nocivo
nozzle *n* esguicho
nuance *n* nuance
nuclear *adj* nuclear
nude *adj* nu
nudism *n* nudismo
nudist *n* nudista
nudity *n* nudez
nuisance *n* amolação
null *adj* nulo
nullify *v* anular
numb *adj* entorpecido
number *n* número
numbness *n* entorpecimento
numerous *adj* numeroso
nun *n* freira
nurse *n* enfermeiro; ama
nurse *v* cuidar, amamentar
nursery *n* berçário
nurture *v* nutrir
nut *n* noz; porca
nutrition *n* nutrição
nutritious *adj* nutritivo
nut-shell *n* casca de noz
nutty *adj* pirado, doido

oak *n* carvalho
oar *n* remo
oasis *n* oásis
oath *n* juramento
obedience *n* obediência
obedient *adj* obediente
obese *adj* obeso
obey *v* obedecer
object *v* objetar
object *n* objeto
objection *n* objeção
objective *n* objetivo
obligate *v* obrigar, coagir
obligation *n* obrigação
obligatory *adj* obrigatório
oblige *v* obrigar
obliged *adj* obrigado, forçado
oblique *adj* oblíquo, indireto
obliterate *v* apagar, arrasar
oblivion *n* oblívio
oblivious *adj* esquecido
oblong *adj* retangular
obnoxious *adj* detestável
obscene *adj* obsceno
obscenity *n* obscenidade
obscure *adj* obscuro
obscurity *n* obscuridade
observation *n* observação
observatory *n* observatório

N
O

observe *v* observar
obsess *v* obsedar, obcecar
obsession *n* obsessão
obsolete *adj* obsoleto
obstacle *n* obstáculo
obstinacy *n* obstinação
obstinate *adj* obstinado
obstruct *v* obstruir
obstruction *n* obstruição
obtain *v* obter
obvious *adj* óbvio
obviously *adv* obviamente
occasion *n* ocasião
occasionally *adv* ocasionalmente
occult *adj* oculto
occupant *n* ocupante
occupation *n* ocupação
occupy *v* ocupar
occur *v* ocorrer
occurrence *n* ocorrência
ocean *n* oceano
October *n* Outubro
octopus *n* polvo
odd *adj* estranho, ímpar
oddity *n* pessoa excêntrica
odds *n* probabilidade
odious *adj* odioso
odometer *n* hodômetro
odor *n* odor, cheiro
odyssey *n* odisséia
of *pre* detestável
offend *v* ofender

offense *n* ofensa
offensive *adj* ofensivo
offer *v* oferecer
offer *n* oferta
offering *n* oferenda
office *n* escritório
officer *n* funcionário
official *adj* oficial
officiate *v* oficiar
offset *v* compensar
offspring *n* descendência
often *adv* freqüentemente
oil *n* óleo; petróleo
ointment *n* ungüento
okay *adv* tudo bem
old *adj* velho, antigo
old age *n* velhice
old-fashioned *adj* fora de moda
olive *n* oliva, azeitona
Olympics *n* Olimpíada
omelet *n* omelete
omen *n* presságio
ominous *adj* agourento
omission *n* omissão
omit *v* omitir
on *pre* sobre, em
once *adv* uma vez
once *c* uma vez que
one *adj* um
oneself *pre* si, si mesmo
ongoing *adj* em curso
onion *n* cebola

onlooker *n* espectador
only *adv* apenas, só
onset *n* início
onslaught *n* ataque
onwards *adv* para a frente
opaque *adj* opaco
open *v* abrir
open *adj* aberto
open up *v* abrir
opening *n* abertura
open-minded *adj* liberal
openness *n* franqueza
opera *n* ópera
operate *v* operar
operation *n* operação
opinion *n* opinião
opium *n* ópio
opponent *n* oponente
opportune *adj* oportuno
opportunity *n* oportunidade
oppose *v* opor
opposite *adj* oposto
opposite *adv* em frente a
opposite *n* contrário
opposition *n* oposição
oppress *v* oprimir
oppression *n* opressão
opt for *v* optar por
optical *adj* óptico
optician *n* óptico
optimism *n* otimismo
optimistic *adj* otimista

option *n* opção
optional *adj* opcional
opulence *n* opulência
or *c* ou, senão
oracle *n* oráculo
orally *adv* oralmente
orange *n* laranja
orangutan *n* orangutango
orbit *n* órbita
orchard *n* pomar
orchestra *n* orquestra
ordain *v* ordenar
ordeal *n* provação
order *n* ordem, pedido
ordinarily *adv* comumente
ordinary *adj* comum, medíocre
ordination *n* ordenação
ore *n* minério
organ *n* órgão
organism *n* organismo
organist *n* organista
organization *n* organização
organize *v* organizar
orient *n* oriente
oriental *adj* oriental
orientation *n* orientação
oriented *adj* orientado
origin *n* origem
original *adj* original
originally *adv* originalmente
originate *v* originar
ornament *n* ornamento**

O

ornamental *adj* ornamental
orphan *n* órfão
orphanage *n* orfanato
orthodox *adj* convencional
ostentatious *adj* ostentoso
ostrich *n* avestruz
other *adj* outro
otherwise *adv* senão
otter *n* lontra
ought to *iv* dever
ounce *n* onça
our *adj* nosso, nossa
ours *pro* nosso, nossa
ourselves *pro* nos
oust *v* desalojar
out *adv* fora, longe
outbreak *n* deflagração
outburst *n* explosão
outcast *adj* proscrito
outcome *n* resultado
outcry *n* protesto
outdated *adj* obsoleto
outdo *v* exceder
outdoor *adv* de sair
outdoors *adv* fora
outer *adj* externo
outfit *n* traje
outgoing *adj* extrovertido
outgrow *v* superar
outing *n* saída, passeio
outlast *v* sobreviver
outlet *n* saída

outline *n* contorno, resumo
outline *v* delinear, esboçar
outlive *v* sobreviver
outlook *n* panorama, vista
outmoded *adj* antiquado
outnumber *v* exceder
outpouring *n* efusão, expansão
output *n* produção
outrage *n* ultraje, atentado
outrageous *adj* abusivo
outrun *v* correr mais
outset *n* início
outshine *v* eclipsar
outside *adv* fora, por fora
outsider *n* forasteiro
outskirts *n* arredores
outspoken *adj* franco
outstanding *adj* notável, saliente
outstretched *adj* distendido
outward *adj* exterior, de ida
outweigh *v* pesar mais
oval *adj* oval
ovary *n* ovário
ovation *n* ovação
oven *n* forno
over *pre* acima de
overall *adv* macacão
overbearing *adj* arrogante
overboard *adv* ao mar
overcast *adj* nublado
overcharge *v* cobrar caro
overcoat *n* sobretudo

overcome *v* comovido
overcrowded *adj* superlotado
overdo *v* exagerar
overdone *adj* cozido demais
overdose *n* overdose
overdue *adj* atrasado
overestimate *v* superestimar
overflow *v* transbordar
overhaul *v* revisar
overlap *v* sobrepor
overlook *v* olhar de cima
overnight *adv* durante a noite
overpower *v* subjugar
overrate *v* superestimar
override *v* cancelar
overrule *v* invalidar, revogar
overrun *v* infestar, exceder
overseas *adv* além-mar
oversee *v* supervisar
overshadow *v* ofuscar
oversight *n* inadvertência
overstate *v* exagerar
overstep *v* ultrapassar
overtake *v* alcançar
overthrow *v* derrubar, destronar
overthrow *n* derrota
overtime *adv* hora extra
overturn *v* virar, emborcar
overview *n* visão geral
overweight *adj* sobrepeso
overwhelm *v* oprimir, esmagar
owe *v* dever

owing to *adv* devido a
owl *n* coruja
own *v* ter, possuir
own *adj* próprio
owner *n* dono, proprietário
ownership *n* propriedade
ox *n* boi, bovino
oxen *n* bois
oxygen *n* oxigênio
oyster *n* ostra

P

pace *v* andar a passo
pace *n* ritmo
pacify *v* apaziguar
pack *v* empacotar
package *n* pacote
pact *n* pacto
pad *v* rechear, forrar
padding *n* enchimento
paddle *v* remar
padlock *n* cadeado
pagan *adj* pagão
page *n* página; pagem
pail *n* balde
pain *n* dor
painful *adj* doloroso

O

painkiller *n* analgésico
painless *adj* indolor
paint *v* pintar
paint *n* tinta
paintbrush *n* pincel
painter *n* pintor
painting *n* pintura
pair *n* par
pajamas *n* pijama
pal *n* colega, companheiro
palace *n* palácio
palate *n* paladar, palato
pale *adj* pálido
paleness *n* palidez
palm *n* palma
palpable *adj* palpável
paltry *adj* torpe, irrisório
pamper *v* mimar
pamphlet *n* panfleto, folheto
pan *n* panela
pancreas *n* pâncreas
pander *v* alcovitar
pang *n* pontada
panic *n* pânico
panorama *n* panorama
panther *n* pantera
pantry *n* despensa
pants *n* calças
pantyhose *n* meia-calça
papacy *n* papado
paper *n* papel
paperclip *n* clipe de papel

paperwork *n* papelada
parable *n* parábola
parachute *n* pára-quedas
parade *n* parada, desfile
paradise *n* paraíso
paradox *n* paradoxo
paragraph *n* parágrafo
parakeet *n* periquito
parallel *n* paralelo
paralysis *n* paralisia
paralyze *v* paralisar
parameters *n* parâmetros
paramount *adj* supremo
paranoid *adj* paranóico
parasite *n* parasita
paratrooper *n* pára-quedista
parcel *n* pacote
parcel post *n* encomenda postal
parch *v* ressecar
parchment *n* pergaminho
pardon *v* perdoar
pardon *n* perdão, indulto
parenthesis *n* parêntesis
parents *n* pais
parish *n* paróquia
parishioner *n* paroquiano
parity *n* paridade
park *v* estacionar
park *n* parque, jardim
parking *n* estacionamento
parliament *n* parlamento
parochial *adj* paroquial

parrot *n* louro
parsley *n* salsa
parsnip *n* pastinaca
part *v* separar, partir
part *n* parte, papel
partial *adj* parcial
partially *adv* parcialmente
participate *v* participar
participation *n* participação
participle *n* particípio
particle *n* partícula
particular *adj* particular
particularly *adv* particularmente
parting *n* divisão, ruptura
partisan *n* partidário
partition *n* divisória, divisão
partly *adv* em parte
partner *n* parceiro, sócio
partnership *n* parceria
partridge *n* perdiz
party *n* partido, festa
pass *n* passe; garganta
pass *v* passar, aprovar
pass around *v* distribuir
pass away *v* morrer
pass out *v* desmaiar
passage *n* passagem
passenger *n* passageiro
passer-by *n* passante
passion *n* paixão
passionate *adj* apaixonado
passive *adj* passivo

passport *n* passaporte
password *n* senha
past *adj* passado
paste *v* colar
paste *n* cola; pasta; massa
pasteurize *v* pasteurizar
pastime *n* passatempo
pastor *n* pastor
pastoral *adj* pastoral
pasture *n* pasto
pat *n* tapinha
patch *v* remendar
patch *n* remendo
patent *n* patente
patent *adj* patente; óbvio
paternity *n* paternidade
path *n* caminho, trilha
pathetic *adj* patético
patience *n* paciência
patient *adj* paciente
patio *n* pátio, pórtico
patriarch *n* patriarca
patrimony *n* patrimônio
patriot *n* patriota
patriotic *adj* patriótico
patrol *n* patrulha
patron *n* patrono
patronage *n* patrocínio
patronize *v* patrocinar
pattern *n* padrão, modelo
pavement *n* pavimento
pavilion *n* pavilhão

P

paw *n* pata
pawn *v* penhorar
pawnbroker *n* penhorista
pay *n* remuneração
pay *iv* pagar
pay back *v* reembolsar
pay off *v* subornar
pay slip *n* contracheque
payable *adj* pagável
payee *n* recebedor
payment *n* pagamento
payroll *n* folha de pagamento
pea *n* ervilha
peace *n* paz
peaceful *adj* tranqüilo
peach *n* pêssego
peacock *n* pavão
peak *n* pico, apogeu
peanut *n* amendoim
pear *n* pêra
pearl *n* pérola
peasant *n* camponês
pebble *n* pedregulho
peck *v* bicar; beliscar
peck *n* bicada; beijoca
peculiar *adj* estranho, singular
pedagogy *n* pedagogia
pedal *n* pedal
pedantic *adj* pedante
pedestrian *n* pedestre
peel *v* descascar
peel *n* casca

peep *v* espreitar, espiar
peer *n* par do reino, par
pelican *n* pelicano
pellet *n* grânulo; pelota
pen *n* caneta, pena
penalize *v* penalizar
penalty *n* penalty, penalidade
penance *n* penitência
penchant *n* propensão
pencil *n* lápis
pendant *n* pingente
pending *adj* pendente
pendulum *n* pêndulo
penetrate *v* penetrar
penguin *n* pingüim
penicillin *n* penicilina
peninsula *n* península
penitent *n* penitente
penniless *adj* sem um tostão
penny *n* centavo, pêni
pension *n* pensão
pentagon *n* pentágono
pent-up *adj* retido, preso
people *n* pessoas, povo
pepper *n* pimenta, pimentão
per *pre* por
perceive *v* perceber
percent *adv* por cento
percentage *n* percentagem
perception *n* percepção
perennial *adj* perene
perfect *adj* perfeito

P

perfection *n* perfeição
perforate *v* perfurar
perforation *n* perfuração
perform *v* representar; executar
performance *n* desempenho
perfume *n* perfume
perhaps *adv* talvez
peril *n* perigo
perilous *adj* perigoso
perimeter *n* perímetro
period *n* período
perish *v* perecer
perishable *adj* perecível
perjury *n* perjúrio
permanent *adj* permanente
permeate *v* permear
permission *n* permissão
permit *v* permitir
pernicious *adj* pernicioso
perpetrate *v* perpetrar
persecute *v* perseguir
persevere *v* perseverar
persist *v* persistir
persistence *n* persistência
persistent *adj* persistente
person *n* pessoa
personal *adj* pessoal
personality *n* personalidade
personify *v* personificar
personnel *n* pessoal
perspective *n* perspectiva
perspiration *n* perspiração

perspire *v* suar, perspirar
persuade *v* persuadir
persuasion *n* persuasão
persuasive *adj* persuasivo
pertain *v* pertencer, concernir
pertinent *adj* pertinente
perturb *v* perturbar
perverse *adj* perverso
pervert *v* perverter
pervert *adj* pervertido
pessimism *n* pessimismo
pessimistic *adj* pessimista
pest *n* peste
pester *v* importunar
pesticide *n* pesticida
petal *n* pétala
petite *adj* delicada
petition *n* petição
petrified *adj* petrificado
petroleum *n* petróleo
pettiness *n* mesquinharia
petty *adj* mesquinho; trivial
pew *n* banco de igreja
phantom *n* fantasma
pharmacist *n* farmacêutico
pharmacy *n* farmácia
phase *n* fase
pheasant *n* faisão
phenomenon *n* fenômeno
philosopher *n* filósofo
philosophy *n* filosofia
phobia *n* fobia

P

phone *n* telefone
phone *v* telefonar
phony *adj* falso
phosphorus *n* fósforo
photo *n* foto
photocopy *n* fotocópia, xerox
photograph *v* fotografar
photographer *n* fotógrafo
photography *n* fotografia
phrase *n* frase
physically *adv* fisicamente
physician *n* médico
physics *n* física
pianist *n* pianista
piano *n* piano
pick *v* escolher; catar
pick up *v* captar; levantar
pickpocket *n* batedor de carteira
pickup *n* caminhonete
picture *n* foto, retrato,
picture *v* imaginar
picturesque *adj* pitoresco
pie *n* torta
piece *n* pedaço, peça
piecemeal *adv* em partes
pier *n* cais
pierce *v* perfurar, traspassar
piety *n* piedade, devoção
pig *n* porco
pigeon *n* pombo
piggy bank *n* cofre
pile *v* empilhar

pile *n* pilha, estaca
pile up *v* empilhar
pilfer *v* roubar, furtar
pilgrim *n* peregrino
pilgrimage *n* peregrinação
pill *n* pílula
pillage *v* pilhar, saquear
pillar *n* pilar
pillow *n* travesseiro
pillowcase *n* fronha
pilot *n* piloto
pimple *n* espinha, empola
pin *n* alfinete
pincers *n* alicate, pinça
pinch *v* beliscar, apertar
pinch *n* beliscão, pitada
pine *n* pinheiro, pinho
pineapple *n* abacaxi
pink *adj* rosada
pinpoint *v* localizar
pint *n* quartilho
pioneer *n* pioneiro
pious *adj* pio, piedoso
pipe *n* cano; flauta
pipeline *n* duto
piracy *n* pirataria
pirate *n* pirata
pistol *n* pistola
pit *n* buraco, cova
pitchfork *n* forcado
pitfall *n* alçapão
pitiful *adj* lamentável

P

pity *n* pena
placard *n* cartaz
placate *v* aplacar
place *n* lugar, local
placid *adj* plácido
plague *n* praga, peste
plain *n* planície
plain *adj* simples, comum
plainly *adv* simplesmente
plaintiff *n* demandante
plan *v* planejar, projetar
plan *n* plano, planta
plane *n* avião, plano
planet *n* planeta
plant *v* plantar
plant *n* planta
plaster *n* reboco, emplastro
plaster *v* rebocar, emplastrar
plastic *n* plástico
plate *n* prato; chapa; placa
plateau *n* planalto
platform *n* plataforma
platinum *n* platina
platoon *n* pelotão
plausible *adj* plausível
play *v* jogar; tocar
play *n* lazer; peça; jogo
player *n* jogador
playful *adj* brincalhão
playground *n* playground
plea *n* apelo; alegação
plead *v* alegar, suplicar

pleasant *adj* agradável
please *v* agradar, aprazar
pleasing *adj* agradável
pleasure *n* prazer
pleat *n* prega
pleated *adj* pregueado
pledge *v* prometer; penhorar
pledge *n* penhor, sinal
plentiful *adj* pleno, abundante
plenty *adv* bastante, muito
pliable *adj* flexível
pliers *n* alicate
plot *v* tramar; traçar
plot *n* trama; lote
plow *v* arar
ploy *n* estratagema
pluck *v* arrancarcolher
plug *v* tapar; ligar
plug *n* plugue; tampão
plum *n* ameixa
plumber *n* encanador
plumbing *n* encanamento
plummet *v* cair
plump *adj* rechonchudo
plunder *v* saquear
plunge *v* mergulhar, imergir
plunge *n* mergulho, salto
plural *n* plural
plus *adv* mais
plush *adj* felpudo
plutonium *n* plutônio
pneumonia *n* pneumonia

P

pocket *n* bolso, bolsa
poem *n* poema
poet *n* poeta
poetry *n* poesia
poignant *adj* pungente
point *n* ponta, cabo, ponto
point *v* apontar
pointed *adj* pontudo
pointless *adj* sem sentido
poise *n* equilibrar
poison *v* envenenar
poison *n* veneno
poisoning *n* envenenamento
poisonous *adj* venenoso
Poland *n* Polônia
polar *adj* polar
pole *n* pólo
police *n* polícia
policeman *n* policial
policy *n* política
Polish *adj* polonês
polish *n* polimento, lustre
polish *v* polir, lustrar
polite *adj* educado
politeness *n* polidez
politician *n* político
politics *n* política
poll *n* eleição, votação
pollen *n* pólen
pollute *v* poluir
pollution *n* poluição
polygamist *adj* polígamo

polygamy *n* poligamia
pomegranate *n* romã
pomposity *n* pomposidade
pond *n* lagoa
ponder *v* ponderar
pontiff *n* pontífice
pool *n* piscina, bilhar
pool *v* reunir
poor *n* pobre
poorly *adv* mal
popcorn *n* milho
Pope *n* Papa
poppy *n* papoula
popular *adj* popular
popularize *v* popularizar
populate *v* povoar
population *n* população
porcelain *n* porcelana
porch *n* varanda, pórtico
porcupine *n* porco-espinho
pore *n* poro
pork *n* carne de porco
porous *adj* poroso
port *n* porto
portable *adj* portátil
portent *n* presságio
porter *n* carregador
portion *n* porção, parte
portrait *n* retrato
portray *v* retratar
Portugal *n* Portugal
Portuguese *adj* português

P

pose *v* posar
pose *n* pose
posh *adj* chique
position *n* posição
positive *adj* positivo
possess *v* possuir
possession *n* possessão
possibility *n* possibilidade
possible *adj* possível
post *n* poste; posto
post office *n* correio
postage *n* postagem
postcard *n* cartão postal
poster *n* cartaz
posterity *n* posteridade
postman *n* carteiro
postmark *n* carimbo postal
postpone *v* postergar, adiar
postponement *n* adiamento
pot *n* pote
potato *n* batata
potent *adj* potente
potential *adj* potencial
poultry *n* aves domésticas
pound *v* bater, triturar
pound *n* libra
pour *v* escorrer, fluir, vazar
poverty *n* pobreza
powder *n* pó
power *n* poder; potência
powerful *adj* poderoso
powerless *adj* impotente

practical *adj* prático
practice *v* praticar
practice *n* prática
pragmatist *adj* pragmatista
prairie *n* campina
praise *v* elogiar, louvar
praise *n* elogio, louvor
praiseworthy *adj* louvável
prank *n* peça
prawn *n* camarão grande
pray *v* rezar, suplicar
prayer *n* oração, reza
preach *v* pregar
preacher *n* pregador
preaching *n* sermão
preamble *n* prefácio, prólogo
precarious *adj* precário
precaution *n* precaução
precede *v* preceder
precedent *n* precedente
preceding *adj* precedente
precept *n* preceito
precious *adj* precioso
precipice *n* precipício
precipitate *v* precipitar
precise *adj* preciso
precision *n* precisão
precocious *adj* precoce
precursor *n* precussor
predecessor *n* predecessor
predicament *n* predicamento
predict *v* predizer

P

prediction *n* predição
predilection *n* predileção
predisposed *adj* predisposto
predominate *v* predominar
preempt *v* tomar lugar
prefabricate *v* prefabricar
preface *n* prefácio
prefer *v* preferir
preference *n* preferência
prefix *n* prefixo
pregnancy *n* gravidez
pregnant *adj* grávida
prehistoric *adj* pre-histórico
prejudice *n* preconceito
preliminary *adj* preliminar
prelude *n* prelúdio
premature *adj* prematuro
premeditate *v* premeditar
premeditation *n* premeditação
premise *n* premissa
premises *n* dependências
premonition *n* premonição
preoccupation *n* preocupação
preoccupy *v* preocupar
preparation *n* preparação
prepare *v* preparar
preposition *n* preposição
prerequisite *n* pre-requisito
prerogative *n* prerogativa
prescribe *v* prescrever
prescription *n* prescrição
presence *n* presença

present *adj* atual, presente
present *v* apresentar
presentation *n* apresentação
preserve *v* preservar
preside *v* presidir
presidency *n* presidência
president *n* presidente
press *n* pressão, aperto
press *v* apertar, premer
pressing *adj* urgente
pressure *v* pressionar
pressure *n* pressão
prestige *n* prestígio
presume *v* presumir
presumption *n* presunção
presuppose *v* pressupor
presupposition *n* pressuposição
pretend *v* fingir
pretense *n* pretexto
pretension *n* pretensão
pretty *adj* bonito, belo
prevail *v* prevalecer
prevalent *adj* prevalecente
prevent *v* prevenir
prevention *n* prevenção
preventive *adj* preventivo
preview *n* pré-estréia
previous *adj* antecedente
prey *n* presa
price *n* preço
pricey *adj* caro
prick *v* picar

P

pride *n* orgulho
priest *n* padre, sacerdote
priestess *n* sacerdotisa
priesthood *n* sacerdócio
primacy *n* primacia
primarily *adv* principalmente
prime *adj* primeiro
primitive *adj* primitivo
prince *n* príncipe
princess *n* princesa
principal *adj* principal
principle *n* princípio
print *v* imprimir, estampar
print *n* impressão
printer *n* impressora
printing *n* impressão
prior *adj* prioritário
priority *n* prioridade
prism *n* prisma
prison *n* prisão
prisoner *n* prisioneiro
privacy *n* privacidade
private *adj* privado
privilege *n* privilégio
prize *n* prêmio
probability *n* probabilidade
probable *adj* provável
probe *v* sondar, tentar
problem *n* problema
problematic *adj* problemático
procedure *n* procedimento
proceed *v* prosseguir

proceedings *n* ata, processo
proceeds *n* dinheiro, lucro
process *v* processar
process *n* processo
procession *n* procissão
proclaim *v* proclamar
proclamation *n* proclamação
procrastinate *v* procastinar
procreate *v* procriar
procure *v* conseguir
prod *v* cutucar, incitar
prodigious *adj* prodigioso
prodigy *n* prodígio
produce *v* produzir
produce *n* produção
product *n* produto
production *n* produção
productive *adj* produtivo
profane *adj* profano
profess *v* professar
profession *n* profissão
professional *adj* profissional
professor *n* professor
proficiency *n* proficiência
proficient *adj* proficiente
profile *n* perfil
profit *v* lucrar
profit *n* lucro
profitable *adj* lucrativo
profound *adj* profundo
program *n* programa
programmer *n* programador

P

progress *v* progredir

progress *n* progresso

progressive *adj* progressivo

prohibit *v* proibir

prohibition *n* proibição

project *v* projetar

project *n* projeto

projectile *n* projétil

prologue *n* prólogo

prolong *v* prolongar

promenade *n* passeio público

prominent *adj* proeminente

promiscuous *adj* promíscuo

promise *n* promessa

promote *v* promover

promotion *n* promoção

prompt *adj* pronto, pontual

prone *adj* propenso

pronoun *n* pronome

pronounce *v* pronunciar

proof *n* prova

propaganda *n* propaganda

propagate *v* propagar

propel *v* propelir

propensity *n* inclinação

proper *adj* próprio, correto

properly *adv* devidamente

property *n* propriedade

prophecy *n* profecia

prophet *n* profeta

proportion *n* proporção

proposal *n* proposta

propose *v* propor

proposition *n* proposta

prose *n* prosa

prosecute *v* processar

prospect *n* perspectiva

prosper *v* prosperar

prosperity *n* prosperidade

prosperous *adj* próspero

prostate *n* próstata

prostrate *adj* prostrado

protect *v* protegir

protection *n* proteção

protein *n* proteína

protest *v* protestar

protest *n* protesto

protocol *n* protocolo

prototype *n* protótipo

protract *v* prolongar

protracted *adj* prolongado

protrude *v* salientar-se

proud *adj* orgulhoso

proudly *adv* orgulhosamente

prove *v* provar

proven *adj* provado

proverb *n* provérbio

provide *v* prover

providence *n* providência

providing that *c* contanto que

province *n* província

provision *n* cláusula

provisional *adj* provisório

provocation *n* provocação

P

provoke v provocar
prow n proa
prowl v rondar
prowler n gatuno
proximity n proximidade
proxy n procuração
prudence n prodência
prudent adj prudente
prune v podar
prune n ameixa seca
prurient adj pruriente, lascivo
pseudonym n pseudônimo
psychiatrist n psiquiatra
psychiatry n psiquiatria
psychic adj psíquico
psychology n psicologia
psychopath n psicopata
puberty n puberdade
public adj público
publication n publicação
publicity n publicidade
publicly adv publicamente
publish v publicar
publisher n publicador
pudding n pudim
puerile adj pueril
puff n lufada; pompom
puffy adj inchado
pull v puxar; arrancar
pull down v demolir
pull out v tirar; arrancar
pulley n roldana

pulp n polpa; pasta
pulpit n púlpito
pulsate v pulsar
pulse n pulso
pulverize v pulverizar
pump v bombear
pump n bomba
pumpkin n abóbora
punch v socar; furar
punch n soco; murro
punctual adj pontual
puncture n furo
punish v punir
punishable adj punível
punishment n punição
pupil n pupila; aluno
puppet n marionete
puppy n cachorrinho filhote
purchase v comprar
purchase n compra
pure adj puro
puree n purê
purgatory n purgatório
purge n purgatório
purge v purgar, depurar
purification n purificação
purify v purificar
purity n pureza
purple adj violeta, púrpura
purpose n propósito
purposely adv de propósito
purse n bolsa

P

pursue *v* seguir; ocupar-se
pursuit *n* perseguição
pus *n* pus
push *v* empurrar
pushy *adj* insistente
put *iv* pôr, colocar
put aside *v* por de lado
put away *v* guardar
put off *v* adiar
put out *v* apagar
put up with *v* agüentar
putrid *adj* pútrido, podre
puzzle *n* quebra-cabeças
puzzling *adj* enigmático
pyramid *n* pirâmide
python *n* píton

quagmire *n* pântano; confusão
quail *n* codorna
quake *v* tremer
qualify *v* qualificar
quality *n* qualidade
qualm *n* escrúpulo
quandary *n* dilema
quantity *n* quantidade
quarrel *v* querelar

quarrel *n* briga
quarrelsome *adj* briguento
quarry *n* pedreira; caça
quarter *n* quarto; bairro
quarterly *adj* trimestral
quarters *n* quartel
quash *v* anular, aniquilar
queen *n* rainha
queer *adj* estranho
quell *v* esmagar, mitigar
quench *v* saciar, apagar
quest *n* busca
question *v* perguntar
question *n* pergunta
questionable *adj* discutível
questionnaire *n* questionário
queue *n* fila
quick *adj* rápido
quicken *v* apressar
quickly *adv* rapidamente
quicksand *n* areia movediça
quiet *adj* quieto, tranqüilo
quietness *n* quietude, calma
quilt *n* acolchoado
quit *iv* abandonar, deixar
quite *adv* totalmente
quiver *v* tremer, estremecer
quiz *v* examinar; caçoa
quotation *n* citação
quote *v* citar; cotar
quotient *n* quociente

R

rabbi *n* rabino
rabbit *n* coelho
rabies *n* raiva
race *v* correr
race *n* corrida; raça
racism *n* racismo
racist *adj* racista
racket *n* raquete
racketeering *n* mafioso
radar *n* radar
radiation *n* radiação
radiator *n* radiador
radical *adj* radical
radio *n* rádio
radish *n* rabanete
radius *n* raio
raffle *n* rifa
raft *n* abundância
rag *n* trapo, pano
rage *n* fúria
ragged *adj* andrajoso
raid *n* reide
raid *v* assaltar
raider *n* assaltante
rail *n* grade, trilho
railroad *n* ferrovia
rain *n* chuva
rain *v* chover
rainbow *n* arco-íris

raincoat *n* capa de chuva
rainfall *n* precipitação
rainy *adj* chuvoso
raise *n* aumento
raise *v* elevar; criar
raisin *n* uva passa
rake *n* rastelo
rally *n* rally; assembléia
ram *n* carneiro
ram *v* bater
ramification *n* ramificação
ramp *n* rampa
rampage *v* esbravejar
rampant *adj* desenfreado
ranch *n* rancho, fazenda
rancor *n* rancor
randomly *adv* ao acaso
range *n* variedade; alcance
rank *n* linha, classe
rank *v* classificar-se
ransack *v* vasculhar; saquear
ransom *v* resgatar
rape *v* estuprar, violar
rape *n* estupro, violação
rapid *adj* rápido
rapist *n* estuprador
rapport *n* concordância
rare *adj* raro
rarely *adv* raramente
rascal *n* velhaco, maroto
rash *n* erupção
raspberry *n* framboesa

R

rat *n* rato
rate *n* avaliar
rather *adv* antes
ratification *n* ratificação
ratify *v* ratificar
ratio *n* proporção
ration *v* racionar
ration *n* ração
rational *adj* racional, sensato
rationalize *v* racionalizar
rattle *v* chocalhar
ravage *v* devastar
ravage *n* devastação
rave *v* delirar
raven *n* corvo
ravine *n* ravina
raw *adj* cru, em carne viva
ray *n* raio
raze *v* arrasar
razor *n* navalha, barbeador
reach *v* alcançar, estender
reach *n* alcance
react *v* reagir
reaction *n* reação
read *iv* ler; registrar
reader *n* leitor
readiness *n* prontidão, presteza
reading *n* leitura
ready *adj* pronto, disposto
real *adj* real, verdadeiro
realism *n* realismo
reality *n* realidade

realize *v* realizar; compreender
really *adv* realmente
realm *n* reino; setor
realty *n* bens imóveis
reap *v* colher, ceifar
reappear *v* reaparecer
rear *v* criar; empinar
rear *n* retaguarda, fundos
rear *adj* traseiro
reason *v* raciocinar
reason *n* razão
reasonable *adj* razoável
reasoning *n* raciocínio
reassure *v* tranqüilizar
rebate *n* reembolso
rebel *v* rebelar-se
rebel *n* rebelde
rebellion *n* rebelião
rebirth *n* renascimento
rebound *v* ricochetear
rebuff *v* repelir
rebuff *n* repulsa
rebuild *v* reconstruir
rebuke *v* repreender
rebuke *n* repreensão
rebut *v* refutar
recall *v* lembrar
recant *v* retratar
recap *v* recapitular
recapture *v* recapturar
recede *v* retroceder
receipt *n* recibo**

R

receive *v* receber
recent *adj* recente
reception *n* recepção
receptionist *n* recepcionista
receptive *adj* receptivo
recess *n* recesso, recreio
recession *n* recessão
recharge *v* recarregar
recipe *n* receita
reciprocal *adj* recíproco
recital *n* recital
recite *v* recitar
reckless *adj* temerário
reckon *v* considerar
reckon on *v* contar com
reclaim *v* reclamar
recline *v* recostar
recluse *n* recluso
recognition *n* reconhecimento
recognize *v* reconhecer
recollect *v* recordar
recollection *n* recordação
recommend *v* recomendar
recompense *v* recompensar
recompense *n* recompensa
reconcile *v* reconciliar
reconsider *v* reconsiderar
reconstruct *v* reconstruir
record *v* gravar; registrar
record *n* disco, antecedentes
recorder *n* gravador
recording *n* gravação

recount *n* relatar
recoup *v* recobrar
recourse *n* recurso
recover *v* recuperar
recovery *n* recuperação
recreate *v* recriar, restaurar
recreation *n* recreação
recruit *v* recrutar
recruit *n* recruta
recruitment *n* recrutamento
rectangle *n* retângulo
rectangular *adj* retangular
rectify *v* retificar
rector *n* diretor
rectum *n* reto
recuperate *v* recuperar
recur *v* repetir
recurrence *n* recorrência
recycle *v* reciclar
red *adj* vermelho
red tape *n* burocacia
redden *v* avermelhar
redeem *v* redimir
redemption *n* redenção
red-hot *adj* em brasa
redo *v* refazer
redouble *v* redobrar
redress *v* compensar
reduce *v* reduzir
redundant *adj* redundante
reed *n* junco
reef *n* recife

R

reel *n* carretel; reel
reelect *v* reeleger
reenactment *n* reapresentação
reentry *n* reentrada
refer to *v* referir-se a
referee *n* árbitro
reference *n* referência
referendum *n* referenda
refill *v* reabastecer
refinance *v* refinanciar
refine *v* refinar
refinery *n* refinaria
reflect *v* refletir
reflection *n* reflexo, reflexão
reflexive *adj* reflexivo
reform *v* reformar
reform *n* reforma
refrain *v* abster
refresh *v* refrescar
refreshing *adj* refrescante
refreshment *n* lanche
refrigerate *v* refrigerar
refuel *v* reabastecer
refuge *n* refúgio
refugee *n* refugiado
refund *v* reembolsar
refund *n* reembolso
refurbish *v* redecorar
refusal *n* recusa
refuse *v* recusar
refuse *n* lixo, refugo
refute *v* refutar

regain *v* recobrar
regal *adj* régio
regard *v* considerar
regarding *pre* com respeito a
regardless *adv* indiferente a
regards *n* saudações
regeneration *n* regeneração
regent *n* regente
regime *n* regime
regiment *n* regimento
region *n* região
regional *adj* regional
register *v* registrar
registration *n* inscrição
regret *v* lamentar
regret *n* pesar
regrettable *adj* lamentável
regularity *n* regularidade
regularly *adv* relgularmente
regulate *v* regular
regulation *n* regulação
rehabilitate *v* rehabilitar
rehearsal *n* ensaio
rehearse *v* ensaiar
reign *v* reinar
reign *n* reino
reimburse *v* reembolsar
reimbursement *n* reembolso
rein *v* tomar as rédeas
rein *n* rédeas
reindeer *n* rena
reinforce *v* reforçar

R

reinforcements *n* reforço
reiterate *v* reiterar
reject *v* rejeitar
rejection *n* rejeição
rejoice *v* regozijar
rejoin *v* reunir, retorquir
rejuvenate *v* rejuvenecer
relapse *n* recaída
related *adj* aparentado
relationship *n* relacionamento
relative *adj* relativo
relative *n* parente
relax *v* relaxar
relaxation *n* relaxamento
relaxing *adj* relaxante
relay *v* transmitir
release *v* soltar, divulgar
relegate *v* relegar
relent *v* ceder, apiadar-se
relentless *adj* implacável
relevant *adj* relevante
reliable *adj* confiável
reliance *n* dependência
relic *n* vestígio, relíquia
relief *n* alívio, auxílio
relieve *v* aliviar, substituir
religion *n* religião
religious *adj* religioso
relinquish *v* renunciar a
relish *v* saborear
relive *v* reviver, recordar
relocate *v* mudar

relocation *n* relocação
reluctant *adj* relutante
rely on *v* contar com
remain *v* permanecer
remainder *n* resto
remaining *adj* restante
remains *n* sobras, restos
remake *v* refazer
remark *v* observar, comentar
remark *n* observação
remarkable *adj* notável
remarry *v* casar de novo
remedy *v* remediar
remedy *n* remédio
remember *v* lembrar
remembrance *n* lembrança
remind *v* fazer lembrar
reminder *n* lembrete
remission *n* remissão
remit *v* remeter
remittance *n* remetência
remnant *n* remanescente
remodel *v* remodelar
remorse *n* remorso
remorseful *adj* cheio de remorso
remote *adj* remoto
removal *n* remoção
remove *v* remover
remunerate *v* remunerar
renew *v* renovar
renewal *n* renovação
renounce *v* renunciar

R

renovate *v* renovar
renovation *n* renovação
renowned *adj* famoso
rent *v* alugar
rent *n* aluguel
reorganize *v* reorganizar
repair *v* reparar
reparation *n* reparação
repatriate *v* repatriar
repay *v* pagar
repayment *n* reembolso
repeal *v* revogar
repeal *n* revogação
repeat *v* repetir
repel *v* repelir
repent *v* arrepender
repentance *n* arrependimento
repetition *n* repetição
replace *v* substituir
replacement *n* substituto
replay *n* repetir
replenish *v* reabastecer
replete *adj* repleto
replica *n* réplica
replicate *v* replicar
reply *v* responder
reply *n* resposta
report *v* relatar; denunciar
report *n* relatório, boato
reportedly *adv* supostamente
reporter *n* repórter
repose *v* repousar

repose *n* repouso
represent *v* representar
repress *v* reprimir
repression *n* repressão
reprieve *n* comutar, suspender
reprint *v* reimprimir
reprint *n* reimpressão
reprisal *n* represália
reproach *v* reprovar
reproach *n* reprovação
reproduce *v* reproduzir
reproduction *n* reprodução
reptile *n* réptil
republic *n* república
repudiate *v* repudiar
repugnant *adj* repugnante
repulse *v* repelir
repulse *n* repulsa
repulsive *adj* repulsivo
reputation *n* reputação
reputedly *adv* supostamente
request *v* pedir, solicitar
request *n* petição
require *v* requerer
requirement *n* requerimento
rescue *v* resgatar
rescue *n* resgate
research *v* pesquisar
research *n* pesquisa
resemblance *n* semelhança
resemble *v* parecer-se com
resent *v* ressentir

R

resentment *n* ressentimento
reservation *n* reserva
reserve *v* reservar
reservoir *n* represa, açude
reside *v* residir
residence *n* residência
residue *n* resíduo
resign *v* resignar
resignation *n* resignação
resilient *adj* resiliente
resist *v* resistir
resistance *n* resistência
resolute *adj* resoluto
resolution *n* resolução
resolve *v* resolver
resort *v* freqüentar, recorrer
resounding *adj* ressonante
resource *n* recurso
respect *v* respeitar
respect *n* respeito
respectful *adj* respeitoso
respective *adj* respectivo
respiration *n* respiração
respite *n* pausa, trégua
respond *v* responder
response *n* resposta
responsibility *n* responsabilidade
responsible *adj* responsável
responsive *adj* responsivo
rest *v* descansar
rest *n* descanso
restaurant *n* restaurante

restful *adj* repousado
restitution *n* restituição
restless *adj* inquieto
restoration *n* restauração
restore *v* restaurar
restrain *v* reter, refrear
restraint *n* contenção
restrict *v* restringir
result *n* resultado
resume *v* resumir
resumption *n* ressunção
resurface *v* ressurgir
resurrection *n* ressurreição
resuscitate *v* ressuscitar
retain *v* reter, guardar
retaliate *v* retaliar, vingar
retaliation *n* retaliação
retarded *adj* retardado
retention *n* retenção
retire *v* retirar-se
retirement *n* retiro, retirada
retract *v* retratar
retreat *v* fugir; retirar-se
retreat *n* escape; retiro
retrieval *n* retorno
retrieve *v* recobrar
retroactive *adj* retroativo
return *v* retornar
return *n* retorno
reunion *n* reunião
reveal *v* revelar
revealing *adj* revelador

R

revel *v* divertir-se
revelation *n* revelação
revenge *v* vingar
revenge *n* vingança
revenue *n* imposto, renda
reverence *n* reverência
reverse *n* reverso, inverter
reversible *adj* reversível
revert *v* reverter
review *v* rever; criticar
review *n* revisão; crítica
revise *v* revisar
revision *n* revisão
revive *v* reviver, renovar
revoke *v* revogar
revolt *v* revoltar
revolt *n* revolta
revolting *adj* revoltante
revolve *v* revolver
revolver *v* revólver
revue *n* revista
revulsion *n* revulsão
reward *v* recompensar
reward *n* recompensa
rewarding *adj* recompensador
rheumatism *n* reumatismo
rhinoceros *n* rinoceronte
rhyme *n* rima
rhythm *n* ritmo
rib *n* costela
ribbon *n* fita
rice *n* arroz

rich *adj* rico; saboroso
rid of *iv* livrar-se de
riddle *n* enigma
ride *iv* montar
ridge *n* cordilheira
ridicule *v* ridicularizar
ridicule *n* escárnio
ridiculous *adj* ridículo
rifle *n* rifle
rift *n* greta, falha
right *adv* exatamente
right *adj* direito, certo
right *n* direito
rigid *adj* rígido
rigor *n* rigor
rim *n* beira; aba
ring *iv* tocar, telefonar
ring *n* anel, ringue
ringleader *n* líder
rinse *v* enxaguar
riot *v* amotinar
riot *n* distúrbio
rip *v* rasgar
rip off *v* roubar
ripe *adj* maduro
ripen *v* amadurecer
ripple *n* ondulação
rise *iv* levantar-se
risk *v* arriscar
risk *n* risco
risky *adj* arriscado
rite *n* rito**

R

rival *n* rival
rivalry *n* rivalidade
river *n* rio
rivet *v* rebitar
riveting *adj* rebitagem
road *n* estrada
roam *v* vagar
roar *v* rugir
roar *n* rugido
roast *v* assar
roast *n* carne assada
rob *v* roubar
robber *n* ladrão
robbery *n* roubo
robe *n* roupão, manto
robust *adj* robusto
rock *n* pedra, rocha
rocket *n* foguete
rocky *adj* rochoso
rod *n* barra; vara
rodent *n* roedor
roll *v* girar, rolar
romance *n* romance
roof *n* teto
room *n* quarto, espaço
roomy *adj* espaçoso
rooster *n* galo
root *n* raiz
rope *n* corda
rosary *n* rosário
rose *n* rosa
rosy *adj* rosado

rot *v* apodrecer
rot *n* podridão
rotate *v* rodar, girar
rotation *n* rotação
rotten *adj* podre
rough *adj* áspero
round *adj* redondo
roundup *n* captura
rouse *v* despertar
rousing *adj* excitante
route *n* rota
routine *n* rotina
row *v* remar; brigar
row *n* fila; disputa
rowdy *adj* desordeiro
royal *adj* real
royalty *n* realeza
rub *v* esfregar, coçar
rubber *n* borracha
rubbish *n* lixo, entulho
rubble *n* cascalho, entulho
ruby *n* rubi
rudder *n* leme, timão
rude *adj* rude
rudeness *n* rudeza
rudimentary *adj* rudimentar
rug *n* tapete
ruin *v* arruinar
ruin *n* ruínas
rule *v* mandar
rule *n* regra, regulamento
ruler *n* régua; rei

R

rum *n* rum
rumble *v* ribombar
rumble *n* ruido sudo
rumor *n* rumor
run *iv* correr; executar
run away *v* fugir, escapar
run into *v* encontrar por acaso
run out *v* sair; esgotar
run over *v* atropelar
run up *v* acumular
runner *n* corredor
rupture *n* ruptura
rupture *v* romper
rural *adj* rural
ruse *n* artimanha
rush *v* apressar
Russia *n* Rússia
Russian *adj* russo
rust *v* enferrujar
rust *n* ferrugem
rustic *adj* rústico
rust-proof *adj* inoxidável
rusty *adj* enferrujado
ruthless *adj* cruel, brutal
rye *n* centeio

R
S

S

sabotage *v* sabotar
sabotage *n* sabotagem
sack *v* saquear, pilhar
sack *n* saco; saque
sacrament *n* sacramento
sacred *adj* sagrado
sacrifice *n* sacrifício
sacrilege *n* sacrilégio
sad *adj* triste
sadden *v* entristecer
saddle *n* sela, assento
sadist *n* sádico
sadness *n* tristeza
safe *adj* seguro
safeguard *n* salvaguarda
safety *n* segurança
sail *v* velejar
sail *n* vela
sailboat *n* barco a vela
sailor *n* marinheiro
saint *n* santo
salad *n* salada
salary *n* salário
sale *n* venda
sale slip *n* recibo
salesman *n* vendedor
saliva *n* saliva, cuspe
salmon *n* salmão
saloon *n* salão, bar

salt *n* sal
salty *adj* salgado
salvage *v* salvar
salvation *n* salvação
same *adj* igual, mesmo
sample *n* amostra
sanctify *v* santificar
sanction *v* sancionar
sanction *n* sanção
sanctity *n* santidade
sanctuary *n* santuário
sand *n* areia
sandal *n* sandália
sandpaper *n* lixa
sandwich *n* sanduíche
sane *adj* são
sanity *n* sanidade
sap *n* seiva
sap *v* solapar
sapphire *n* safira
sarcasm *n* sarcasmo
sarcastic *adj* sarcástico
sardine *n* sardinha
satanic *adj* satânico
satellite *n* satélite
satire *n* sátira
satisfaction *n* satisfação
satisfactory *adj* satisfatório
satisfy *v* satisfazer
saturate *v* saturar
Saturday *n* sábado
sauce *n* molho

saucepan *n* caçarola
saucer *n* pires
sausage *n* salsicha
savage *adj* selvagem
savagery *n* selvageria
save *v* salvar; economizar
savings *n* economia
savior *n* salvador
savor *v* saborear
saw *iv* serrar
saw *n* serrote
say *iv* dizer
saying *n* adágio; dito
scaffolding *n* andaime
scald *v* escaldar
scale *v* escamar, descascar
scale *n* balança; escama
scalp *n* escalpo
scam *n* fraude
scan *v* examinar
scandal *n* escândalo
scandalize *v* escandalizar
scapegoat *n* bode expiatório
scar *n* cicatriz
scarce *adj* escasso, raro
scarcely *adv* apenas
scarcity *n* escassez
scare *v* assustar
scare *n* susto
scare away *v* espantar
scarf *n* cachecol
scary *adj* assustador

S

scatter *v* dispersar
scenario *n* situaçao
scene *n* cenário, cena
scenery *n* vista, panorama
scenic *adj* pitoresco
scent *n* essência
schedule *v* programar
schedule *n* horario
scheme *n* projeto, trama
schism *n* cisma, separação
scholar *n* sabio; bolsista
scholarship *n* bolsa de estudos
school *n* escola
science *n* ciência
scientific *adj* científico
scientist *n* cientista
scissors *n* tesoura
scoff *v* zombar, troçar
scold *v* repreender
scolding *n* repreensão
scooter *n* patinete
scope *n* alcance
scorch *v* abrasar
score *n* contagem
score *v* marcar ponto
scorn *v* desprezar
scornful *n* zombador
scorpion *n* escorpião
scoundrel *n* canalha
scour *v* limpar, esfregar
scourge *n* flagelo
scout *n* escoteiro

scramble *v* precipitar-se
scrambled *adj* disperso; mexido
scrap *n* pedaço, sobra
scrap *v* brigar
scrape *v* arranhar, raspar
scratch *v* arranhar; riscar
scratch *n* arranhão
scream *v* gritar
scream *n* grito
screech *v* guinchar
screen *n* biombo, cortina
screen *v* projetar
screw *v* parafusar
screw *n* parafuso
screwdriver *n* chave de fenda
scribble *v* rabiscar
script *n* script, texto
scroll *n* rolo
scrub *v* esfregar
scruples *n* escrúpulos
scrupulous *adj* escrupuloso
scrutiny *n* escrutínio
scuffle *n* luta
sculptor *n* escultor
sculpture *n* escultura
sea *n* mar
seafood *n* frutos do mar
seagull *n* gaivota
seal *v* selar, vedar
seal *n* selo; foca
seal off *v* interditar
seam *n* costura, junta

S

seamless *adj* sem costura

seamstress *n* costureira

search *v* procurar, revistar

search *n* busca

seashore *n* praia

seasick *adj* mareado

seaside *adj* beira-mar

season *n* temporada; estação

seasonal *adj* sazonal

seasoning *n* tempero

seat *n* assento; lugar

seated *adj* sentado

secede *v* apartar-se

secluded *adj* retirado, isolado

seclusion *n* isolamento

second *n* segundo

secondary *adj* secundário

secrecy *n* secredo

secret *n* secredo

secretary *n* secretário

secretly *adv* secretamente

sect *n* seita

section *n* seção

sector *n* setor

secure *v* segurar

secure *adj* seguro

security *n* seguridade

sedate *v* sedar

sedation *n* sedação

seduce *v* seduzir

seduction *n* sedução

see *iv* ver

seed *n* semente

seedless *adj* sem semente

seedy *adj* abatido

seek *iv* buscar

seem *v* parecer

see-through *adj* transparente

segment *n* segmento

segregate *v* segregar

segregation *n* segregação

seize *v* agarrar; capturar

seizure *n* apreensão, convulsão

seldom *adv* raramente

select *v* selecionar

selection *n* seleção

self-conscious *adj* tímido

self-esteem *n* auto-estima

self-evident *adj* evidente

self-interest *n* interesse próprio

selfish *adj* egoísta

selfishness *n* egoísmo

self-respect *n* respeito próprio

sell *iv* vender

seller *n* vendedor

sellout *n* liquidação

semblance *n* aparência

semester *n* semestre

seminary *n* seminário

senate *n* Senado

senator *n* senador

send *iv* enviar, mandar

sender *n* remetente

senile *adj* senil

S

senior *adj* mais velho, superior
seniority *n* velhice
sensation *n* sensação
sense *v* sentir
sense *n* senso, sentido
senseless *adj* desacordado
sensible *adj* sensível, sensato
sensitive *adj* sensível, sensitivo
sensual *adj* sensual
sentence *v* sentenciar
sentence *n* sentença, veredicto
sentiment *n* sentimento
sentimental *adj* sentimental
sentry *n* sentinela, vigia
separate *v* separar
separate *adj* separado
separation *n* separação
September *n* Setembro
sequel *n* seqüencia, resultado
sequence *n* seqüencia
serenade *n* serenata
serene *adj* sereno
serenity *n* serenidade
sergeant *n* sargento
series *n* série
serious *adj* sério; grave
seriousness *n* seriedade
sermon *n* sermão
serpent *n* serpente
serum *n* soro
servant *n* servo, criado
serve *v* servir; ser útil

service *n* serviço
service *v* prestar serviço
session *n* sessão
set *n* jogo, conjunto
set *iv* pôr, colocar
set about *v* começar
set off *v* sair a caminho
set out *v* começar
set up *v* montar
setback *n* revés
setting *n* ambiente
settle *v* assentar
settle down *v* instalar-se
settle for *v* aceitar
settlement *n* assentamento
settler *n* colono
setup *n* emboscada
seven *adj* sete
seventeen *adj* dezessete
seventh *adj* sétimo
seventy *adj* setenta
sever *v* decepar, romper
several *adj* vários
severance *n* rompimento
severe *adj* severo; sério
severity *n* severidade
sew *v* costurar, coser
sewage *n* esgoto
sewer *n* cano de esgoto
sewing *n* costura
sex *n* sexo
sexuality *n* sexualidade

S

shabby *adj* maltrapilho
shack *n* cabana, choça
shackle *n* algema, cadeia
shade *n* sombra
shadow *n* sombra
shady *adj* sombrio; duvidoso
shake *iv* sacudir, agitar
shaky *adj* trêmulo
shallow *adj* raso, baixio
sham *n* fingimento
shambles *n* matadouro
shame *v* envergonhar
shame *n* vergonha
shameful *adj* vergonhoso
shameless *adj* descarado
shape *v* formar, moldar
shape *n* forma
share *v* dividir, partilhar
share *n* parte, porção
shareholder *n* acionista
shark *n* tubarão
sharp *adj* afiado; esperto
sharpen *v* afiar; aguçar
sharpener *n* apontador
shatter *v* quebrar
shave *v* barbear
she *pro* ela
shear *iv* tosquiar
shed *iv* derramar
sheep *n* ovelha
sheets *n* lençóis
shelf *n* estante

shell *n* concha, casca
shellfish *n* marisco
shelter *v* acolher
shelter *n* cobertura
shelves *n* estante
shepherd *n* pastor
sherry *n* xerez
shield *v* defender
shield *n* escudo
shift *n* turno; movimento
shift *v* trocar; mover
shine *iv* brilhar
shiny *adj* brilhante
ship *n* navio
shipment *n* carregamento
shipwreck *n* naufrágio
shipyard *n* estaleiro
shirk *v* esquivar, evitar
shirt *n* camisa
shiver *v* tremer, tiritar
shiver *n* tremor, calafrio
shock *v* chocar; eletrocutar
shock *n* choque; meda
shocking *adj* chocante
shoddy *adj* vulgar, barato
shoe *n* sapato
shoe polish *n* graxa de sapato
shoe store *n* loja de sapatos
shoelace *n* cordão de sapato
shoot *iv* atirar; disparar
shoot down *v* derrubar
shop *v* fazer compras

S

shop *n* loja
shoplifting *n* furto em loja
shopping *n* compra, compras
shore *n* margem, praia
short *adj* curto, pequeno
shortage *n* falta, deficiência
shortcoming *n* desvantagem
shortcut *n* atalho
shorten *v* encurtar
shorthand *n* taquigrafia
short-lived *adj* efêmero, fugaz
shortly *adv* logo, em breve
shorts *n* calças curtas
shortsighted *adj* míope, vista curta
shot *n* tiro; foto; chance
shotgun *n* espingarda de caça
shoulder *n* ombro
shout *v* gritar
shout *n* grito
shouting *n* gritaria, clamor
shove *v* empurrar
shove *n* empurrão
shovel *n* pá
show *iv* mostrar, exibir
show off *v* exibir, destacar
show up *v* aparecer
showdown *n* lucha final
shower *n* chuveiro
shrapnel *n* metralha
shred *v* cortar em pedaços
shred *n* pedaço, tira

shrewd *adj* perspicaz, astuto
shriek *v* gritar
shriek *n* berro, grito
shrimp *n* camarão
shrine *n* relicário
shrink *iv* encolher
shroud *n* mortalha
shrouded *adj* envolvido
shrub *n* arbusto
shrug *v* encolher os ombros
shudder *n* tremor, calafrio
shudder *v* estremecer
shuffle *v* embaralhar
shun *v* evitar
shut *iv* fechar, cerrar
shut off *v* parar, desligar
shut up *v* calar
shy *adj* tímido
shyness *n* timidez
sick *adj* doente
sicken *v* adoecer
sickening *adj* nauseante
sickle *n* foice, alfanje
sickness *n* doença
side *n* lado, declive
sideburns *n* costeleta
sidestep *v* tirar o corpo fora
sidewalk *n* calçada
sideways *adv* de lado
siege *n* sítio, cerco
siege *v* sitiar, cercar
sift *v* peneirar

S

sigh *n* suspiro
sigh *v* suspirar
sight *n* visão
sightseeing *v* excursionar
sign *v* assinalar
sign *n* sinal
signal *n* sinal
signature *n* assinatura
significance *n* significância
significant *adj* significante
signify *v* significar
silence *n* silêncio
silence *v* silenciar
silent *adj* silencioso
silhouette *n* silhueta
silk *n* seda
silly *adj* tolo, bobo
silver *n* prata
silversmith *n* prateiro
silverware *n* prataria
similar *adj* similar
similarity *n* similaridade
simmer *v* ferver
simple *adj* simples
simplicity *n* simplicidade
simplify *v* simplificar
simply *adv* simplesmente
simulate *v* simular
simultaneous *adj* simultâneo
sin *v* pecar
sin *n* pecado
since *c* desde; visto que

since *pre* desde
since then *adv* desde então
sincere *adj* sincero
sincerity *n* sinceridade
sinful *adj* pecador
sing *iv* cantar
singer *n* cantor
single *n* solteiro
single *adj* só, único
singlehanded *adj* sozinho
single-minded *adj* obcecado
singular *adj* singular
sinister *adj* sinistro, fúnebre
sink *iv* afundar; baixar
sinner *n* pecador
sip *v* sorver
sip *n* golinho
sir *n* senhor
siren *n* sirene
sirloin *n* lombo
sissy *adj* efeminado
sister *n* irmã; freira
sister-in-law *n* cunhada
sit *iv* sentar
site *n* lugar, local; site
sitting *n* sessão
situated *adj* situado
situation *n* situação
six *adj* seis
sixteen *adj* dezesseis
sixth *adj* sexto
sixty *adj* sessenta

S

sizable *adj* considerável
size *n* tamanho
size up *v* medir; avaliar
skate *v* patinar
skate *n* skate; patim
skeleton *n* esqueleto
skeptic *adj* cético
sketch *v* esboçar
sketch *n* croqui, esboço
sketchy *adj* incompleto
ski *v* esquiar
skill *n* habilidade
skillful *adj* habilidoso
skim *v* escumar; desnatar
skin *v* esfolar, descascar
skin *n* pele
skinny *adj* magro, magricela
skip *v* saltitar, pular
skip *n* pulo
skirmish *n* escaramuça
skirt *n* saia
skull *n* crânio, caveira
sky *n* céu
skylight *n* clarabóia
skyscraper *n* arranha-céu
slab *n* laje; fatia grossa
slack *adj* frouxo, folgado
slacken *v* afrouxar, folgar
slacks *n* calça comprida
slam *v* bater, trombar
slander *n* calúnia, difamação
slanted *adj* inclinado, oblíquo

slap *n* tapa
slap *v* estapear, dar tapa
slash *n* talho, vergastada
slash *v* talhar, açoitar
slate *n* ardósia; lousa
slaughter *v* massacrar
slaughter *n* massacre
slave *n* escravo
slavery *n* escravatura
slay *iv* matar
sleazy *adj* decrépito
sleep *iv* dormir
sleep *n* sono, descanso
sleeve *n* manga
sleeveless *adj* sem manga
sleigh *n* trenó
slender *adj* esguio, escasso
slice *v* fatiar, cortar
slice *n* fatia, talhada
slide *iv* deslizar
slightly *adv* ligeiramente
slim *adj* fraco, escasso
slip *v* escorregar; decair
slip *n* lapso
slipper *n* pantufa
slippery *adj* escorregadio
slit *iv* fender, rachar
slob *adj* preguiçoso
slogan *n* slogan
slope *n* declive
sloppy *adj* mole, desleixado
slot *n* fenda

slow *adj* lento, vagaroso
slow down *v* ir mais devagar
slow motion *n* câmera lenta
slowly *adv* lentamente
sluggish *adj* lerdo
slum *n* bairro pobre
slump *v* baixar, despencar
slump *n* recessão
slur *v* insultar, manchar
sly *adj* maldoso
smack *n* palmada; toque
smack *v* dar uma palmada
small *adj* pequeno
smallpox *n* varíola
smart *adj* elegante, esperto
smash *v* esmagar; colidir
smear *n* mancha; difamação
smear *v* sujar, ofender
smell *iv* cheirar
smelly *adj* fedido
smile *v* sorrir
smile *n* sorriso
smith *n* ferreiro
smoke *v* fumar
smoked *adj* defumado
smoker *n* fumante
smooth *v* alisar, suavizar
smooth *adj* suave, sereno
smoothly *adv* suavemente
smoothness *n* suavidade
smother *v* sufocar
smuggler *n* contrabandista

snail *n* caracol
snake *n* serpente
snapshot *n* instantâneo
snare *v* pegar em armadilha
snare *n* armadilha
snatch *v* arrebatar
sneak *v* esgueirar-se
sneeze *v* espirrar
sneeze *n* espirro
sniff *v* fungar, farejar
sniper *n* atirador de tocaia
snitch *v* delatar, furtar
snooze *v* cochilar
snore *v* roncar
snore *n* ronco
snow *v* nevar
snow *n* neve
snowfall *n* nevada
snowflake *n* floco de neve
snub *v* ofender
snub *n* ofensa
soak *v* saturar, encharcar
soak in *v* penetrar, entrar
soak up *v* absorver
soar *v* voar alto
sob *v* soluçar
sob *n* soluço
sober *adj* sóbrio
so-called *adj* suposto
sociable *adj* sociável
socialism *n* socialismo
socialist *adj* socialista

S

socialize *v* socializar
society *n* sociedade
sock *n* meia
soda *n* soda
sofa *n* sofá
soft *adj* suave, brando
soften *v* amaciar, suavizar
softly *adv* suavemente
softness *n* suavidade
soggy *adj* ensopado
soil *v* sujar, engraxar
soil *n* terra
soiled *adj* sujo
solace *n* consolação
solar *adj* solar
solder *v* soldar
soldier *n* soldado
sold-out *adj* esgotado
sole *n* sola; solha
sole *adj* único, sozinho
solely *adv* unicamente
solemn *adj* solene
solicit *v* solicitar
solid *adj* sólido
solidarity *n* solidariedade
solitary *adj* solitário
solitude *n* solidão
soluble *adj* solúvel
solution *n* solução
solve *v* solver, resolver
solvent *adj* solvente
somber *adj* sombrio

some *adj* algum; pouco
somebody *pro* alguém
someday *adv* algum dia
somehow *adv* de alguma forma
someone *pro* alguém
something *pro* alguma coisa
sometimes *adv* às vezes
someway *adv* de algum jeito
somewhat *adv* um pouco
son *n* filho
song *n* canção
son-in-law *n* genro
soon *adv* logo, em breve
soothe *v* aliviar, acalmar
sorcerer *n* feiticeiro
sorcery *n* feitiçaria
sore *n* ferida, dor
sore *adj* dolorido
sorrow *n* desgosto, pesar
sorrowful *adj* lamentável
sorry *adj* arrependido
sort *n* tipo
sort out *v* classificar
soul *n* alma
sound *n* som
sound *v* soar; parecer
sound out *v* sondar, investigar
soup *n* sopa
sour *adj* azedo, irritado
source *n* fonte, origem
south *n* sul
southbound *adv* para o sul

S

southeast *n* sudeste
southern *adj* meridional
southerner *n* sulista
southwest *n* sudoeste
souvenir *n* suvenir
sovereign *adj* soberano
sovereignty *n* soberania
soviet *adj* soviético
sow *iv* semear
spa *n* balneário
space *n* espaço
space out *v* espaçar
spacious *adj* espaçoso
spade *n* pá; espadas
Spain *n* Espanha
span *v* abarcar
span *n* vão; duração
Spaniard *n* espanhol
Spanish *adj* espanhol
spank *v* bater, surrar
spanking *n* surra
spare *v* poupar, economizar
spare *adj* livro, parco
sparingly *adv* frugalmente
spark *n* faísca, chispa
spark off *v* levar a, causar
spark plug *n* vela de ignição
sparkle *v* cintilar, faiscar
sparrow *n* pardal
sparse *adj* escasso, disperso
spasm *n* espasmo
speak *iv* falar, dizer

speaker *n* locutor
spear *n* lança
spearhead *v* liderar
special *adj* especial
specialize *v* especializar
specialty *n* especialidade
species *n* espécie
specific *adj* específico
specimen *n* espécime
speck *n* ponto, mancha
spectacle *n* espetáculo
spectator *n* espectador
speculate *v* especular
speculation *n* especulação
speech *n* fala; palestra
speechless *adj* sem fala
speed *iv* acelerar
speed *n* velocidade
speedily *adv* velozmente
speedy *adj* rápido, veloz
spell *iv* soletrar; enfeitiçar
spell *n* encanto, ataque
spelling *n* ortografia
spend *iv* passar, gastar
spending *n* gasto, despesa
sperm *n* esperma
sphere *n* esfera
spice *n* tempero
spicy *adj* picante; malicioso
spider *n* aranha
spider web *n* teia de aranha
spill *iv* derramar

S

spill *n* derramamento
spin *iv* girar; protelar
spine *n* espinha
spineless *adj* fraco
spinster *n* solteirona
spirit *n* espírito
spiritual *adj* espiritual
spit *iv* cuspir
spite *n* malvadeza
spiteful *adj* maldoso
splash *v* salpicar
splendid *adj* esplêndido
splendor *n* esplendor
splint *n* tala
splinter *n* farpa, estilhaço
splinter *v* fragmentar
split *n* fenda, brecha
split *iv* fender, separar
split up *v* repartir, separar
spoil *v* estragar; mimar
spoils *n* despojo
sponge *n* esponja
sponsor *n* patrocinador
spontaneity *n* espontaneidade
spontaneous *adj* espontâneo
spooky *adj* espectral
spool *n* carretel, bobina
spoon *n* colher
spoonful *n* colherada
sporadic *adj* esporádico
sport *n* esporte
sporty *adj* berrante

S

spot *v* localizar
spot *n* ponto, lugar; mancha
spotless *adj* imaculado
spotlight *n* refletor
spouse *n* esposo, cônjuge
sprain *v* torcer, deslocar
sprawl *v* esparramar
spray *v* borrifar
spread *iv* espalhar; difundir
spring *iv* saltar; brotar
spring *n* primavera; mola
springboard *n* trampolim
sprinkle *v* borrifar, salpicar
sprout *v* germinar, brotar
spruce up *v* embelezar
spur *v* esporear; incitar
spur *n* espora; estímulo
spy *v* espiar
spy *n* espiar
squalid *adj* esquálido
squander *v* dissipar, gastar
square *adj* quadrado, reto
square *n* quadrado; praça
squash *v* achatar, esmagar
squeak *v* guinchar
squeaky *adj* rechinante
squeamish *adj* melindroso
squeeze *v* espremer, apertar
squeeze in *v* enfiar, meter
squeeze up *v* comprimir, apertar
squid *n* lula
squirrel *n* esquilo

stab v apunhalar

stab n facada

stability n estabilidade

stable adj estável, fixo

stable n estábulo

stack v amontoar

stack n pilha, monte

staff n equipe, bastão

stage n estágio, etapa

stage v encenar, dirigir

stagger v cambalear

staggering adj cambaleante

stagnant adj estagnado

stagnate v estagnar

stagnation n estagnação

stain v manchar, colorir

stain n mancha

stair n degrau

staircase n escadaria

stairs n escadaria

stake n estaca, poste, risco

stake v apostar; sustentar

stale adj passado, fedido

stalemate n empate; sem saída

stalk v seguir, espreitar

stalk n caule, talo

stall n estande

stall v enguiçar; atrasar

stammer v tartamudear

stamp v selar, sapatear

stamp n selo, carimbo

stamp out v erradicar

stampede n fuga precipitada

stand iv pôr de pé, manter

stand n estrado

stand for v rumar para

stand out v sobressair

stand up v estar en pé

standard n norma; criterio

standardize v padronizar

standing n reputaçao

standpoint n ponto de vista

standstill adj de paralisação

staple v grampear

staple n grampo; fibra

stapler n grampeador

star n estrela

starch n amido

starchy adj engomado;rígido

stare v fitar, encarar

stark adj completo; rígido

start v começar

start n começo

startle v alarmar

startled adj temeroso

starvation n fome, inanição

starve v morrer de fome

state n estado; classe

state v declarar

statement n declaração

station n estação

stationary adj fixo, imóvel

stationery n papelaria

statistic n estatística

S

statue *n* estátua
status *n* estado; condição
statute *n* estatuto, lei
staunch *adj* leal, sólido
stay *v* permanecer
stay *n* estadia
steady *adj* firme, estável
steak *n* bife
steal *iv* roubar, furtar
stealthy *adj* clandestino
steam *n* vapor, energia
steel *n* aço
steep *adj* excessivo
stem *n* tronco; raiz
stem *v* derivar
stench *n* fedor
step *n* passo; degrau
step down *v* abdicar
step out *v* apear, descer
step up *v* aumentar
stepbrother *n* meio-irmão
step-by-step *adv* passo a passo
stepdaughter *n* enteada
stepfather *n* padrasto
stepladder *n* escadinha
stepmother *n* madrasta
stepsister *n* meia-irmã
stepson *n* enteado
sterile *adj* estéril
sterilize *v* esterilizar
stern *n* popa
stern *adj* austero, duro

sternly *adv* severamente
stew *n* guisado
stewardess *n* aeromoça
stick *n* vara
stick *iv* aferrar-se
stick around *v* esperar
stick out *v* ressaltar
stick to *v* aderir, apegar-se
sticker *n* adesivo, etiqueta
sticky *adj* pegajoso; difícil
stiff *adj* duro, rígido
stiffen *v* endurecer
stiffness *n* dureza
stifle *v* reprimir, asfixiar
stifling *adj* sufocante
still *adj* tranqüilo; imóvel
still *n* calma
stimulant *n* estimulante
stimulate *v* estimular
stimulus *n* estímulo
sting *iv* picar, enganar
sting *n* picada
stinging *adj* picante, doloroso
stingy *adj* mesquinho
stink *iv* feder
stink *n* fedor
stinking *adj* fedorento
stipulate *v* estipular
stir *v* movimentar; mexer
stir up *v* agitar, incitar
stitch *v* suturar; costurar
stitch *n* ponto; sutura

S

stock *v* armazenar

stock *n* estoque; reserva

stocking *n* meia

stockpile *n* estoque, reserva

stockroom *n* almoxarifado

stoic *adj* estóico

stomach *n* esgômago

stone *n* pedra; caroço

stone *v* apedrejar

stool *n* tamborete

stop *v* parar

stop *n* parada; pausa

stop by *v* fazer uma visitinha

stop over *v* fazer escala

storage *n* armazenagem

store *v* armazenar

store *n* loja

stork *n* cegonha

storm *n* tempestade

stormy *adj* tempestuoso

story *n* estória

stove *n* fogão

straight *adj* reto, liso

straighten out *v* resolver

strain *v* tensionar

strain *n* peso; esforço

strained *adj* coado; hostil

strainer *n* coador, filtro

strait *n* estreito

stranded *adj* encalhado

strange *adj* estranho

stranger *n* estranho

strangle *v* estrangular

strap *n* tira, correia

strategy *n* estratégia

straw *n* palha

strawberry *n* morango

stray *adj* perdido

stray *v* errar; desviar

stream *n* corrente, riacho

street *n* rua

streetcar *n* bonde

streetlight *n* poste de luz

strength *n* força

strengthen *v* fortalecer

strenuous *adj* vigoroso

stress *n* estresse; acento

stressful *adj* estressante

stretch *n* trecho

stretch *v* estirar

stretcher *n* esticador

strict *adj* estrito, rígido

stride *iv* andar a passos largos

strife *n* briga, rixa

strike *n* greve; golpe

strike *iv* chocar, bater, atacar

strike back *v* revidar

strike up *v* iniciar

striking *adj* impressionante

string *n* pavio; corda; série

stringent *adj* rigoroso; apertado

strip *n* tira, faixa

strip *v* despir; tirar

stripe *n* listra; tira; franja

S

striped *adj* listrado, riscado

strive *iv* aspirar, esforçar-se

stroke *n* pancada, apoplexia

stroll *v* passear

strong *adj* forte

structure *n* estrutura

struggle *v* lutar, esforçar-se

struggle *n* luta, esforço

stub *n* toco; canhoto

stubborn *adj* teimoso

student *n* estudante

study *v* estudar

stuff *n* coisa; material

stuff *v* encher, entulhar

stuffing *n* recheio

stuffy *adj* malventilado

stumble *v* tropeçar

stun *v* atordoar, pasmar

stunning *adj* maravilhoso

stupendous *adj* estupendo

stupid *adj* estúpido

stupidity *n* estupidez

sturdy *adj* resistente

stutter *v* gaguejar

style *n* estilo

subdue *v* subjugar

subdued *adj* suave; quietoo

subject *v* sujeitar

subject *n* sujeito; assunto

sublime *adj* sublime

submerge *v* submergir

submissive *adj* submisso

submit *v* submeter

subpoena *v* intimar

subpoena *n* intimação

subscribe *v* subscrever

subscription *n* subscrição

subsequent *adj* subseqüente

subsidiary *adj* subsidiário

subsidize *v* subsidiar

subsidy *n* subsídio

subsist *v* subsistir

substance *n* substância

substandard *adj* sub-norma

substantial *adj* substancial

substitute *v* substituir

substitute *n* substituto

subtitle *n* subtítulo

subtle *adj* sutil, delicado

subtract *v* subtrair

subtraction *n* subtração

suburb *n* subúrbio

subway *n* metrô; túnel

succeed *v* suceder

success *n* sucesso

successful *adj* bem sucedido

successor *n* sucessor

succulent *adj* suculento

succumb *v* sucumbir

such *adj* tal; semelhante

suck *v* chupar, sugar

sucker *n* chupador; ventosa

sudden *adj* repentino

suddenly *adv* de repente

S

sue *v* processar
suffer *v* sofrer
suffer from *v* sofrer de
suffering *n* sofrimento
sufficient *adj* suficiente
suffocate *v* sufocar, asfixiar
sugar *n* açúcar
suggest *v* sugerir
suggestion *n* sugestão
suggestive *adj* sugestivo
suicide *n* suicídio
suit *n* paletó; processo
suitable *adj* apropriado
suitcase *n* mala, maleta
sulfur *n* enxofre
sullen *adj* mal-humorado
sum *n* soma, total
sum *v* somar
summarize *v* sumariar, resumir
summary *n* sumário
summer *n* verão
summit *n* pico, cume, ápice
summon *v* convocar
sumptuous *adj* suntuoso
sun *n* sol
sun block *n* protetor solar
sunburn *n* queimadura de sol
Sunday *n* Domingo
sundown *n* pôr-do-sol
sunglasses *n* óculos escuros
sunken *adj* afundado, submerso
sunny *adj* ensolarado

sunrise *n* nascer do sol
sunset *n* ocaso, pôr-do-sol
superb *adj* soberbo
superfluous *adj* supérfluo
superior *adj* superior
superiority *n* superioridade
supermarket *n* supermercado
superpower *n* superpotência
supersede *v* substituir, suplantar
superstition *n* superstição
supervise *v* supervisar
supervision *n* supervisão
supper *n* jantar, ceia
supple *adj* flexível, maleável
supplier *n* abastecedor
supplies *n* suprimento
supply *v* fornecer
support *v* apoio, suporte
supporter *n* defensor, partidário
suppose *v* supor
supposing *c* se, supondo que
supposition *n* suposição
suppress *v* suprimir
supremacy *n* supremacia
supreme *adj* supremo
surcharge *n* sobrecarga
sure *adj* certo
surely *adv* certamente
surf *v* surfar
surface *n* superfície
surgeon *n* cirurgião
surgical *adv* cirúrgico

S

surname *n* sobrenome

surpass *v* superar

surplus *n* excesso

surprise *v* surpreender

surprise *n* surpresa

surrender *v* entregar, render

surrender *n* entrega, rendição

surround *v* cercar, rodear

surroundings *n* arredores

surveillance *n* vigilância

survey *n* inspeção

survival *n* sobrevivência

survive *v* sobreviver

survivor *n* sobrevivente

susceptible *adj* suscetível

suspect *v* suspeitar

suspect *n* suspeito

suspend *v* suspender

suspenders *n* suspensório

suspense *n* suspense

suspension *n* suspenção

suspicion *n* suspeição

suspicious *adj* suspeitoso

sustain *v* sustentar

sustenance *n* sustento

swallow *v* engolir, tragar

swamp *n* pântano, brejo

swamped *adj* inundado, cheio

swan *n* cisne

swap *v* trocar, barganhar

swap *n* troca, permuta

swarm *n* enxame; multidão

sway *v* oscilar; inclinar

swear *iv* jurar; blasfemar

sweat *n* suor

sweat *v* suar

sweater *n* suéter, pulôver

Sweden *n* Suécia

Swedish *adj* sueco

sweep *iv* varrer

sweet *adj* doce

sweeten *v* adoçar

sweetheart *n* querido, amor

sweetness *n* doçura

sweets *n* bombom, doce

swell *iv* inchar

swelling *n* inchação

swift *adj* rápido

swim *iv* nadar

swimmer *n* nadador

swimming *n* natação; tontura

swindle *v* fraudar

swindle *n* engano, fraude

swindler *n* trapaceiro

swing *iv* balançar

swing *n* balanço; impulso

Swiss *adj* suíço

switch *v* mudar, trocar

switch *n* troca; chave

switch off *v* apagar

switch on *v* acender; abrir

Switzerland *n* Suíça

swivel *v* rodar, girar

swollen *adj* inchado

S

sword *n* espada
swordfish *n* peixe-espada
syllable *n* sílaba
symbol *n* símbolo
symbolic *adj* simbólico
symmetry *n* simetria
sympathize *v* simpatizar
sympathy *n* simpatia
symphony *n* sinfonia
symptom *n* sintoma
synagogue *n* sinagoga
synchronize *v* sincronizar
synod *n* sínodo
synonym *n* sinônimo
synthesis *n* síntese
syphilis *n* sífilis
syringe *n* seringa
syrup *n* xarope, melado
system *n* sistema
systematic *adj* sistemático

T

table *n* mesa
tablecloth *n* toalha de mesa
tablespoon *n* colher de sopa
tablet *n* tablete, pastilha
tack *n* tacha

tackle *v* cuidar de; obstruir
tact *n* tato; diplomacia
tactful *adj* delicado, discreto
tactical *adj* tático
tactics *n* tática
tag *n* etiqueta
tail *n* rabo, raseiro
tail *v* seguir de perto
tailor *n* alfaiate
tainted *adj* manchado
take *iv* pegar; tomar
take apart *v* desmontar
take away *v* roubar, tomar
take back *v* devolver
take in *v* ingerir, receber
take off *v* decolar; safar-se
take over *v* assumir
tale *n* conto; narração
talent *n* talento
talk *v* conversar
talkative *adj* falante
tall *adj* alto
tame *v* domar, amansar
tangent *n* tangente
tangerine *n* tangerina
tangible *adj* tangível
tangle *n* nó, confusão
tank *n* tanque
tanned *adj* bronzeado
tantamount to *adj* equivalente a
tantrum *n* acesso de raiva
tap *n* tapa

S
T

tap into v utilizar
tape n fita, trena
tape recorder n gravador
tapestry n tapeçaria
tar n alcatrão
tarantula n tarântula
tardy adv atrasado
target n alvo, meta
tariff n tarifa
tarnish v empanar, manchar
tart n torta de frutas
tartar n tártaro
task n tarefa
taste v provar
taste n gosto
tasteful adj gostoso
tasteless adj sem gosto
tasty adj gostoso
tavern n taverna
tax n imposto
tea n chá
teach iv ensinar
teacher n professor
team n time
teapot n chaleira
tear iv rasgar; demolir
tear n lágrima; rasgão
tearful adj lacrimoso
tease v importunar, irritar
teaspoon n colher de chá
technical adj técnico
technicality n detalhe técnico

technician n técnico
technique n técnica
technology n tecnologia
tedious adj tedioso
tedium n tédio
teenager n adolescente
teeth n dentes
telegram n telegrama
telepathy n telepatia
telephone n telefone
telescope n telescópio
televise v televisionar
television n televisão
tell iv contar, distingüir
teller n caixa; narrador
telling adj eficaz, notável
temper n temperamento
temperature n temperatura
tempest n tempestade
temple n templo; têmpora
temporary adj temporário
tempt v tentar
temptation n tentação
tempting adj tentador
ten adj dez
tenacity n tenacidade
tenant n inquilino;
tendency n tendência
tender adj tenro, delicado
tenderness n carinho, ternura
tennis n tênis
tenor n tenor

T

tense *adj* tenso

tension *n* tensão

tent *n* barraca, tenda

tentacle *n* tentáculo

tentative *adj* tentativo

tenth *adj* décimo

tenuous *adj* tênuo, delgado

tepid *adj* tépido

term *n* vocábulo; período

terminate *v* terminar

terminology *n* terminologia

termite *n* cupim

terms *n* condições

terrace *n* terraço

terrain *n* terreno

terrestrial *adj* terrestre

terrible *adj* terrível

terrific *adj* tremendo

terrify *v* aterrorizar

terrifying *adj* horripilante

territory *n* território

terror *n* terror

terrorism *n* terrorismo

terrorist *n* terrorista

terrorize *v* aterrorizar

terse *adj* conciso

test *v* testar

test *n* teste

testament *n* testamento

testify *v* testificar

testimony *n* testemunha

text *n* texto

textbook *n* livro escolar

texture *n* textura

thank *v* agradecer

thankful *adj* agradecido

thanks *n* graças

that *adj* esse; aquele

thaw *v* descongelar

thaw *n* degelo

theater *n* teatro

theft *n* roubo

theme *n* tema

themselves *pro* eles mesmos

then *adv* então; e depois

theologian *n* teólogo

theology *n* teologia

theory *n* teoria

therapy *n* terapia

there *adv* lá, ali

therefore *adv* portanto

thermometer *n* termômetro

thermostat *n* termostato

these *adj* estes

thesis *n* tese

they *pro* eles

thick *adj* grosso

thicken *v* engrossar

thickness *n* grossura

thief *n* ladrão

thigh *n* coxa

thin *adj* fino, magro

thing *n* coisa

think *iv* pensar

T

thinly *adv* delgadamente
third *adj* terceiro
thirst *v* ter sede
thirsty *adj* sedento
thirteen *adj* treze
thirty *adj* trinta
this *adj* este
thorn *n* espinho
thorny *adj* espinhoso
thorough *adj* completo
those *adj* aqueles, esses
though *c* apesar
thought *n* idéia
thoughtful *adj* cuidadoso
thousand *adj* mil
thread *v* roscar
thread *n* linha, corda, rosca
threat *n* ameaça
threaten *v* ameaçar
three *adj* três
thresh *v* trilhar
threshold *n* limiar
thrifty *adj* frugal
thrill *v* excitar, tremer
thrill *n* tremor; emoção
thrive *v* prosperar
throat *n* garganta
throb *n* pulsação
throb *v* pulsar, palpitar
thrombosis *n* trombose
throne *n* trono
throng *n* multidão

through *pre* através, por
throw *iv* jogar, lançar
throw away *v* jogar fora
throw up *v* vomitar
thug *n* criminoso
thumb *n* polegar
thumbtack *n* tacha, tachinha
thunder *n* trovão
thunderbolt *n* raio
thunderstorm *n* tempestade
Thursday *n* Quinta-feira
thus *adv* portanto, até
thwart *v* impedir
thyroid *n* tireóide
tickle *v* coçar; divertir
tickle *n* cócegas
ticklish *adj* coceguento
tide *n* maré; tendência
tidy *adj* limpo, arrumado
tie *v* amarrar; empatar
tie *n* laço; empate
tiger *n* tigre
tight *adj* apertado
tighten *v* apertar, arroxar
tile *n* azulejo, telha
till *pre* até
till *v* arar, lavrar
tilt *v* inclinar; atacar
timber *n* madeira
time *n* tempo
time *v* cronometrar
timeless *adj* eterno, infitito

T

timely *adj* oportuno

times *n* vezes

timetable *n* tabela de horário

timid *adj* tímido

timidity *n* timidez

tin *n* lata; estanho

tiny *adj* minúsculo

tip *n* ponta; pista

tiptoe *n* ponta do pé

tired *adj* cansado

tiredness *n* cansaço

tireless *adj* incansável

tiresome *adj* cansativo

tissue *n* tecido

title *n* título

to *pre* para, a

toad *n* sapo

toast *v* tostar; brindar

toast *n* torrada; brinde

toaster *n* torradeira

tobacco *n* tabaco

today *adv* hoje

toddler *n* criança pequena

toe *n* dedo do pé

toenail *n* unha do pé

together *adv* junto

toil *v* labutar

toilet *n* banheiro

token *n* sinal, ficha

tolerable *adj* tolerável

tolerance *n* tolerância

tolerate *v* tolerar

toll *n* badalada; pedágio

toll *v* tocar sino

tomato *n* tomate

tomb *n* tumba

tombstone *n* lápide

tomorrow *adv* amanhã

ton *n* tonelada

tone *n* tom

tongs *n* alicate, tenaz

tongue *n* língua

tonic *n* tônico

tonight *adv* hoje à noite

tonsil *n* amígdala

too *adv* também; demais

tool *n* ferramenta

tooth *n* dente

toothache *n* dor de dente

toothpick *n* palito de dente

top *n* topo, alto

topic *n* tópico

topple *v* ruir, tombar

torch *n* tocha

torment *v* tormentar

torment *n* tormento

torrent *n* torrente

torrid *adj* tórrico

torso *n* busto, torso

tortoise *n* tartaruga

torture *v* torturar

torture *n* tortura

toss *v* jogar, lançar

total *adj* total

T

totalitarian *adj* totalitário

totality *n* totalidade

touch *n* toque, tato

touch *v* tocar

touch on *v* mencionar

touch up *v* retocar

touching *adj* comovente

tough *adj* duro, resistente

toughen *v* endurecer

tour *n* viagem, circuito

tourism *n* turismo

tourist *n* turista

tournament *n* torneio

tow *v* rebocar

tow truck *n* guincho

towards *pre* rumo a, para

towel *n* toalha

tower *n* torre

towering *adj* elevado

town *n* cidade

town hall *n* prefeitura

toxic *adj* tóxico

toxin *n* toxina

toy *n* brinquedo

trace *v* traçar, rastrear

track *n* rasto, pista

track *v* rastrear, perseguir

traction *n* tração

tractor *n* trator

trade *n* negócio; escambo

trade *v* negociar; permutar

trademark *n* marca registrada

trader *n* comerciante

tradition *n* tradição

traffic *n* tráfico

traffic *v* negociar

tragedy *n* tragédia

tragic *adj* trágico

trail *v* perseguir; rastejar

trail *n* caminho, rastro

trailer *n* reboque

train *n* trem

train *v* treinar

trainee *n* estagiário

trainer *n* treinador

training *n* treinamento

trait *n* característica

traitor *n* traidor

trajectory *n* trajetória

tram *n* bonde; vagão

trample *v* pisar, pisotear

trance *n* transe

tranquility *n* tranqüilidade

transaction *n* transação

transcend *v* transcender

transcribe *v* transcrever

transfer *v* transferir

transfer *n* transferência

transform *v* transformar

transformation *n* transformação

transfusion *n* transfusão

transient *adj* transitório

transit *n* trânsito

transition *n* transição**

translate *v* traduzir

translator *n* tradutor

transmit *v* transmitir

transparent *adj* transparente

transplant *v* transplantar

transport *v* transportar

trap *n* cilada

trash *n* lixo

trash can *n* lixeira

traumatic *adj* traumático

traumatize *v* traumatizar

travel *v* viajar

traveler *n* viajante

tray *n* bandeja

treacherous *adj* traiçoeiro

treachery *n* traição

tread *iv* andar, pisar

treason *n* traição

treasure *n* tesouro

treasurer *n* tesoureiro

treat *v* tratar, prazer

treat *n* presente

treatment *n* tratamento

treaty *n* tratado

tree *n* árvore

tremble *v* tremer

tremendous *adj* tremendo

tremor *n* tremor

trench *n* trincheira

trend *n* tendência

trendy *adj* moderno

trespass *v* transgredir

trial *n* julgamento

triangle *n* triângulo

tribe *n* tribo

tribulation *n* tribulação

tribunal *n* tribunal

tribute *n* tributo

trick *v* enganar

trick *n* truque, fraude

trickle *v* gotejar, pingar

tricky *adj* complicado

trigger *v* causar, provocar

trigger *n* gatilho

trim *v* aparar, arrumar

trimester *n* trimestre

trimmings *n* restos; adorno

trip *n* viagem

trip *v* tropeçar

triple *adj* triplo

tripod *n* tripé

triumph *n* triunfo

triumphant *adj* triunfante

trivial *adj* trivial, banal

trivialize *v* banalizar

trolley *n* carrinho; bonde

troop *n* tropa

trophy *n* troféu

tropic *n* trópico

tropical *adj* tropical

trouble *n* preocupação

trouble *v* preocupar

troublesome *adj* preocupante

trousers *n* calça comprida

T

trout *n* truta

truce *n* trégua

truck *n* caminhão, troca

trucker *n* motorista

trumped-up *adj* forjado

trumpet *n* trombeta

trunk *n* baú; tronco

trust *v* confiar

trust *n* confiança

truth *n* verdade

truthful *adj* verdadeiro

try *v* tentar

tub *n* tina, banheira

tuberculosis *n* tuberculose

Tuesday *n* Terça-feira

tuition *n* custo da instrução

tulip *n* tulipa

tumble *v* cair, tombar

tummy *n* barriga

tumor *n* tumor

tumult *n* tumulto

tumultuous *adj* tumultuoso

tuna *n* atum; boceta

tune *n* tom

tune up *v* afinar, ajustar

tunic *n* túnica

tunnel *n* túnel

turbine *n* turbina

turbulence *n* turbulência

turf *n* turfa, turfe

Turk *adj* turco

Turkey *n* Turquia

turmoil *n* tumulto

turn *n* giro, curva; vez

turn *v* girar, virar

turn back *v* voltar, retornar

turn down *v* rejeitar

turn in *v* entregar

turn off *v* desligar; afastar

turn on *v* ligar; abrir

turn out *v* apagar

turn over *v* denunciar, inverter

turn up *v* surgir; tornar-se

turret *n* torre

turtle *n* tartaruga

tusk *n* presa, dente

tutor *n* tutor

tweezers *n* pinça

twelfth *adj* duodécimo

twelve *adj* doze

twentieth *adj* vigésimo

twenty *adj* vinte

twice *adv* duas vezes

twilight *n* crepúsculo

twin *n* gêmeo

twinkle *v* cintilar, brilhar

twist *v* torcer, trançar

twist *n* giro; torção

twisted *adj* torcido

twister *n* ciclone

two *adj* dois

tycoon *n* magnata

type *n* tipo

type *v* tipificar

T

typical *adj* típico
tyranny *n* tirania
tyrant *n* tirano

U

ugliness *n* fealdade
ugly *adj* feio
ulcer *n* úlcera
ultimate *adj* último, máximo
ultimatum *n* ultimato
ultrasound *n* ultrassom
umbrella *n* guarda-chuva
umpire *n* árbitro
unable *adj* incapaz
unanimity *n* unanimidade
unarmed *adj* desarmado
unassuming *adj* despretensioso
unattached *adj* desligado, solto
unavoidable *adj* inevitável
unaware *adj* insconsciente
unbearable *adj* insuportável
unbeatable *adj* imbatível
unbelievable *adj* inacreditável
unbiased *adj* imparcial
unbroken *adj* contínuo, intacto
unbutton *v* desabotoar
uncertain *adj* incerto

uncle *n* tio
uncomfortable *adj* desconfortável
uncommon *adj* incomum
unconscious *adj* inconsciente
uncover *v* descobrir
undecided *adj* indeciso
undeniable *adj* inegável
under *pre* debaixo
undercover *adj* secreto
underdog *n* perdedor
undergo *v* submeter-se
underground *adj* subterrâneo
underlie *v* fundamentar
underline *v* sublinhar
underlying *adj* fundamental
undermine *v* minar, corroer
underneath *pre* por baixo
understand *v* entender
understandable *adj* compreensível
understanding *adj* compreensivo
undertake *v* empreender
underwear *n* roupa interior
underwrite *v* subscrever
undeserved *adj* imerecido
undesirable *adj* indesejável
undisputed *adj* inconteste
undo *v* desfazer
undoubtedly *adv* certamente
undress *v* despir
undue *adj* indevido
unearth *v* desenterrar
uneasiness *n* desconforto

T
U

uneasy *adj* desconfortável
uneducated *adj* inculto, rude
unemployed *adj* desempregado
unemployment *n* desemprego
unending *adj* interminável
unequal *adj* desigual
unequivocal *adj* inequívoco
uneven *adj* desnivelado
uneventful *adj* monótono
unexpected *adj* inesperado
unfailing *adj* infalível
unfair *adj* injusto
unfairly *adv* injustamente
unfairness *n* injustiça
unfaithful *adj* infiel
unfamiliar *adj* estranho
unfasten *v* desatar
unfavorable *adj* desfavorável
unfit *adj* inadequado
unfold *v* desdobrar
unforeseen *adj* imprevisto
unforgettable *adj* inesquecível
unfounded *adj* infundado
unfriendly *adj* inamistoso
unfurnished *adj* sem móveis
ungrateful *adj* ingrato
unhappiness *n* infelicidade
unhappy *adj* infeliz
unharmed *adj* ileso
unhealthy *adj* doentio
unheard-of *adj* desconhecido
unhurt *adj* ileso

unification *n* unificação
uniform *n* uniforme
uniformity *n* uniformidade
unify *v* unificar
unilateral *adj* unilateral
union *n* união
unique *adj* único
unit *n* unidade
unite *v* unir
unity *n* união
universal *adj* universal
universe *n* universo
university *n* universidade
unjust *adj* injusto
unjustified *adj* injustificado
unknown *adj* desconhecido
unlawful *adj* proibido
unleaded *adj* sem chumbo
unleash *v* desatar
unless *c* a menos que
unlike *adj* distinto
unlikely *adj* improvável
unlimited *adj* inlimitado
unload *v* descarregar
unlock *v* destrancar
unlucky *adj* azarado
unmarried *adj* solteiro
unmask *v* desmascarar
unmistakable *adj* inequívoco
unnecessary *adj* desnecessário
unnoticed *adj* despercebível
unoccupied *adj* desocupado

U

unpack _v_ desempacotar
unpleasant _adj_ desagradável
unplug _v_ desligar
unpopular _adj_ impopular
unpredictable _adj_ imprevisível
unprofitable _adj_ não lucrativo
unprotected _adj_ desprotegido
unravel _v_ desenredar
unreal _adj_ irreal
unrealistic _adj_ irreal
unreasonable _adj_ irracional
unrelated _adj_ desvinculado
unreliable _adj_ falível
unrest _n_ inquietação
unsafe _adj_ inseguro
unselfish _adj_ altruísta
unspeakable _adj_ indizível
unstable _adj_ móvel
unsteady _adj_ instável
unsuccessful _adj_ malsucedido
unsuitable _adj_ inadequado
unsuspecting _adj_ inocente
unthinkable _adj_ impensável
untie _v_ desatar, soltar
until _pre_ até
untimely _adj_ inoportuno
untouchable _adj_ intocável
untrue _adj_ falso
unusual _adj_ incomum
unveil _v_ desvelar
unwillingly _adv_ de má vontade
unwind _v_ desenrolar

unwise _adj_ insensato
unwrap _v_ abrir
upbringing _n_ formação
upcoming _adj_ vindouro
update _v_ atualizar
upgrade _v_ melhorar
upheaval _n_ revolta
uphill _adv_ para cima
uphold _v_ suster, defender
upholstery _n_ tapeçaria
upkeep _n_ manutenção
upon _pre_ sobre, em
upper _adj_ superior
upright _adj_ ereto; correto
uprising _n_ revolta
uproar _n_ ruído, baderna
uproot _v_ desarraigar
upset _v_ preocupar
upstairs _adv_ em cima
uptight _adj_ tenso
up-to-date _adj_ atualizado
upwards _adv_ para cima
urban _adj_ urbano
urge _n_ ânsia, ímpeto
urge _v_ urgir
urgency _n_ urgência
urgent _adj_ urgente
urinate _v_ urinar
urine _n_ urina
urn _n_ urna
us _pro_ nos, nós
usage _n_ uso

use *v* usar
use *n* uso, usança
used to *adj* acostumado
useful *adj* útil
usefulness *n* utilidade
useless *adj* imprestável
user *n* usuário
usual *adj* usual
usurp *v* usurpar
utensil *n* utensílio
uterus *n* útero
utilize *v* utilizar
utmost *adj* maior
utter *v* expressar

V

vacancy *n* vacância
vacant *adj* vago, livre
vacate *v* vagar, desocupar
vacation *n* férias
vaccinate *v* vacinar
vaccine *n* vacina
vacillate *v* vacilar
vagrant *n* errante
vague *adj* vago, turvo
vain *adj* vão
vainly *adv* futilmente

valiant *adj* valente
valid *adj* válido
validate *v* validar
validity *n* validade
valley *n* valente
valuable *adj* valioso
value *n* valor
valve *n* válvula
vampire *n* vampiro
van *n* furgão
vandal *n* vândalo
vandalism *n* vandalismo
vandalize *v* vandalizar
vanguard *n* vanguarda
vanish *v* desvanecer
vanity *n* vaidade
vanquish *v* vencer
vaporize *v* vaporizar
variable *adj* variável
varied *adj* variado
variety *n* variedade
various *adj* vários
varnish *v* envernizar
varnish *n* verniz, brilho
vary *v* variar
vase *n* vaso
vast *adj* vasto
veal *n* vitela
veer *v* desviar
vegetable *v* vegetal, verdura
vegetarian *adj* vegetariano
vegetation *n* vegetação

vehicle *n* veículo
veil *n* véu
vein *n* veia
velocity *n* velocidade
velvet *n* veludo
venerate *v* venerar
vengeance *n* vingança
venison *n* veado
venom *n* veneno
vent *n* escape
ventilate *v* ventilar
ventilation *n* ventilação
venture *v* aventurar
venture *n* aventura; risco
verb *n* verbo
verbally *adv* verbalmente
verbatim *adv* literalmente
verdict *n* veredicto
verge *n* margem; borda
verification *n* verificação
verify *v* verificar
versatile *adj* versátil
verse *n* verso
versed *adj* versado
version *n* versão
versus *pre* versus
vertebra *n* vértebra
very *adj* muito
vessel *n* vaso, navio
vest *n* vestes
vestige *n* vestígio
veteran *n* veterano

veterinarian *n* veterinário
veto *v* vetar, proibir
viaduct *n* viaduto
vibrant *adj* vibrante
vibrate *v* vibrar
vibration *n* vibração
vice *n* vice; vício
vicinity *n* vizinhança
vicious *adj* vicioso; violento
victim *n* vítima
victimize *v* vitimar
victor *n* vencedor
victorious *adj* vitorioso
victory *n* vitória
view *n* vista; opinião
view *v* ver, observar
viewpoint *n* ponto de vista
vigil *n* vigília
village *n* vila
villager *n* aldeão
villain *n* vilão
vindicate *v* vindicar
vindictive *adj* vindicativo
vine *n* vinha
vinegar *n* vinagre
vineyard *n* vinhedo
violate *v* violar
violence *n* violência
violent *adj* violento
violet *n* violeta
violin *n* violino
violinist *n* violinista

viper *n* víbora
virgin *n* virgem
virginity *n* virgindade
virile *adj* viril
virility *n* virilidade
virtually *adv* virtualmente
virtue *n* virtude
virtuous *adj* virtuoso
virulent *adj* virulento
virus *n* vírus
visibility *n* visibilidade
visible *adj* visível
vision *n* visão
visit *n* visita
visit *v* visitar
visitor *n* visitante
visual *adj* visual
visualize *v* visualizar
vital *adj* vital
vitality *n* vitalidade
vitamin *n* vitamina
vivacious *adj* vivaz
vivid *adj* vívido
vocabulary *n* vocabulário
vocation *n* vocação
vogue *n* voga, moda
voice *n* voz
void *adj* inválido
volatile *adj* volátil
volcano *n* vulcão
volleyball *n* vôleibol
voltage *n* voltagem

volume *n* volume
volunteer *n* voluntário
vomit *v* vomitar
vomit *n* vômito
vote *v* votar
vote *n* voto
voting *n* votação
vouch for *v* garantir
voucher *n* recibo; fiador
vow *v* prometer, jurar
vowel *n* vogal
voyage *n* viajem por mar
voyager *n* viajor, viajante
vulgar *adj* vulgar
vulgarity *n* vulgaridade
vulnerable *adj* vulnerável
vulture *n* ave de rapina

wafer *n* bolacha
wag *v* menear
wage *n* salário, soldo
wagon *n* vagão, carroça
wail *v* choramingar
wail *n* lamento
waist *n* cintura
wait *v* esperar

waiter *n* garçom
waiting *n* espera
waitress *n* garçonete
waive *v* desistir; protelar
wake up *iv* despertar
walk *v* caminhar
walk *n* caminhadao
walkout *n* greve
wall *n* parede
wallet *n* carteira
walnut *n* noz
walrus *n* morsa
waltz *n* valsa
wander *v* vagar, errar
wanderer *n* vagabundo
wane *v* minguar
want *v* querer
war *n* guerra
ward *n* ala de hospital
warden *n* encarregado
wardrobe *n* guarda-roupa
warehouse *n* depósito
warm *adj* cálido, cordial
warm up *v* esquentar; animar
warmth *n* calor; cordialidade
warn *v* advertir, avisar
warning *n* aviso, advertência
warp *v* entortar, distorcer
warped *adj* empenado, curvo
warrant *v* garantir, atestar
warrant *n* ordem de prisão
warranty *n* garantia

warrior *n* guerreiro
warship *n* navio de guerra
wart *n* verruga
wary *adj* cuidadoso, alerta
wash *v* lavar
washable *adj* lavável
wasp *n* vespa
waste *v* desperdiçar
waste *n* desperdício
waste basket *n* cesta de lixo
wasteful *adj* esbanjador
watch *n* relógio
watch *v* vigiar
watch out *v* estar alerta
watchful *adj* vigilante
watchmaker *n* relojoeiro
water *n* água
water *v* aguar, regar
water down *v* diluir
water heater *n* aquecedor de água
waterfall *n* catarata, cascata
watermelon *n* melancia
waterproof *adj* à prova d'água
watertight *adj* impenetrável
watery *adj* aguado
watt *n* watt
wave *n* onda, ondulação
waver *v* oscilar
wavy *adj* ondulado
wax *n* cera
way *n* caminho; forma

way in *n* entrada
way out *n* saída
we *pro* nós
weak *adj* fraco
weaken *v* enfraquecer
weakness *n* fraqueza
wealth *n* riqueza
wealthy *adj* opulento
weapon *n* arma
wear *n* vestimenta; gasto
wear *iv* vestir; esgotar
wear down *v* gastar; cansar
wear out *v* desgastar
weary *adj* esgotado, farto
weather *n* tempo, clima
weave *iv* tecer
web *n* teia, rede
web site *n* página da Internet
wed *iv* casar
wedding *n* casamento
wedge *n* cunha
Wednesday *n* Quarta-feira
weed *n* mato
weed *v* extirpar
week *n* semana
weekday *adj* dia da semana
weekend *n* fim de semana
weekly *adv* semanalmente
weep *iv* chorar
weigh *v* pesar
weight *n* peso
weird *adj* estranho

welcome *v* receber
welcome *n* boas-vindas
weld *v* soldar
welder *n* soldador
welfare *n* bem-estar
well *n* poço
well-known *adj* conhecido
well-to-do *adj* próspero
west *n* Oeste
westbound *adv* rumo oeste
western *adj* faroeste
westerner *adj* ocidental
wet *adj* molhado
whale *n* baleia
wharf *n* cais
what *adj* que, qual, quais
whatever *adj* qualquer um
wheat *n* trigo
wheel *n* roda
wheelbarrow *n* carrinho de mão
wheelchair *n* cadeira de rodas
wheeze *v* chiar; resfolegar
when *adv* quando
whenever *adv* sempre que
whereabouts *n* paradeiro
whereas *c* enquanto que
whereupon *c* e portanto
wherever *c* qualquer lugar
whether *c* se; quer
which *adj* qual
while *c* enquanto, durante
whim *n* sarilho; capricho

W

whine *v* ganir
whip *v* bater, chicotear
whip *n* chicote
whirl *v* rodopiar, girar
whirlpool *n* redemoinho
whiskers *n* bigode
whisper *v* sussurrar
whisper *n* cochicho
whistle *v* assobiar
whistle *n* assobio
white *adj* branco
whiten *v* branquear
whittle *v* retalhar
who *pro* quem, qual
whoever *pro* quem quer que seja
whole *adj* inteiro
wholehearted *adj* de todo coração
wholesale *n* atacado
wholesome *adj* são, sadio
whom *pro* a quem
why *adv* por quê
wicked *adj* mau, malvado
wickedness *n* maldade
wide *adj* vasto, amplo
widely *adv* amplamente
widen *v* alargar, ampliar
widespread *adj* expandido
widow *n* viúva
widower *n* viúvo
width *n* largura
wield *v* manejar

wife *n* esposa, mulher
wig *n* peruca
wiggle *v* menear
wild *adj* selvagem
wild boar *n* javali
wilderness *n* deserto, selva,
will *n* vontade; testamento
willfully *adv* de propósito
willing *adj* disposto
willingly *adv* de bom grado
willingness *n* disposição
willow *n* salgueiro
wily *adj* astuto
wimp *adj* fraco, débil
win *iv* vencer, ganhar
wind *n* vento
wind up *v* enrolar; dar corda
winding *adj* tortuoso
windmill *n* moinho de vento
window *n* janela
windpipe *n* traquéia
windshield *n* pára-brisa
windy *adj* ventoso; vaidoso
wine *n* vinho
winery *n* lagar, vinícola
wing *n* asa, ala
wink *n* pestanejo
wink *v* piscar; cintilar
winner *n* vencedor, ganhador
winter *n* inverno
wipe *v* secar, limpar
wipe out *v* eliminar, extingüir

wire *n* arame; telegrama

wireless *adj* sem fio

wisdom *n* sabedoria

wise *adj* sábio

wish *v* desejar

wish *n* desejo

wit *n* talento

witch *n* bruxa, feiticeira

witchcraft *n* bruxaria, feitiçaria

with *pre* com

withdraw *v* retirar, retrair

withdrawal *n* retirada

withdrawn *adj* retraído

wither *v* murchar

withhold *iv* recusar; reter

within *pre* dentro de

without *pre* sem

withstand *v* resistir

witness *n* testemunha

witty *adj* vivo, engenhoso

wives *n* esposas

wizard *n* mago

wobble *v* oscilar

woes *n* desgraças

wolf *n* lobo

woman *n* mulher

womb *n* ventre

women *n* mulheres

wonder *v* perguntar-se

wonder *n* maravilha

wonderful *adj* maravilhoso

wood *n* madeira

wooden *adj* de madeira

wool *n* lã

woolen *adj* de lã

word *n* palavra; recado

wording *n* redação

work *n* trabalho, obra

work *v* trabalhar, funcionar

work out *v* exercitar-se, malhar

workable *adj* viável

workbook *n* caderno

worker *n* trabalhador

workshop *n* oficina

world *n* mundo

worldly *adj* mundano

worldwide *adj* mundial

worm *n* verme

worn-out *adj* gasto; esgotado

worrisome *adj* inquietante

worry *v* preocupar-se

worry *n* preocupação

worse *adj* pior

worsen *v* piorar

worship *n* culto, adoração

worst *adj* pior

worth *adj* digno de

worthless *adj* sem valor

worthwhile *adj* vale a pena

worthy *adj* digno, merecedor

would-be *adj* pretenso

wound *n* ferida

wound *v* ferir

woven *adj* tecido

W

wrap *v* embrulhar
wrap up *v* agasalhar
wrapping *n* embrulho
wrath *n* ira
wreath *n* coroa
wreck *v* arruinar, destroçar
wreckage *n* destroços
wrench *n* chave inglesa
wrestle *v* lutar
wrestler *n* lutador
wrestling *n* luta livre
wretched *adj* desgraçado
wring *iv* torcer, contorcer
wrinkle *v* enrugar
wrinkle *n* ruga
wrist *n* pulso, munheca
write *iv* escrever
write down *v* anotar
writer *n* escritor
writhe *v* contorcer-se
writing *n* escrita, escrito
written *adj* escrito
wrong *adj* errado

X-mas *n* Natal
X-ray *n* Raio X

yacht *n* iate
yam *n* inhame
yard *n* jarda; pátio
yarn *n* fio, lã; história
yawn *n* bocejo
yawn *v* bocejar
year *n* ano
yearly *adv* anualmente
yearn *v* anelar
yeast *n* levedura
yell *v* gritar
yellow *adj* amarelo
yes *adv* sim
yesterday *adv* ontem
yet *c* já; ainda
yield *v* dar lucro
yield *n* produção, lucro
yoke *n* jugo, canga
yolk *n* gema
you *pro* você, tu; vós; te, ti

young *adj* jovem
youngster *n* menino; jovem
your *adj* seu, teu
yours *pro* seu, teu
yourself *pro* você mesmo
youth *n* juventude
youthful *adj* juvenil

zap *v* destruir
zeal *n* zelo
zealous *adj* zeloso
zebra *n* zebra
zero *n* zero
zest *n* gosto, sabor
zinc *n* zinco
zipper *n* zíper
zone *n* zona
zoo *n* zoológico
zoology *n* zoologia

Portuguese-English

Bilingual Dictionaries, Inc.

Abbreviations

English - Portuguese

a - article - artigo
adj - adjective - adjetivo
adv - adverb - advérvio
c - conjunction - conjunção
e - exclamation - exclamação
f - feminine (noun) - feminino (sustantivo)
m - masculine (noun) - masculino (sustantivo)
pre - preposition - preposição
pro - pronoun - pronome
v - verb - verbo

abacaxi *f* pineapple
abade *m* abbot
abadia *f* abbey
abafar *v* muffle
abaixar-se *v* bend down
abaixo *adv* below
abajur *f* lamp
abandonado *adj* derelict
abandonar *v* abandon
abandono *m* abandonment
abarcar *v* span
abarrotado *adj* crowded
abarrotar *v* cram
abastecedor *m* supplier
abastecer *v* cater to
abatedouro *f* butchery
abater *v* cut down
abatido *adj* dejected
abdicação *nf* abdication
abdicar *v* abdicate
abdômen *m* abdomen
abdução *f* abduction
abduzir *v* abduct
abelha *f* bee
abençoado *adj* blessed
abençoar *v* bless
aberração *f* aberration
aberto *adj* open
abertura *f* opening

abismal *adj* abysmal
abismo *m* abyss
abóbora *f* pumpkin
abolir *v* abolish
abominação *f* loathing
abominar *v* abhor, loathe
abordagem *m* approach
abortar *v* abort
aborto *m* abortion
abraçar *v* embrace, hug
abraço *m* embrace
abrasar *v* scorch
abreviação *f* abbreviation
abreviar *v* abbreviate
abridor de lata *m* can opener
Abril *m* April
abrir *v* open, unwrap
abrir à força *v* break open
abrogar *v* abrogate
abruptamente *adv* abruptly
absoluto *adj* absolute
absolver *v* acquit
absolvição *f* acquittal
absolvisão *v* absolve
absorto *adj* engrossed
absorvente *adj* absorbent
absorver *v* absorb
abster *v* refrain
abster (se) *v* abstain
abstinência *f* abstinence
abstrato *adj* abstract
absurdo *adj* absurd

abundância _f_ abundance
abundante _adj_ plentiful
abundar _v_ abound
abusar _v_ abuse
abusivo _adj_ abusive
abuso _m_ abuse
acabar _v_ finish
academia _f_ academy
acadêmico _adj_ academic
acalmar _v_ appease, soothe
acampamento _m_ camp
acampar _v_ camp
ação _f_ action, deed
acariciar _v_ caress
acarinhar _v_ cherish
acarretar _v_ entail
acatar _v_ comply
aceitação _f_ acceptance
aceitar _v_ accept
aceitável _adj_ acceptable
acelerador _m_ accelerator
acelerar _v_ accelerate, speed
acenar _v_ beckon
acender _v_ kindle, switch on
acender-se _v_ flare-up
acento _m_ accent
acerca de _pre_ about
acessível _adj_ accessible
acesso _m_ access
acesso de raiva _m_ tantrum
achatar _v_ squash
acidental _adj_ accidental

acidente _m_ accident
acidez _f_ acidity
ácido _m_ acid
acima _pre_ above
acima de _pre_ over
acionista _m_ shareholder
aclamar _v_ acclaim
aclimatar _v_ acclimatize
aço _m_ steel
açoitar _v_ flog
acolchoado _f_ quilt
acolher _v_ shelter
acomodar _v_ accommodate
acompanhar _v_ accompany
aconchegante _adj_ cozy
aconchegar _v_ cuddle
aconselhar _v_ advise
aconselhável _adj_ advisable
acontecer _v_ happen
acontecimento _m_ happening
acordado _adj_ awake
acordar _v_ awake
acordeão _m_ accordion
acordo _m_ accord, deal
acorrentar _v_ chain
acostumado _adj_ used to
acostumar _v_ accustom
açougueiro _m_ butcher
acre _nm_ acre
acreditar _v_ believe
acreditável _adj_ believable
acrobata _m_ acrobat

açúcar *m* sugar
acumular *v* accumulate
acusação *f* accusation
acusar *v* accuse
acústico *adj* acoustic
adamantino *adj* adamant
adaptação *f* adaptation
adaptador *m* adapter
adaptar *v* adapt
adaptável *adj* adaptable
adega *f* cellar
adejar *v* flutter
adequado *adj* adequate
aderir *v* adhere, stick to
adesivo *adj* adhesive
adiamento *nm* postponement
adiante *pre* along
adiante *adv* forward
adiar *v* adjourn
adição *f* addition
adicional *adj* additional
adicionar *v* add
adivinhação *m* guess
adivinhar *v* guess
adjacente *adj* adjacent
adjetivo *m* adjective
administração *f* management
administrar *v* administer
administrar mal *v* mismanage
admiração *f* admiration
admirador *m* admirer
admirar *v* admire

admirável *adj* admirable
admissão *f* admittance
admissível *adj* admissible
admitir *v* admit
admoestação *f* admonition
admoestar *v* admonish
adoção *f* adoption
adoçar *v* sweeten
adoecer *v* sicken
adolescência *nf* adolescence
adolescente *m* adolescent
adoração *f* worship
adorar *v* adore
adorável *adj* adorable, lovable
adormecido *adj* asleep
adornar *v* adorn
adorno *m* trimmings
adotar *v* adopt
adotivo *adj* adoptive
adquirir *v* acquire
adulação *f* flattery
adular *v* flatter
adulterar *v* adulterate
adultério *m* adultery
adulto *m* adult, grown-up
Advento *m* Advent
advérbio *m* adverb
adversário *m* adversary
adversidade *f* adversity
adverso *adj* adverse
advertir *v* warn
advogado *m* attorney

aeromoça *nf* stewardess
aeronave *m* aircraft
aeroporto *m* airport
afagar *v* fondle
afável *adj* affable
afeição *f* affection
afeiçoado *m* attachment
aferrar-se *v* stick
afetar *v* affect
afetuoso *adj* affectionate
afiado *adj* sharp
afiar *v* sharpen
afiliar(se) *v* affiliate
afinar *v* tune up
afinidade *f* affinity
afirmação *f* assertion
afirmar *v* affirm, claim
afirmativo *adj* affirmative
afivelar *v* buckle up
afixar *v* affix
aflição *f* affliction
afligir *v* distress, afflict
aflitivo *adj* distressing
afluência *f* influx
afogar *v* drown
afortunado *adj* fortunate
afrodisíaco *adj* aphrodisiac
afronta *f* affront
afrontar *v* affront
afrouxar *v* loose
afundar *v* sink
agachar-se *v* crouch

agarrar *v* cling, grab, seize
agasalhar *v* wrap up
agência *f* agency
agenda *f* agenda
agente *m* agent
ágil *adj* agile
agir *v* act
agitado *adj* hectic
agitador *m* agitator
agitar *v* stir up
aglomerado *m* cluster
aglomerar *v* agglomerate
aglomerar-se *v* crowd
agnóstico *nm* agnostic
agonia *f* agony, anguish
agonizante *adj* agonizing
agonizar *v* agonize
agora *adv* now
Agosto *m* August
agourento *adj* ominous
agradar *v* ingratiate, please
agradável *adj* pleasant
agradecer *v* thank
agradecido *adj* thankful
agravação *f* aggravation
agravar *v* aggravate
agregado *adj* attached
agregar *v* aggregate
agressão *f* aggression
agressivo *adj* aggressive
agressor *m* aggressor
agrícola *adj* agricultural

agricultura _m_ agriculture
água _f_ water
aguaceiro _m_ downpour
aguado _adj_ watery
agudo _adj_ acute
agüentar _v_ endure, put up with
águia _f_ eagle
agulha _m_ needle
ainda mais _c_ even more
aipo _m_ celery
ajoalhar _v_ kneel
ajuda _f_ help
ajudante _m_ aide
ajudar _m_ help
ajuntar _v_ assemble
ajustar _v_ adjust, fit
ajustável _adj_ adjustable
ajuste _m_ adjustment
ala _f_ wing
ala de hospital _f_ ward
alargar _v_ broaden
alarmante _adj_ alarming
alarmar _v_ startle
alarme _f_ alarm
alavanca _nf_ lever
albergue _m_ inn
alcachofra _f_ artichoke
alcançar _v_ attain, reach
alcançável _adj_ attainable
alcance _m_ reach, scope
alçapão _m_ pitfall
alcatrão _m_ tar

alcoólico _adj_ alcoholic
alcoolismo _m_ alcoholism
alcovitar _v_ pander
aldeão _m_ villager
aldeia _f_ hamlet
alegação _f_ allegation
alegar _v_ allege
alegoria _adj_ allergic
alegre _adj_ joyful
alegremente _adv_ joyfully
alegria _nm_ joy
aleijado _adj_ cripple
aleijar _v_ cripple, maim
além de _pre_ besides
além de _adv_ beyond
além disso _adv_ furthermore
Alemanha _f_ Germany
alemão _adj_ German
além-mar _adv_ overseas
alergia _f_ allergy
alerta _f_ alert
alfabetizado _adj_ literate
alfabeto _m_ alphabet
alface _nf_ lettuce
alfaiate _m_ tailor
alfândega _f_ customs
alfinete _m_ pin
álgebra _f_ algebra
algema _f_ shackle, handcuffs
algemar _v_ handcuff
algodão _m_ cotton
alguém _pro_ somebody

algum *adj* any, some
algum dia *adv* someday
alguma coisa *pro* something
alho *m* garlic
aliado *adj* allied
aliado *m* ally
aliança *f* alliance
aliar *v* ally
aliás *adv* incidentally
alibre *m* caliber
alicate *n* pincers, tongs
alienado *adj* estranged
alimentar *v* feed
alimento *m* nourishment
alinhamento *m* alignment
alinhar *v* align
alisar *v* smooth
alistar *v* draft
alistar-se *v* enlist
aliviar *v* relieve, soothe
alívio *m* relief
alma *m* soul
almanaque *m* almanac
almirante *m* admiral
almoço *m* lunch
almofada *f* cushion
almôndega *nf* meatball
almoxarifado *m* stockroom
alojamento *m* lodging
alojar *v* lodge
alpinismo *m* climbing
altamente *adv* highly

altar *m* altar
alteração *f* alteration
alterar *v* alter
altercação *m* altercation
alternado *adj* alternate
alternar *v* alternate
alternativa *f* alternative
Alteza *f* Highness
altitude *f* altitude
altivo *adj* haughty
alto *adv* loud
alto *adj* high, tall
alto-falante *m* loudspeaker
altruísta *adj* unselfish
altura *f* height
alugar *v* rent
aluguel *f* rent
alumínio *m* aluminum
aluno *m* pupil
alusão *f* allusion
alvejante *m* bleach
alvejar *v* bleach
alvo *m* butt
alvo de riso *m* laughing stock
alvorada *f* dawn
alvoroço *m* fuss
amado *adj* beloved
amador *adj* amateur
amadurecer *v* ripen
amaldiçoar *v* cuss
amanhã *adv* tomorrow
amante *f* lover, mistress

amar _v_ love
amarelo _adj_ yellow
amargamente _adv_ bitterly
amargo _adj_ bitter
amargor _m_ bitterness
amargurar _v_ embitter
amarrar _v_ moor, tie, bind
amassar _v_ crease
amável _adj_ amiable
ambição _f_ ambition
ambicioso _adj_ ambitious
ambiente _m_ environment
ambíguo _adj_ ambiguous
ambivalente _adj_ ambivalent
ambos _adj_ both
ambulância _f_ ambulance
ameaça _f_ threat
ameaçar _v_ threaten
amêijoa _f_ clam
ameixa _f_ plum
ameixa seca _f_ prune
amêndoa _f_ almond
amendoim _nm_ peanut
americano _adj_ American
amido _m_ starch
amiga _f_ girlfriend
amigável _adj_ amicable
amígdala _f_ tonsil
amigo _m_ friend
amizade _f_ friendship
amnésia _f_ amnesia
amolação _m_ nuisance

amônia _f_ ammonia
amontoar _v_ heap, stack
amor _m_ love
amora _f_ blackberry
amordaçar _v_ gag
amorfo _adj_ amorphous
amoroso _adj_ loving
amortecer _v_ cushion
amortizar _v_ amortize
amostra _f_ sample
amotinar _v_ riot
amplamente _adv_ widely
ampliação _f_ enlargement
ampliar _v_ widen, enlarge
amplificador _m_ amplifier
amplificar _v_ amplify
amplo _adj_ ample, wide
amputação _f_ amputation
amputar _v_ amputate
amuado _adj_ grumpy
amurada _f_ bulwark
analfabeto _adj_ illiterate
analgésico _m_ painkiller
analisar _v_ analyze
análise _m_ analysis
analogia _f_ analogy
anão _m_ dwarf, midget
anarquia _f_ anarchy
anarquista _m_ anarchist
anatomia _f_ anatomy
ancestral _m_ ancestor
anchova _f_ anchovy

âncora *m* anchor

ancorar *v* land

andaime *m* scaffolding

andar a passo *v* pace

andrajoso *adj* ragged

anedota *f* anecdote

anel *m* ring

anelar *v* yearn

anemia *f* anemia

anêmico *adj* anemic

anestesia *f* anesthesia

anexar *v* annex

anexo *m* attachment

anfíbio *adj* amphibious

anfiteatro *m* amphitheater

anfitriã *f* hostess

anfitrião *m* host

angariar votos *v* canvas

angelical *adj* angelic

angina *f* angina

Anglicano *adj* Anglican

ângulo *f* angle

ângulo *m* corner

animação *f* animation

animal *m* animal

animar *v* cheer up

animosidade *f* animosity

aniquilação *f* annihilation

aniquilar *v* annihilate

anistia *f* amnesty

aniversário *m* anniversary

anjo *m* angel

ano *m* year

ano bissexto *m* leap year

anonimidade *f* anonymity

anônimo *adj* anonymous

anormal *adj* abnormal

anormalidade *f* abnormality

anotação *f* annotation

anotar *v* note

ânsia *f* urge

ansiar *v* crave

ansiedade *f* anxiety

ansioso *adj* anxious

antagonizar *v* antagonize

antecedente *m* antecedent

antecedente *adj* previous

antecedentes *m* record

antecipação *f* anticipation

antecipar *v* anticipate

antena *f* antenna

antes *adv* before

antes de *pre* before

antibiótico *m* antibiotic

antídoto *m* antidote

antigamente *adv* formerly

antigo *adj* ancient

antiguidade *nf* antiquity

antílope *m* antelope

antipatia *f* antipathy

antiquado *adj* outmoded

anual *adj* annual

anualmente *adv* yearly

anulação *f* annulment

anular *v* annul, quash
anunciador *m* announcer
anunciar *v* announce
anúncio *m* announcement
ao acaso *adv* randomly
ao lado *adv* aside
ao lado *pre* beside
ao longo de *pre* alongside
ao mar *adv* overboard
apagador *f* eraser
apagar *v* put out, switch off
apaixonado *adj* passionate
apalpar *v* feel
apanhar *v* catch
aparar *v* trim
aparecer *v* appear, show up
aparecimento *f* appearance
aparelho *m* device, gadget
aparência *m* guise
aparentado *adj* related
aparente *adj* apparent
aparentemente *adv* apparently
aparição *f* apparition
apartamento *m* apartment
apartar-se *v* drift apart
apatia *f* apathy
apavorante *adj* appalling
apaziguamento *m* appeasement
apaziguar *v* pacify
apear *v* step out
apedrejar *v* stone
apelar *v* appeal

apelido *m* nickname
apelo *m* appeal, plea
apenas *adv* scarcely
apêndice *m* appendix
apendicite *m* appendicitis
aperitivo *m* aperitif, appetizer
apertado *adj* tight
apertar *v* tighten, press
aperto *m* grip, press
aperto de mão *m* handshake
apesar *c* though
apesar de *c* despite
apesar de tudo *adv* nevertheless
apesar disso *c* nonetheless
apetite *m* appetite
ápice *m* apex, summit
aplacar *v* placate
aplanar *v* flatten
aplaudir *v* applaud
aplauso *m* applause
aplicação *f* application
aplicante *m* applicant
aplicar *v* apply
aplicável *adj* applicable
apocalipse *m* apocalypse
apodrecer *v* rot
apoiar *v* aid, bolster
apoiar-se *v* lean on
apoio *m* aid
apologia *f* apology
apontador *m* sharpener
apontar *v* appoint, assign

apoplexia *f* stroke
aposta *f* bet
apostar *v* bet, gamble
apostólico *adj* apostolic
apóstolo *m* apostle
apóstrofe *m* apostrophe
apreciação *f* appreciation
apreciar *v* appreciate
apreender *v* apprehend
apreensão *m* arrest, seizure
apreensivo *adj* apprehensive
aprender *v* learn
aprendiz *m* apprentice
apresentação *f* presentation
apresentar *v* present
apresentar-se *v* come forward
apressadamente *adv* hastily
apressado *adj* hasty
apressar *v* hurry, rush
apressar-se *v* hurry up
aprisionar *v* imprison
aprofundar *v* deepen
apropriado *adj* suitable
aprovação *f* approval
aprovar *v* approve
aproximado *adj* close
aproximar(se) *v* approach
aptidão *f* aptitude
apto *adj* good
apunhalar *v* stab
apurar *v* ascertain
aquário *m* aquarium

aquático *adj* aquatic
aquecedor *m* heater
aquecimento *m* heating
aqueduto *m* aqueduct
aqueles *adj* those
aqui *adv* here
aquisição *f* acquisition
ar *m* air
Árabe *adj* Arabic
arame *m* wire
aranha *f* spider
arar *v* plow, till
arauto *m* herald
arbitragem *m* arbitration
arbitrar *v* arbitrate
arbitrário *adj* arbitrary
arbusto *m* bush, shrub
arcaico *adj* archaic
arcebispo *m* archbishop
arco *m* arc, arch
arco-íris *m* rainbow
ardente *adj* ardent
ardor *m* ardor
ardósia *f* slate
árduo *adj* arduous
área *f* area
areia *f* sand
areia movediça *f* quicksand
arena *f* arena
argila *nf* clay
árido *adj* arid, barren
aristocracia *f* aristocracy

aristocrata *m* aristocrat
aritmética *f* arithmetic
arma *f* weapon
arma de fogo *f* firearm
arma de mão *f* handgun
armação *m* frame
armadilha *f* snare
armado *adj* armed
armadura *f* armor
armamentos *m* armaments
armar *v* arm
armário *m* closet
armazém *m* depot
armazenagem *m* storage
armazenar *v* hoard, stock
armistício *m* armistice
aromático *adj* aromatic
arpão *nm* harpoon
Arqueologia *f* archaeology
arquiteto *m* architect
arquitetura *nf* architecture
arquivar *v* file
arquivo *m* file
arrancar *v* pull
arrancarcolher *v* pluck
arranha-céu *m* skyscraper
arranhão *m* scratch
arranhar *v* claw
arranjar *v* arrange
arranjo *m* arrangement
arrasar *v* obliterate
arrastar *v* drag

arrebatar *v* snatch
arredores *m* surroundings
arrefecer *v* chill
arrendador *m* lessor
arrendamento *m* lease
arrendar *v* lease
arrendatário *m* lessee
arrepender *v* repent
arrependido *adj* sorry
arrependimento *m* repentance
arriscado *adj* risky
arriscar *v* risk
arrogância *f* arrogance
arrogante *adj* arrogant
arrombar *v* burglarize
arrotar *v* burp
arroto *m* belch
arroz *m* rice
arruaceiro *m* hoodlum
arruinar *v* ruin
arrumado *adj* neat
arsão *m* arson
arsenal *m* arsenal
arsênico *m* arsenic
arte *m* art, craft
artéria *f* artery
artesão *m* artisan
artico *adj* arctic
articulação *f* articulation
articular *v* articulate
artífice *m* craftsman
artificial *adj* artificial

artigo *m* article, item
artilharia *f* artillery
artimanha *f* ruse
artista *f* artist
artístico *adj* artistic
artrite *f* arthritis
árvore *m* tree
ás *n* ace
às vezes *adv* sometimes
ascender *v* ascend
ascensão *nf* ascendancy
ascético *adj* ascetic
asfalto *m* asphalt
asfixiar *v* asphyxiate
asilo *m* asylum
asma *f* asthma
asmático *adj* asthmatic
aspargo *m* asparagus
aspecto *m* aspect, look
áspero *adj* coarse, rough
aspiração *f* aspiration
aspirar *v* aspire
aspirina *f* aspirin
assado à carvão *adj* charbroil
assaltante *m* assailant
assaltar *v* assail, assault
assalto *n* assault, holdup
assar *v* bake, roast
assassinar *v* assassinate
assassinato *m* murder
assassínio *f* assassination
assassino *m* murderer

assediar *v* beset
assédio *m* harassment
assegurar *v* ensure
assembléia *f* assembly
assentamento *n* settlement
assentar *v* settle
assento *m* seat
assimilação *f* assimilation
assimilar *v* assimilate
assinalar *v* sign
assinatura *f* signature
assistência *f* attendance
assistir *v* assist
assoalho *m* floor
assobiar *v* whistle
assobio *m* whistle
associação *f* association
associar *v* associate
assomar *v* loom
assombro *m* amazement
assombroso *adj* amazing
assumir *v* take over
assunto *m* issue, matter
assunto *n* subject
assustador *adj* daunting, frightening, scary
assustar *v* frighten
asterisco *m* asterisk
asteróide *m* asteroid
astrologia *f* astrology
astrólogo *m* astrologer
astronauta *m* astronaut

astronomia *n* astronomy
astronômico *adj* astronomic
astrônomo *m* astronomer
astuto *adj* astute
astutu *adj* foxy
atacado *adj* wholesale
atacante *m* attacker
atacar *v* attack, lash out
atacar de surpresa *v* ambush
atalho *m* shortcut
ataque *m* attack
ataúde *m* casket
até *pre* till, until, until
até agora *adv* hitherto
ateísmo *m* atheism
atenção *f* attention
atencioso *adj* caring, considerate
atendente de bar *nm* bartender
atender *v* attend
atento *adj* attentive
atenuado *adj* attenuating
atenuante *adj* extenuating
atenuar *v* attenuate
aterrissagem *m* landing
aterrissar *v* land
aterrorizar *v* terrify
atestar *v* attest
ateu *m* atheist
atirador *m* marksman
atirador de tocaia *m* sniper
atitude *nf* attitude
ativação *m* activation

ativamente *adv* busily
ativar *v* activate
atividade *f* activity
ativo *adj* active
atleta *m* athlete
atlético *adj* athletic
atmosfera *f* atmosphere
atmosférico *adj* atmospheric
atolar *v* bog down
atômico *adj* atomic
átomo *m* atom
ator *n* actor
atordoar *v* stun
atração *f* attraction
atraente *adj* attractive
atrair *v* attract, lure
atrapalhado *adj* clumsy
atrás *adv* back
atrás *pre* behind
atrasado *adv* late
atrasado *adj* overdue
atrasar *v* delay
atraso *n* delay
atrativo *adj* compelling
através de *pre* across
atrevido *adj* cheeky, daring
atribuição *f* assignment
atribuir *v* attribute
atril *m* lectern
atriz *f* actress
atrocidade *f* atrocity
atrofia *f* atrophy

atropelar *v* run over
atroz *adj* atrocious
atual *adj* present
atualizado *adj* up-to-date
atualizar *v* update
atualmente *adv* nowadays
atum *m* tuna
aturdir *v* baffle
audacidade *adj* audacious
audaz *f* audacity
audiência *f* audience
auditório *m* auditorium
audível *adj* audible
auge *m* peak
aumentar *v* increase
aumento *m* increase, raise
ausência *f* absence
ausente *adj* absent
auspicioso *adj* auspicious
austeridade *m* austerity
austero *adj* austere
autenticar *v* authenticate
autenticidade *f* authenticity
autêntico *adj* authentic
autirizar *v* license
auto-estima *f* self-esteem
auto-estrada *f* freeway
autógrafo *m* autograph
automático *adj* automatic
automóvel *m* auto
autonomia *f* autonomy
autônomo *adj* autonomous

autópsia *f* autopsy
autor *m* author
autoridade *f* authority
autoritário *adj* authoritarian
autorização *f* authorization
autorizar *v* authorize
auxiliar *v* aid
auxiliar *adj* auxiliary
auxiliar *nm* helper
auxílio *m* aid
avalanche *f* avalanche
avaliação *m* appraisal
avaliar *v* assess, deem
avalista *m* guarantor
avançar *v* advance
avanço *m* advance
avarento *m* miser
avareza *f* avarice
avaro *adj* avaricious
ave de rapina *f* vulture
avelã *m* hazelnut
avenida *f* avenue
avental *m* apron
aventura *nf* adventure
aventurar *v* venture
avermelhar *v* redden
aversão *f* aversion
aves domésticas *f* poultry
avestruz *m* ostrich
aviação *f* aviation
aviador *m* flier, aviator
avião *m* airplane

avidez *f* eagerness
ávido *adj* eager
aviso *m* warning
avô *m* grandfather
avós *m* grandparents
axila *f* armpit
axioma *f* axiom
azarado *adj* unlucky
azedo *adj* sour
azia *f* heartburn
azul *adj* blue
azul marinho *adj* navy blue
azulejo *m* tile

B

babá *nf* babysitter, nanny
bacalhau *m* cod
bacia *nf* basin
bactéria *f* bacteria
bagagem *m* luggage
bagunça *f* mess
bagunçado *adj* messy
bagunçar *v* mess up
baía *f* bay
bainha *f* hem
baioneta *f* bayonet
bairro *m* neighborhood

bairro pobre *m* slum
baixa *f* casualty
baixar *v* get down
baixar preço *v* mark down
baixo *adj* low
bala *f* bullet
balança *f* scale
balançar *v* balance, swing
balanço *m* balance, swing
balão *m* balloon
balbuciar *v* babble
balcão *m* balcony
balde *m* bucket, pail
baleia *f* whale
balneário *m* spa
balsa *f* ferry
bálsamo *m* balm
bambu *m* bamboo
banalidade *f* banality
banalizar *v* trivialize
banana *f* banana
banca de jornal *f* newsstand
banco *m* bank, bench
banco de dados *m* database
banco de igreja *m* pew
banda *f* band
bandagem *m* bandage
bandeira *f* flag
bandeja *f* tray
bandido *m* bandit
banhar *v* bathe
banheira *f* bathtub

banheiro *m* bathroom
banir *v* banish
banquete *m* banquet
baque *m* bump
bar *m* bar
barata *f* cockroach
barato *adj* cheap
barbado *adj* bearded
barbarismo *m* barbarism
bárbaro *m* barbarian
bárbaro *adj* barbaric
barbear *v* shave
barbeiro *m* barber
barcaça *f* barge
barco *m* boat
barco a vela *m* sailboat
barganha *f* bargain
barômetro *m* barometer
barra *f* bar
barraca *n* booth, tent
barrar *v* bar
barreira *f* barrier
barricada *f* barricade
barriga *f* belly
barril *m* barrel
base *f* base, basis
basear *v* base
básico *adj* basic
basquetebol *nm* basketball
bastante *adj* plenty
bastão *m* bat
bastardo *m* bastard

batalha *nf* battle
batalhão *m* battalion
batalhar *nf* battle
batata *f* potato
batata frita *f* fries
bater *v* beat, hit, strike
bater em retirada *v* bow out
bater papo *v* chat
batismo *m* baptism
batizar *v* baptize
baú *m* chest, trunk
bazar *m* bazaar
bêbado *adj* drunk
bebê *m* baby, infant
bebedor *m* drinker
beber *v* drink
bebida *f* drink
bebida alcoólica *f* booze
beco *m* alley
beijar *v* kiss
beijo *m* kiss
beira *f* rim, edge, brink
beira-mar *f* seaside
beisebol *m* baseless
beleza *f* beauty
belga *adj* Belgian
Bélgica *f* Belgium
beliche *m* berth
belicoso *adj* fiery
beliscão *m* pinch
beliscar *v* pinch
bem *adj* fine

bem sucedido *adj* successful
bem-estar *m* welfare
bênção *f* blessing
beneficiar *v* benefit
beneficiário *m* beneficiary
benefício *m* benefit
benéfico *adj* beneficial
benevolência *f* benevolence
benevolente *adj* benevolent
benfeitor *m* benefactor
bengala *f* cane
benigno *adj* benign
bens imóveis *m* realty
berçário *m* nursery
berço *m* cradle, crib
berrante *adj* loud
berro *m* shriek
besouro *m* beetle
besta *f* beast
besteira *f* garbage
bestial *adj* bestial
bestialidade *f* bestiality
beterraba *f* beet
bexiga *f* bladder
bezerro *m* calf
Bíblia *f* bible
bíblico *adj* biblical
bibliografia *f* bibliography
biblioteca *f* library
bibliotecário *m* librarian
bicada *f* peck
bicar *v* peck

bicicleta *f* bicycle, bike
bico *m* beak, bill
bife *m* steak
bigamia *f* bigamy
bigode *m* mustache
bigorna *f* anvil
bilhão *m* billion
bilhar *m* billiards
bilheteria *f* box office
bilíngue *adj* bilingual
bilionário *m* billionaire
bílis *f* bile
bimestral *adj* bimonthly
binóculo *m* binoculars
biografia *f* biography
biologia *f* biology
biológico *adj* biological
biombo *m* screen
bisão *m* bison
biscoito *m* cookie
bispo *m* bishop
bizarro *adj* bizarre
blasfemar *v* blaspheme
blasfêmia *f* blasphemy
blecaute *m* blackout
blefar *v* bluff
bloco *m* block
bloquear *v* block, blockade
bloqueio *m* blockade
blusa *f* blouse
boa forma *f* fitness
boas-vindas *f* welcome

boato *m* hearsay
bobão *adj* moron
bobina *f* spool
boca *f* mouth
bocado *m* morsel
bocejar *v* yawn
bocejo *m* yawn
bochecha *f* cheek
bode expiatório *m* scapegoat
boi *m* ox
bóia *f* buoy
boicotar *m* boycott
boina *f* beret
bois *m* oxen
bola *f* ball
bolacha *f* biscuit, wafer
boletim *m* bulletin
bolha *f* blister, bubble
bolo *m* cake
bolo de apostas *m* jackpot
bolota *f* acorn
bolsa *f* bag, purse
bolsa de estudos *f* scholarship
bolsa de mão *f* handbag
bolso *m* pocket
bom *adj* good
bomba *f* bomb, pump
bombardear *v* bomb
bombardeio *m* bombing
bombear *v* pump
bombeiro *m* fireman
bondade *f* goodness

bonde *m* tram
bondoso *adv* kindly
boneca *m* doll
bonito *adj* beautiful
bônus *m* bonus
borboleta *f* butterfly
borda *f* verge, brim
bordado *m* embroidery
bordar *v* embroider
borracha *f* rubber
borrifar *v* spray
bosta *f* crap
bota *f* boot
botânica *f* botany
botão *m* button
boxe *m* boxing
boxeador *m* boxer
bracelete *m* bracelet
braço *m* arm
branco *adj* white
brando *adj* mild, soft
branquear *v* whiten
brasa *f* embers
bravo *adj* brave
bravura *f* bravery
brecar *v* brake
brecha *f* split
brefemente *adv* briefly
breve *adj* brief
brevidade *f* brevity
briga *f* brawl, quarrel
brigada *f* brigade

brigão *m* brawler

brigar *v* scrap

briguento *adj* belligerent, quarrelsome

brilhar *v* shine, glow

brilho *m* brightness

brincadeira *n* fun, game

brincalhão *adj* playful

brincar *v* joke, play

brinco *m* earring

brindar *v* toast

brinquedo *m* toy

brisa *f* breeze

Britanha *f* Britain

britânico *adj* British

broca *f* drill

bronquite *f* bronchitis

bronze *m* bronze

bronzeado *adj* tanned

brotar *v* spring

broto *m* bud

brusco *adj* brusque

brutal *adj* brutal

brutalidade *f* brutality

brutalizar *v* brutalize

bruto *adj* brute

bruxa *f* witch

bruxaria *f* witchcraft

búfalo *m* buffalo

bulbo *m* bulb

bulevar *m* boulevard

bulldozer *v* bulldoze

buraco *m* hole

burguês *adj* bourgeois

burocracia *f* bureaucracy

burocrata *m* bureaucrat

burro *m* donkey

busca *f* search

buscar *v* seek

busto *m* bust

búteo *m* buzzard

butim *m* booty

buzina *f* horn

buzinar *v* honk

C

cabana *f* cabin, hut

cabeça *f* head

cabecear *v* nod

cabeleireiro *m* hairdresser

cabelo *m* hair

cabide *m* hanger

cabina do piloto *f* cockpit

cabine *m* cubicle

cabo *m* cape, corporal

cabra *f* goat

cabrito *f* kid

caça *n* hunting

caçador *m* hunter

B
C

C

caçar *v* hunt
caçarola *f* casserole
cacau *f* cocoa
cacetear *v* bludgeon
cachecol *m* scarf
cacho *m* bunch
cachorro *m* dog
cada *adj* each
cadáver *m* corpse
cadeado *m* padlock
cadeia *f* jail
cadeira *f* chair
cadeira de rodas *f* wheelchair
caderno *m* notebook
caducar *v* lapse
café *m* coffee
café da manhã *m* breakfast
cafeína *f* caffeine
cagado *adj* crappy
cãibra *nf* cramp
caída *f* descent
cair *v* fall
cais *m* pier, wharf
caixa *f* box, cashier
caixa de correio *f* mailbox
caixão *m* coffin
cajado *m* crook
cal *f* lime
calabouço *m* dungeon
calafrio *m* shiver
calamidade *f* calamity
calar *v* shut up

calça comprida *nf* trousers
calçada *f* sidewalk
calçado *m* footwear
calcanhar *m* heel
calcário *m* limestone
calças *f* pants
calças curtas *f* shorts
calcinha *f* briefs
calculadora *f* calculator
calcular *v* calculate
calcular mal *v* miscalculate
cálculo *m* calculation
caldeira *f* boiler
caldo *m* broth
calendário *m* calendar
calibrar *v* calibrate, gauge
cálice *m* chalice
cálido *adj* warm
caligrafia *f* handwriting
calma *m* still
calmaria *f* calm, lull
calmo *adj* calm, cool
calombo *m* knob
calor *m* heat, warmth
caloria *f* calorie
calúnia *f* calumny
cama *f* bed
camada *f* coat, layer
camarada *m* comrade
camaradagem *n* fellowship
camarão *m* shrimp
camarote *m* cabin

cambaleante *adj* staggering
cambalear *v* stagger
camelo *m* camel
câmera *f* camera
câmera lenta *f* slow motion
caminhada *f* hike
caminhadao *m* walk
caminhão *m* truck
caminhar *v* hike, walk
caminho *m* path, way
caminhonete *f* pickup
camisa *f* shirt
camisa de malha *f* jersey
camisola *f* nightgown
campainha *f* bell, buzzer
campainha de porta *f* doorbell
campanário *m* belfry
campanha *f* campaign
campeão *m* champion
campina *f* prairie
campo *m* field
campo minado *m* minefield
camponês *m* peasant
camuflagem *m* camouflage
camuflar *v* camouflage
cana *f* cane
canal *m* canal, channel
canalha *m* scoundrel
canário *m* canary
canção *f* song
cancelamento *f* cancellation
cancelar *v* call off, cancel

câncer *m* cancer
canceroso *adj* cancerous
candelabro *m* chandelier
candidato *m* candidate
candidatura *f* candidacy
cândido *adj* candid
caneca *f* mug
canela *f* cinnamon
caneta *f* pen
cangaru *m* kangaroo
canhão *m* cannon
canibal *m* cannibal
canino *m* fang
cano *m* pipe
cano de esgoto *m* sewer
canoa *nf* canoe
canonizar *v* canonize
cansaço *m* tiredness
cansado *adj* tired
cansar *v* wear down
cansativo *adj* exhausting, tiresome
cantar *v* sing
cantar (galo) *v* crow
cântaro *m* jug
canteiro *m* border
cântico *m* chant
cantina *f* canteen
canto *f* edge
cantor *m* singer
cão de caça *m* hound
caos *m* chaos

caótico *adj* chaotic

capa *f* cloak, cape

capa de chuva *f* raincoat

capacete *m* helmet

capacho *m* mat

capacidade *f* capacity

capanga *m* thug, bully

capaz *adj* capable

capela *nf* chapel

capelão *m* chaplain

capitalismo *m* capitalism

capitalize *v* capitalize

capitão *m* captain

capitular *v* capitulate

capítulo *m* chapter

capotar *v* capsize

capricho *m* whim

cápsula *f* capsule

captar *v* pick up

captura *f* capture

capturar *v* capture

capuz *f* hood

caracol *m* snail

característico *adj* characteristic

caranguejo *m* crab

caratê *m* karate

caráter *m* character

carbonizar *v* char

carburador *m* carburetor

carcaça *f* carcass

carcereiro *m* jailer

cardíaco *adj* cardiac

cardiologia *f* cardiology

careca *adj* bald

careta *f* grimace

carga *f* freight, cargo

cariar *v* decay

caricatura *f* caricature

carícia *f* caress

caridade *f* charity

caridoso *adj* charitable

cárie *f* cavity

carimbo postal *m* postmark

carisma *m* charisma

carismático *adj* charismatic

carnal *adj* carnal

carne *f* flesh, meat

carne assada *f* roast

carne de porco *f* pork

carne de vaca *f* beef

carneiro *m* ram

carnificina *f* carnage

caro *adj* expensive

caroço *m* core

carpete *f* carpet

carpintaria *f* carpentry

carpinteiro *m* carpenter

carrear *v* haul

carregado *adj* loaded

carregador *m* porter

carregamento *n* shipment

carregar *v* carry, cart

carreira *f* career

carretel *m* reel

C

carrinho *m* trolley
carrinho de mão *m* wheelbarrow
carro *m* car
carro fúnebre *m* hearse
carroça *f* cart
carruagem *m* carriage
carta *f* letter
cartão *f* card
cartão postal *f* postcard
cartaz *f* placard
carteira *f* wallet
carteiro *m* mailman
cartucho *m* cartridge
carvalho *m* oak
carvão *m* coal
carvão vegetal *m* charcoal
casa *f* home, house
casa de campo *f* cottage
casaco *m* coat
casado *adj* married
casal *m* couple
casamento *m* marriage
casar *v* marry, wed
casar de novo *v* remarry
casca *f* bark, peel
casca de noz *f* nut-shell
cascalho *m* rubble
cascata *f* cascade
casco *m* hull
caseiro *adj* homely
caso *m* case
caspa *f* dandruff

cassetete *m* baton
cassino *m* casino
casta *f* caste
castanha *f* chestnut
castelo *m* castle
castiçal *m* candlestick
castidade *f* chastity
castigar *v* chastise
castigo *m* chastisement
casto *adj* chaste
castor *m* beaver
cataclismo *m* cataclysm
catacumba *f* catacomb
catalogar *v* catalog
catálogo *m* catalog
catapora *f* chicken pox
catar *v* pick
catarata *f* cataract
catástrofe *f* catastrophe
catecismo *m* catechism
catedral *f* cathedral
categoria *f* class, grade
cativante *adj* enthralling
cativar *v* captivate
cativeiro *m* bondage
catividade *f* captivity
cativo *m* captive
Catolicismo *m* Catholicism
católico *adj* catholic
catorze *adj* fourteen
caubói *m* cowboy
causa *f* cause

causar *v* cause
cavalaria *f* cavalry
cavaleiro *m* knight
cavalheiro *m* gentleman
cavalo *m* horse
cavar *v* dig
caverna *f* cavern
cavidade *f* cavity
caxumba *f* mumps
cebola *f* onion
ceder *v* relent
cedo *adv* early
cegamente *adv* blindly
cegar *v* blind
cego *adj* blind
cegonha *f* stork
cegueira *f* blindness
ceia *f* supper
ceifar *v* reap
celebração *f* celebration
celebrar *v* celebrate
celebridade *f* celebrity
celeiro *m* barn
celestial *adj* celestial
celibatário *adj* celibate
celibato *m* celibacy
cem *adj* hundred
cemitério *m* cemetery
cenário *m* scene
cenoura *f* carrot
censo *m* census
censura *f* censorship

censurar *v* censure
centavo *m* cent, penny
centeio *m* rye
centenário *m* centenary
centésimo *m* hundredth
centímetro *m* center
central *adj* central
centralizar *v* centralize
centro *v* center
cera *f* wax
cera do ouvido *f* earwax
cerâmica *f* ceramic
cerca *f* fence
cercar *v* circle
cerco *m* siege
cereal *m* cereal
cerebral *adj* cerebral
cérebro *m* brain
cereja *f* cherry
cerimônia *f* ceremony
cerrar *v* clench
certamente *adv* surely
certeza *f* certainty
certificado *m* certificate
certificar *v* certify
certo *adj* clear, sure, certain
cerveja *f* beer
cervejaria *f* brewery
cessar *v* cease
cessar-fogo *m* cease-fire
cesta *f* basket
cesta de lixo *f* waste basket

cético *adj* skeptic
céu *m* heaven, sky
cevada *n* barley
chá *m* tea
chacal *m* jackal
chalé *m* chalet
chaleira *f* kettle, teapot
chama *f* flame
chamada *f* call
chamar *v* call
chamativo *adj* eye-catching, lurid
chaminé *f* chimney
chance *f* chance
chanceler *m* chancellor
chantagear *v* blackmail
chantagem *m* blackmail
chapéu *m* cap, hat
charada *f* charade
charme *m* charm
charuto *m* cigar
chave *f* key, switch
chave de fenda *f* screwdriver
chave inglesa *nf* wrench
chaveiro *m* key ring
checar *v* check
check-in *v* check in
chefe *m* boss, chief, chef
chegada *f* arrival
chegar *v* arrive
cheio *adj* full
cheirar *v* smell
cheque *n* check

chiar *v* creak
chiclete *m* bubble gum
chicote *m* lash, whip
chicotear *v* whip, lash
chimpanzé *m* chimpanzee
chique *adj* posh
chispa *f* spark
choça *f* shack
chocalhar *v* rattle
chocante *adj* shocking
chocolate *m* chocolate
chofer *m* chauffeur
choque *m* shock
choramingar *v* wail
chorar *v* cry, weep
chover *v* rain
chover granizo *v* hail
chumbado *adj* leaded
chupador *m* sucker
chupar *v* suck
churrasco *m* barbecue
chutar *v* kick
chuva *nf* rain
chuveiro *m* shower
chuviscar *v* drizzle
chuvisco *m* drizzle
chuvoso *adj* rainy
cianeto *m* cyanide
cicatriz *f* scar
ciclista *m* cyclist
ciclo *m* cycle
ciclone *m* cyclone

C

cidadania *f* citizenship
cidadão *m* citizen
cidade *m* city
cidade natal *f* hometown
ciência *f* science
científico *adj* scientific
cientista *m* scientist
cigano *m* gypsy
cigarro *m* cigarette
cilada *f* trap
cilada de morte *f* death trap
cilindro *m* cylinder
cílio *m* eyelash
cimento *m* cement
cinco *adj* five
cinema *m* cinema
cínico *adj* cynic
cinismo *m* cynicism
cinqüenta *adj* fifty
cintilar *v* sparkle
cinto *m* belt
cintura *f* waist
cinzas *f* ash
cinzeiro *m* ashtray
cinzel *m* chisel
cinzento *adj* grayish
cipreste *m* cypress
circo *m* circus
circuito *m* circuit, tour
circulação *f* circulation
circular *adj* circular
circular *v* circulate

circular *f* newsletter
círculo *m* circle
circuncisão *f* circumcision
circuncisar *v* circumcise
circunstância *f* circumstance
cirurgião *m* surgeon
cirúrgico *adv* surgical
cisma *m* schism
cisne *m* swan
cisterna *f* cistern
cisto *m* cyst
citação *f* quotation
citar *v* quote
ciúme *m* jealousy
cívico *adj* civic
civil *adj* civil
civilização *f* civilization
civilizar *v* civilize
clã *m* clan
clamar *v* clamor
clandestino *adj* clandestine
clara *f* egg white
clarabóia *f* skylight
claramente *adv* clearly
clarear *v* brighten
clareza *f* clarity
clarinete *m* clarinet
claro *adj* clear
classe *f* class, rank
clássico *adj* classic
classificar *v* classify
classificar-se *v* rank

claustro *m* cloister
cláusula *f* clause
clavícula *f* collarbone
clemência *f* clemency
clerical *adj* clerical
clérigo *m* clergyman
clero *m* clergy
clicar *v* click
cliente *m* customer
clientela *f* clientele
clima *m* climate
climático *adj* climatic
clímax *m* climax
clínica *f* clinic
clipe de papel *m* paperclip
clonagem *m* cloning
clonar *v* clone
clube *m* club
coabitar *v* cohabit
coação *f* coercion
coado *adj* strained
coador *m* strainer
coagir *v* coerce
coagulação *f* coagulation
coagular *v* coagulate
coágulo *m* clot
coalhar *v* curdle
coalisão *f* coalition
coberta *f* cover
cobertor *f* blanket
cobertura *f* cover, shelter
cobiçar *v* covet

cobrar *v* charge
cobrar caro *v* overcharge
cobre *f* copper
cobrir *v* cover
cocaína *f* cocaine
coçar *v* itch
cócegas *f* tickle
coceguento *adj* ticklish
coceira *f* itchiness
cochicho *f* whisper
cochilar *v* doze, snooze
cochilo *f* doze
coco *f* coconut
codificar *v* codify
código *f* key, code
codorna *f* quail
coeficiente *f* coefficient
coelho *m* rabbit
coerente *adj* coherent
coesão *f* cohesion
coexistir *v* coexist
cofre *m* chest, safe, piggy bank
cogumelo *m* mushroom
coincidência *f* coincidence
coincidente *adj* coincidental
coincidir *v* coincide, concur
coisa *f* thing, stuff
cola *f* glue, paste
colaboração *f* collaboration
colaborador *m* collaborator
colaborar *v* collaborate
colapso *m* breakdown

C

C

colar *v* glue, paste
colar *m* necklace
colateral *adj* collateral
colcha *f* bedspread
colchão *m* mattress
colchete *m* bracket
coleção *f* collection
colega *m* pal, colleague
coleira *n* leash
cólera *f* cholera
colesterol *m* cholesterol
coletar *v* collect
coletor *m* collector
colheita *f* harvest
colher *v* harvest
colher *f* spoon
colher de chá *f* teaspoon
colherada *f* spoonful
cólica *m* colic
colidir *v* crash, collide
colina *m* hill
colisão *f* collision
colméia *f* beehive, hive
colo *m* lap
cólon *m* colon
colônia *f* cologne, colony
colonial *adj* colonial
colonização *f* colonization
colonizar *v* colonize
colono *m* settler
colorido *adj* colorful
colorir *m* color

colossal *adj* colossal
coluna *f* column
com *pre* with
com exceção *pre* barring
com respeito a *pre* regarding
coma *f* coma
comandante *m* commander
comando *m* commandment
comardar *v* command
combate *m* combat
combatente *m* combatant
combater *v* combat
combinação *f* combination
combinar *v* combine
comboio *m* convoy
combustão *f* combustion
combustível *m* fuel
começar *v* start
começar a fazer *v* get down to
começo *m* start
comédia *f* comedy
comediante *m* comedian
comemorar *v* commemorate
comentar *v* comment
comentário *m* comment
comer *v* eat
comercial *adj* commercial
comerciante *m* businessman
comércio *m* commerce
comestível *adj* edible
cometa *m* comet
cometer *v* commit

cômico *adj* comical
comida *f* food
comissão *nf* commission
comitê *m* committee
como *c* as
como *adv* how
como *pre* like
comoção *f* commotion
comoda *f* dresser
comovente *adj* touching
comovido *v* overcome
compactar *v* compact
compacto *adj* compact
compaixão *f* compassion
companheiro *f* companion
companhia *f* company
comparação *f* comparison
comparar *v* compare
comparável *adj* comparable
compartimento *m* compartment
compassivo *adj* compassionate
compasso *m* compass
compatível *adj* compatible
compatriota *m* countryman
compêndio *m* compendium
compensação *f* compensation
compensar *v* compensate
competência *f* competence
competente *adj* competent
competição *f* competition
competidor *m* competitor
competir *v* compete

competitivo *adj* competitive
compilar *v* compile
complemento *m* complement
completamente *adv* completely
completar *v* complete
completo *adj* complete
complexão *nf* complexion
complexidade *f* complexity
complexo *adj* complex
complicação *f* complication
complicado *adj* tricky
complicar *v* complicate
componente *m* component
compor *v* compose
comporta *m* floodgate
comportamento *m* behavior
comportar-se *v* behave
composição *f* composition
compositor *n* composer
composto *adj* composed
composto *m* compost
compostura *f* composure
compra *f* purchase
comprador *m* buyer
comprar *v* buy
compras *f* shopping
compreender *v* realize
compreensível *adj* understandable
compreensivo *adj* understanding
compressão *f* compression
comprido *adj* lengthy

comprimir *v* compress
comprometido *adj* committed
compromisso *m* commitment
compulsão *f* compulsion
compulsivo *adj* compulsive
compulsório *adj* compulsory
computador *f* computer
computar *v* compute
comum *adj* common, ordinary
comumente *adv* ordinarily
comunhão *f* communion
comunicação *f* communication
comunicar *v* communicate
comunidade *f* community
comunismo *m* communism
comunista *adj* communist
comutar *v* commute
conceber *v* conceive
conceder *v* grant
conceito *m* concept
concentração *f* concentration
concentrar *v* concentrate
concêntrico *adj* concentric
concepção *f* conception
concerto *m* concert
concessão *f* concession
concha *nf* shell
conciência *f* conscience
conciliação *f* compromise
conciliar *v* conciliate
conciliatório *adj* conciliatory
conciso *adj* concise

concluir *v* conclude
conclusão *f* conclusion
conclusivo *adj* conclusive
concordância *nf* rapport
concordar *v* agree
concreto *m* concrete
concreto *adj* concrete
concussão *m* concussion
condado *m* county
condenação *f* condemnation
condenado *adj* doomed
condenar *v* condemn
condensação *f* condensation
condensar *v* condense
condescender *v* condescend
condessa *f* countess
condição *f* condition
condicionador *m* conditioner
condicional *adj* conditional
condições *f* terms
condimento *m* condiment
condolências *f* condolences
conducente *adj* conducive
conduta *f* conduct
conduto *m* chute, duct
condutor *m* conductor
conduzir *v* conduct, lead
cone *m* cone
conectar *v* connect
conexão *f* connection
conferência *f* conference
conferenciar *v* confer

confessar *v* confess
confessor *m* confessor
confiança *f* trust, faith
confiante *adj* confident
confiar *v* confide, trust
confiável *adj* reliable
confidencial *adj* confidential
confidente *m* confidant
confinamento *m* confinement
confinar *v* confine
confirmação *f* confirmation
confirmar *v* confirm
confiscar *v* confiscate
confisco *f* confiscation
confissão *f* confession
confissional *m* confessional
conflitante *adj* conflicting
conflitar *v* conflict
conflito *m* conflict
conformar *v* conform
conforme *c* as
conformidade *f* conformity
conformista *adj* conformist
confortável *adj* comfortable
conforto *m* comfort
confrontação *f* confrontation
confrontar *v* confront
confundir *v* confuse
confusão *f* confusion
confuso *adj* confusing
congelador *m* freezer
congelar *v* freeze

congestão *f* congestion
congestionado *adj* congested
congregação *f* congregation
congregar *v* congregate
congresso *m* congress
conhaque *m* brandy
conhecido *m* acquaintance
conhecido *adj* well-known
conhecimento *m* knowledge
conjectura *f* conjecture
conjugal *adj* conjugal
conjugar *v* conjugate
cônjuge *m* spouse
conjunção *f* conjunction
conjuntamente *adv* jointly
conjunto *m* set
conotar *v* connote
conquista *f* conquest
conquistador *m* conqueror
conquistar *v* conquer
consagração *f* consecration
consagrar *v* consecrate
consanguíneo *adj* akin
consciência *f* consciousness
consciente *adj* aware
consecutivo *adj* consecutive
conseguir *v* procure
conselheiro *m* adviser
conselho *m* advice, council
consenso *m* consensus
consentimento *m* consent
consentir *v* consent

consequência *f* consequence
consequente *adj* consequent
conserva *f* conserve
conservação *f* conservation
conservador *adj* conservative
conservar *v* conserve
consideração *f* consideration
considerar *v* consider
considerável *adj* considerable
consistência *f* consistency
consistente *adj* consistent
consistir *v* consist
consoante *f* consonant
consolação *f* consolation
consolar *v* console
consolidar *v* consolidate
conspiração *f* conspiracy
conspirador *m* conspirator
conspirar *v* conspire
constância *f* constancy
constante *adj* constant
constelação *f* constellation
consternação *f* dismay
consternado *adj* aghast
consternar *v* dismay
constipação *f* constipation
constipado *adj* constipated
constipar *v* constipate
constituição *f* constitution
constituir *v* constitute
constranger *v* constrain
construção *f* construction

construir *iv* build
construtivo *adj* constructive
construtor *m* builder
cônsul *m* consul
consulado *m* consulate
consultar *v* consult
consumidor *m* consumer
consumir *v* consume
consumo *m* consumption
conta *f* account, bill
contactar *v* contact
contador *m* accountant
contadoria *f* bookkeeping
contagem *f* count, score
contagioso *adj* contagious
contaminação *f* contamination
contaminar *v* contaminate
contanto que *c* providing that
contar *v* count, tell
contar com *v* expect, rely on
contato *m* contact
contemplar *v* contemplate
contenção *m* restraint
contendor *m* contender
contentar *v* content
contente *adj* content
conter *v* contain, hold
conter-se *v* compose
conteúdo *m* contents
contexto *m* context
contíguo *adj* adjoining
continental *adj* continental

continente *m* continent
contingência *f* contingency
contingente *adj* contingent
continuação *f* continuation
continuamente *adv* ceaselessly
continuar *v* continue
continuidade *f* continuity
contínuo *adj* continuous
conto *m* tale
contorcer *iv* wring
contorcer-se *v* writhe
contornar *v* bypass
contorno *m* contour, outline
contra *pre* against
contrabandista *m* smuggler
contrabando *m* contraband
contração *f* contraction
contracheque *m* pay slip
contradição *f* contradiction
contradizer *v* contradict
contrapartida *f* counterpart
contrariar *v* counter, cross
contrário *adj* contrary
contrário *m* opposite
contrastar *v* contrast
contraste *m* contrast
contratar *v* contract, hire
contrato *m* contract
contribuição *f* contribution
contribuinte *m* contributor
contribuir *v* contribute
contrição *f* contrition

controlar *v* control
controlável *adj* manageable
controle *m* control
controvérsia *f* controversy
controverso *adj* controversial
contudo *c* although
contundir *v* bruise
contusão *f* bruise
convalescente *adj* convalescent
convenção *f* convention
convencer *v* convince
convencido *adj* cocky
convencional *adj* conventional, orthodox
conveniência *f* convenience
conveniente *adj* expedient
convento *m* convent
convergir *v* converge
conversação *f* conversation
conversão *f* conversion
conversar *v* talk
converso *m* convert
converter *v* convert
convés *f* deck
convicção *f* conviction
convidar *v* invite
convincente *adj* convincing
convite *f* invitation
convocar *v* convene, summon
convulsão *f* seizure, convulsion
cooperação *f* cooperation
cooperar *v* cooperate

cooperativo *adj* cooperative
coordenação *f* coordination
coordenador *n* coordinator
coordenar *v* coordinate
copa *f* cup
cópia *f* copy
copiadora *f* copier
copiar *v* copy
coquetel *m* cocktail
cor *m* color
coração *m* heart
coragem *m* courage
corajosamente *adv* bravely
corajoso *adj* courageous
corar *v* flush
corcova *f* hump
corcunda *f* hunchback
corda *f* rope, string
cordão *m* cord, lace
cordeiro *m* lamb
cordial *adj* cordial
cordilheira *f* ridge
corneta *f* cornet
coro *m* choir, chorus
coroa *f* crown, wreath
coroação *f* coronation
coroar *v* crown
corolário *m* corollary
coronário *adj* coronary
coronel *m* colonel
corpo *m* body
corporação *f* corporation

corporal *adj* corporal
corporalmente *adj* bodily
corpulento *adj* corpulent
corpúsculo *m* corpuscle
correção *f* correction
corredor *m* runner, corridor
corregir *v* correct
correia *f* strap
correio *m* post office, mail
correio aéreo *m* airmail
correlacionar *v* correlate
corrente *adj* current
corrente *f* stream
correr *f* race, run
correr mais *v* outrun
correspondente *m* correspondent
correspondente *adj* corresponding
corresponder *v* correspond
correto *adj* correct
corrida *f* race
corrimão *m* handrail
corroborar *v* corroborate
corroer *v* corrode
corromper *v* corrupt
corrupção *f* corruption
corrupto *adj* corrupt
cortador *m* cutter
cortar *v* slice, cut, carve
cortar em pedaços *v* shred
cortar for a *v* cut off
cortar grama *v* mow
cortar no meio *v* halve

corte _m_ cut
corte de cabelo _m_ haircut
cortejar _v_ court
cortês _adj_ courteous
cortesia _f_ courtesy
cortina _f_ curtain, drape
coruja _f_ owl
corvo _m_ crow, raven
coser _v_ sew
cosmético _m_ cosmetic
cósmico _adj_ cosmic
cosmonauta _m_ cosmonaut
costa _f_ coast, back
costeiro _adj_ coastal
costela _f_ rib
costeleta _f_ sideburns
costume _m_ custom
costumeiro _adj_ customary
costura _f_ sewing
costurar _v_ stitch
costureira _f_ seamstress
cotovelo _m_ elbow
couraçado _m_ battleship
couro _m_ leather
couve-flor _f_ cauliflower
covard _m_ coward
covardemente _adv_ cowardly
covardia _f_ cowardice
coxa _f_ thigh
coxeadura _f_ limp
coxear _v_ limp
cozido demais _adj_ overdone

cozinha _f_ cuisine, kitchen
cozinhar _v_ cook
cozinheiro _m_ cook
crachá _f_ badge
crânio _m_ skull
craque _m_ crash
crasso _adj_ crass
cratera _f_ crater
cravo _m_ carnation
credibilidade _f_ credibility
crédito _m_ credit
credor _m_ creed, creditor
crédulo _adj_ gullible
cremar _v_ cremate
crematório _m_ crematorium
crème _f_ cream
cremoso _adj_ creamy
crença _f_ belief
crente _m_ believer
crepúsculo _m_ nightfall
crescente _adj_ increasing
crescer _v_ grow
crescimento _m_ growth
criação _f_ creation
criado _m_ attendant
criador _m_ creator
criança _f_ child, kid
crianças _f_ children
criar _v_ create, rear
criatividade _n_ creativity
criativo _adj_ creative
criatura _f_ creature

crime *m* crime
criminal *adj* criminal
criminoso *m* thug
críquete *m* cricket
crise *f* crisis
crista *f* crest
cristal *m* crystal
cristalino *m* lens
cristão *adj* Christian
Cristianismo *m* Christianity
critério *m* criterion
crítica *f* criticism, review
criticar *v* criticize
crítico *adj* critical
crível *adj* credible
crocante *adj* crispy
crocodilo *m* crocodile
crônica *f* chronicle
crônico *adj* chronic
cronologia *f* chronology
cronometrar *v* time
croqui *m* sketch
crosta *f* crust
crostoso *adj* crusty
cru *adj* raw, crude
crucial *adj* crucial
crucificação *f* crucifixion
crucificar *v* crucify
crucifixo *m* crucifix
cruel *adj* cruel
crueldade *f* cruelty
cruz *f* cross

cruzada *f* crusade
cruzado *m* crusader
cruzar *v* cross
cúbico *adj* cubic
cubo *m* cube
cubo de gelo *m* ice cube
cuidado *m* care, caution
cuidadoso *adj* careful, wary
cuidar *v* care, nurse
cuidar de *v* care for
cuidar-se *v* fend
culminar *v* culminate
culpa *f* blame, fault
culpado *adj* guilty
culpar *v* blame
cultivar *v* cultivate
cultivável *adj* arable
culto *m* cult
cultura *f* cultivation
cultural *adj* cultural
cume *f* summit
cúmplice *m* accomplice
cumplicidade *f* complicity
cumprimentar *v* congratulate
cumprir *v* fulfill
cunha *f* wedge
cunhada *f* sister-in-law
cunhado *m* brotherhood
cunhar moeda *v* mint
cupim *f* termite
cupom *m* coupon
cúpula *f* dome

cura *f* cure
curador *m* curator
curandeiro *m* healer
curar *v* cure, heal
curativo *m* dressing
curável *adj* curable
curiosidade *f* curiosity
curioso *adj* curious
curso *m* course
curto *adj* short
curva *f* curve
curvar *v* curve
curvar-se *v* bow
curvo *adj* warped
cuspir *v* spit
custar *v* cost
custo *m* cost
custódia *f* custody
cutelaria *f* cutlery
cutelo *m* chopper
cutucar *v* prod
czar *m* czar

D

da moda *adj* fashionable
dado *m* dice
dados *m* data
dama de honra *f* bridesmaid
damasco *m* apricot
danação *f* damnation
dança *f* dance, dancing
dançar *v* dance
danificar *v* damage
dano *m* damage, harm
danoso *adj* damaging
dar *v* give
dar à luz *v* bear
dar corda *v* wind up
dar lucro *v* yield
dar risadinhas *v* giggle
dar risinhos *v* chuckle
dar um pulo *v* drop in
dar uma palmada *v* smack
dardo *m* dart
data *f* date
datar *v* date
de *pre* from
de acordo com *pre* according to
de algum jeito *adv* someway
de alguma forma *adv* somehow
de bom grado *adv* willingly
de fato *adv* indeed
de frente *adv* head-on

de improviso *adv* impromptu
de lã *adj* woolen
de lado *adv* sideways
de luxo *adj* deluxe
de má vontade *adv* unwillingly
de madeira *adj* wooden
de novo *adv* again, anew
de paralisação *adj* standstill
de perto *adv* closely
de propósito *adv* purposely, willfully
de repente *adv* suddenly
de sair *adv* outdoor
de trás *adv* backwards
deão *m* dean
debaixo *pre* under
debandar *v* disband
debate *m* debate
debater *v* debate
débil *adj* wimp
débito *m* debit
década *f* decade
decadência *f* decadence
decair *v* decay, go down
decapitar *v* behead
decência *f* decency
decendência *f* ancestry
decente *adj* decent
decepção *f* deception
decepção *m* disappointment
decepcionante *adj* disappointing
decida *f* descent

decidir *v* decide
decifrar *v* decipher
decimal *adj* decimal
décimo *adj* tenth
decisão *f* decision
decisivo *adj* decisive
declaração *f* declaration
declarado *adj* avowed
declarar *v* declare
declinação *f* declension
declinar *v* decline
declínio *m* downturn
declive *m* decline, slope
decolagem *m* lift-off
decolar *v* take off
decompor *v* decompose
decomposição *f* decay
decoração *f* décor
decorar *v* decorate
decoro *m* decorum
decrépito *adj* decrepit
decrescer *v* decrease
decréscimo *m* decrease
decretar *v* decree
decreto *m* decree
dedicação *f* dedication
dedicar *v* dedicate
dedo *m* finger
dedo do pé *m* toe
dedução *f* deduction
deduzir *v* deduce, deduct
deduzível *adj* deductible

defeito *m* defect, flaw

defeituoso *adj* defective

defender *v* defend

defender-se *v* fend off

defensor *v* advocate

defesa *f* defense

deficiência *f* deficiency

deficiente *adj* deficient

deficit *m* deficit

definhar *v* languish

definição *f* definition

definido *adj* definite

definir *v* define

definitivo *adj* definitive

deflagração *f* outbreak

deformar *v* deform

deformidade *f* deformity

defraudar *v* defraud

defumado *adj* smoked

degelo *m* thaw

degeneração *f* degeneration

degenerado *adj* degenerate

degenerar *v* degenerate

degradação *f* degradation

degradante *adj* degrading

degradar *v* degrade, demote

degrau *m* degree

deitar *v* lay, lie

deixar *v* quit, leave

deixar cair *v* drop

dela *pro* hers

delatar *v* snitch

dele *adj* his

dele *pro* his

delegação *f* delegation

delegado *m* delegate

delegar *v* delegate

deleitar *v* delight

deleite *m* delight

deleitoso *adj* delightful

delgadamente *adv* thinly

deliberado *adj* deliberate

deliberar *v* deliberate

delicada *adj* petite

delicadeza *f* delicacy

delicado *adj* delicate

delicioso *adj* delicious

delinear *v* outline

delinquência *f* delinquency

delinquente *m* delinquent

delir *v* delete

delirar *v* rave

delito grave *m* felony

delito leve *m* misdemeanor

demais *adv* too

demanda *f* demand

demandante *m* plaintiff

demandar *v* demand

demissão *f* dismissal

demitir *v* fire

democracia *f* democracy

democrático *adj* democratic

demolição *f* demolition

demolir *v* demolish

demônio *m* demon
demonstrar *v* demonstrate
demonstrativo *adj* demonstrative
demorado *adj* lingering
denegrir *v* denigrate
denominador *m* denominator
denotar *v* denote
densidade *f* density
denso *adj* dense
dentadura *f* dentures
dental *adj* dental
dente *m* tooth, dent
dentes *m* teeth
dentista *m* dentist
dentro de *pre* inside, within
denunciar *v* denounce
deparar com *v* come across
departamento *m* department
dependência *f* reliance
dependências *f* premises
dependente *adj* dependent
depender *v* depend
deplorar *v* deplore
deplorável *adj* deplorable
depois *pre* after
depor *v* depose
deportação *f* deportation
deportar *v* deport
depósito *m* deposit
depravação *f* depravity
depravar *v* deprave
depreciação *f* depreciation

depreciar *v* belittle
depreciativo *adj* derogatory
depressão *f* depression
deprimente *adj* depressing
deprimido *adj* despondent
deprimir *v* depress
depurar *v* purge
derivado *adj* derivative
derivar *v* derive; stem
derramamento *m* spill
derramar *v* shed, spill
derreter *v* melt
derrota *f* defeat
derrotado *adj* beaten
derrotar *v* defeat
derrubar *v* bring down
desabafar-se *v* break out
desabotoar *v* unbutton
desacordado *adj* senseless
desafiador *adj* challenging
desafiante *adj* defiant
desafiar *v* defy, dare
desafio *m* defiance
desagradar *v* displease
desagradável *adj* unpleasant
desagregar *v* desegregate
desajustado *adj* misfit
desalojar *v* oust
desamparado *adj* destitute
desanimador *adj* discouraging
desanimar *v* dishearten
desânimo *m* discouragement

desaparecer *v* disappear
desaparecido *adj* missing
desaparição *f* disappearance
desapontar *v* disappoint, let down
desaprovação *f* disapproval
desaprovar *v* disapprove
desarmado *adj* unarmed
desarmamento *m* disarmament
desarmar *v* disarm
desarraigar *v* uproot
desastre *m* disaster
desastroso *adj* disastrous
desatar *v* loosen, untie
desatino *m* folly
desbotado *adj* faded
descafeinado *adj* decaf
descalço *adj* barefoot
descansar *v* rest
descanso *m* rest
descarado *adj* shameless
descarga *f* discharge
descarregar *v* unload
descarrilhar *v* derail
descartar *v* discard
descartável *adj* disposable
descarte *m* disposal
descascar *v* peel
descendência *f* offspring
descendente *m* descendant
descender *v* descend
descer *v* get off

descoberta *fm* discovery
descobrir *v* discover
desconectar *v* disconnect
desconfiado *adj* distrustful
desconfiança *f* distrust
desconfiar *v* mistrust
desconfortável *adj* uncomfortable
desconforto *m* discomfort
descongelar *v* defrost
desconhecido *adj* unknown
descontar *v* discount
descontente *adj* discontent
descontinuar *v* discontinue
desconto *m* discount
descrédito *v* discredit
descrença *f* disbelief
descrever *v* describe
descrição *f* description
descritivo *adj* descriptive
descuidado *adj* careless
descuido *m* carelessness
desculpa *f* excuse
desculpar *v* excuse
desde *pre* since
desde então *adv* since then
desdém *m* disdain
desdobrar *v* unfold
desejar *v* desire, wish
desejável *adj* desirable
desejo *m* desire, craving
desembarque *v* disembark

desembolsar *v* disburse
desempacotar *v* unpack
desempenho *m* performance
desempregado *adj* jobless
desemprego *m* unemployment
desencantado *adj* disenchanted
desencorajar *v* discourage
desenfreado *adj* rampant
desenhar *v* draw
desenhista *m* draftsman
desenho *m* lay-out
desenredar *v* disentangle
desenrolar *v* unwind
desenterrar *v* unearth
desenvolver *v* develop
desequilíbrio *m* imbalance
deserção *f* defection
deserdar *v* disinherit
desertar *v* defect, desert
deserto *m* desert
desertor *m* deserter
desesperado *adj* desperate
desespero *f* despair
desfalcar *v* embezzle
desfavorável *adj* unfavorable
desfazer *v* undo
desfigurar *v* disfigure
desfiladeiro *m* gorge
desgastar *v* wear out
desgostar *v* dislike
desgosto *m* distaste, sorrow
desgraça *f* disgrace

desgraçado *adj* wretched
desgraçar *v* disgrace
desgraças *f* woes
desidratar *v* dehydrate
designar *v* appoint, assign
desigual *adj* unequal
desigualdade *f* inequality
desilusão *f* disillusion
desimpedir *v* clear
desinfetante *v* disinfectant
desinfetar *v* disinfect
desinflar *v* deflate
desintegração *f* disintegration
desintegrar *v* disintegrate
desintegrar-se *v* crumble
desinteressado *adj* disinterested
desistir *v* back down, desist, give up
deslealdade *f* disloyalty
deslear *adj* disloyal
desligado *adj* unattached
desligar *v* unplug, turn off
deslizar *v* slide
deslocar *v* dislocate, sprain
deslumbrante *adj* dazzling
deslumbrar *v* dazzle
desmaiar *v* faint, pass out
desmaio *m* faint
desmantelar *v* dismantle
desmascarar *v* unmask
desmontar *v* take apart
desmoralizar *v* demoralize

desmoronar v collapse
desnatar v skim
desnecessário adj unnecessary
desnesto adj devious
desnivelado adj uneven
desnutrição f malnutrition
desobedecer v disobey
desobediência f disobedience
desobediente adj disobedient
desocupado adj unoccupied
desocupar v vacate
desodorante m deodorant
desolação f desolation
desolado adj desolate
desonestidade f dishonesty
desonesto adj dishonest
desonra f dishonor
desonroso adj dishonorable
desordeiro adj rowdy
desordem m disorder
desorganizado adj disorganized
desorientado adj disoriented
despachar v dispatch
despedida f farewell
despedir v dismiss, lay off
despejar v dump, evict
despejo m dump
despencar v slump
despensa f pantry
despercebível adj unnoticed
desperdiçar v waste
desperdício m waste

despertar v wake up, arouse
despesa f expense
despir v undress
despojo m spoils
déspota f despot
despótico adj despotic
desprazer n displeasure
despretensioso adj unassuming
desprezar v despise, scorn
desprezível adj despicable
desprezo m contempt
desprotegido adj unprotected
desprovido adj deprived
desqualificar v disqualify
desrespeito m disrespect
destilar v distill
destinatário m addressee
destino m fate, destiny
destituído adj devoid
destrancar v unlock
destroçar v wreck
destroços m wreckage
destronar v overthrow
destruição f destruction
destruidor n destroyer
destruir v destroy
destrutivo adj destructive
desunidade f disunity
desvalorização f devaluation
desvalorizar v devalue
desvanecer v vanish
desvantagem f disadvantage

D

desvelar *v* unveil
desviar *v* divert, bypass
desvinculado *adj* unrelated
desvio *m* detour, deviation
detalhar *v* detail
detalhe *m* detail
detalhe técnico *f* technicality
detectar *v* detect
detector *m* detector
detenção *f* detention
deter *v* deter
detergente *m* detergent
deterioração *f* deterioration
deteriorar *v* deteriorate
determinação *f* determination
determinar *v* determine
detestar *v* detest
detestável *adj* detestable
detestável *pre* of
detetive *m* detective
detonação *f* detonation
detonador *m* detonator
detonar *v* detonate
detrimento *m* detriment
Deus *m* God
deusa *f* goddess
devastação *f* devastation
devastador *adj* devastating
devastar *v* ravage
devedor *m* debtor
dever *m* duty
dever *v* owe, ought to

devidamente *adv* duly
devido *adj* due
devido a *adv* owing to
devoção *f* devotion
devolver *v* give back
devorar *v* devour
devotar *v* devote
devoto *adj* devout
dez *adj* ten
dez centavos *m* dime
Dezembro *m* December
dezenove *adj* nineteen
dezesseis *adj* sixteen
dezessete *adj* seventeen
dezoito *adj* eighteen
dia da semana *adj* weekday
diabete *f* diabetes
diabético *adj* diabetic
diabo *m* devil
diabólico *adj* diabolical
diácono *m* deacon
diagnosticar *v* diagnose
diagnóstico *f* diagnosis
diagonal *adj* diagonal
diagrama *m* diagram
dialeto *m* dialect
diálogo *m* dialogue
diamante *m* diamond
diâmetro *m* diameter
diariamente *adv* daily
diário *m* diary
diarréia *f* diarrhea

dicionário *m* dictionary
dieta *f* diet
difamação *f* slander
difamar *v* defame
diferença *f* difference
diferente *adj* different
diferir *v* differ
difícil *adj* difficult
dificilmente *adv* hardly
dificuldade *f* difficulty
difundir *v* diffuse
digerir *v* digest
digestão *f* digestion
digestivo *adj* digestive
dígito *m* digit, figure
dignatário *m* dignitary
dignidade *f* dignity
dignificar *v* dignify
dilapidado *adj* dilapidated
dilema *m* dilemma
diligência *f* diligence
diligente *adj* diligent
diluir *v* dilute
dilúvio *m* deluge
dimensão *f* dimension
diminuir *v* diminish
Dinamarca *m* Denmark
dinâmico *adj* dynamic
dinamite *f* dynamite
dinastia *f* dynasty
dinheiro *m* money
dinheiro vivo *m* cash

dinossauro *m* dinosaur
diocese *f* diocese
diploma *m* diploma
diplomacia *f* diplomacy
diplomata *f* diplomat
diplomático *adj* diplomatic
dique *m* dike
direção *f* direction
direcionado *adj* bound
direcionado a *adj* bound for
direito *m* right
direito *adj* right, direct
direto *adv* nonstop
diretor *m* director
diretório *m* directory
diretrizes *f* guidelines
dirigente *m* manager
dirigir *v* direct
dirigir-se a *v* head for
disagradável *adj* distasteful
discar *v* dial
discernir *v* discern
discípulo *m* disciple
disco *m* disk, record
discordância *f* disagreement
discordar *v* disagree
discórdia *f* discord
discrepância *f* discrepancy
discreto *adj* discreet
discrição *f* discretion
discriminação *f* discrimination
discriminar *v* discriminate

discussão *f* discussion
discutir *v* argue
discutível *adj* questionable
disfarçar *v* disguise
disfarçar-se *v* masquerade
disfarce *m* disguise
disparar *v* shoot
disparate *m* nonsense
disparidade *f* disparity
dispensação *f* dispensation
dispensar *v* dispense
dispersão *f* dispersal
dispersar *v* disperse, scatter
disperso *adj* scrambled
displicente *adj* carefree
disponível *adj* available
dispor *v* dispose
disposição *f* willingness
dispositivo *m* appliance
disposto *adj* willing
disputa *f* dispute
disputante *m* contestant
disputar *v* contest
disseminar *v* disseminate
dissidente *adj* dissident
dissimular *v* conceal
dissipar *v* dispel, squander
dissolução *f* dissolution
dissoluto *adj* dissolute
dissolver *v* dissolve
dissonante *adj* discordant
dissuadir *v* dissuade

distância *f* distance
distante *adj* distant
distendido *adj* outstretched
distinção *f* distinction
distinguir *v* distinguish
distintivo *adj* distinctive
distinto *adj* distinct
distorção *f* distortion
distorcer *v* distort
distração *f* distraction
distrair *v* distract
distribuição *f* distribution
distribuir *v* distribute
distrito *m* district
distúrbio *m* disturbance
disuso *m* disuse
ditador *m* dictator
ditadura *f* dictatorship
ditar *v* dictate
ditatorial *adj* dictatorial
dito *m* saying
ditongo *m* diphthong
ditoso *adj* blissful
divã *m* couch
divagar *v* digress
divergir *v* dissent
diversão *f* amusement
diversidade *f* diversity
diversificar *v* diversify
diverso *adj* diverse
divertido *adj* amusing
divertimento *m* entertainment

divertir *v* amuse
dívida *f* debt, dues
dividendo *m* dividend
dividir *v* divide
divindade *f* deity
divino *adj* divine
divisão *f* division, parting
divisível *adj* divisible
divisória *f* partition
divorciado *m* divorcee
divorciar *v* divorce
divórcio *m* divorce
divulgar *v* divulge
dizer *v* say
do norte *adj* northern
doação *f* donation
doador *m* donor
dobradiça *f* hinge
dobrar *v* bend, fold
doce *m* sweets
doce *adj* sweet
dócil *adj* docile
docilidade *f* docility, meekness
documentação *f* documentation
documentário *m* documentary
documento *m* document
doçura *f* sweetness
doença *f* disease, illness
doente *adj* ill, sick
doentio *adj* unhealthy
dogmático *adj* dogmatic
dois *adj* two

dois-pontos (:) *m* colon
dólar *m* dollar
dolorido *adj* sore
doloroso *adj* painful
domar *v* tame
domesticar *v* domesticate
doméstico *adj* domestic
dominação *f* domination
dominante *adj* domineering
dominar *v* master
Domingo *m* Sunday
domínio *m* dominion
dona de casa *f* housewife
donar *v* donate
donativo *m* alms
dono *m* owner
donzela *f* maiden
dopar *v* dope
dor *m* ache, pain
dor de cabeça *m* headache
dor de dente *m* toothache
dor de ouvido *m* earache
dormir *v* sleep
dormitório *m* dormitory
dosagem *f* dosage
dossiê *m* dossier
dote *f* dowry
dourado *adj* golden
doutor *m* doctor
doutrina *f* doctrine
doutrinar *v* indoctrinate
doze *adj* twelve

dragão *m* dragon
dramático *adj* dramatic
dramatizar *v* dramatize
drástico *adj* drastic
drenagem *m* drainage
drenar *v* drain
droga *f* drug
drogar *v* drug
duas vezes *adv* twice
dúcia *f* dozen
duelo *m* duel
duodécimo *adj* twelfth
duplicar *v* double
duplo *adj* dual, double
duque *n* duke
duquesa *f* duchess
duração *f* duration, length, span
duradouro *adj* lasting
durante *pre* during
durante a noite *adv* overnight
durar *v* last
durável *adj* durable
dureza *f* hardship
duro *adj* hard, tough
duto *m* pipeline
dúvida *f* doubt
duvidar *v* doubt
duvidoso *adl* doubtful

e *c* and
e portanto *c* whereupon
eclipsar *v* outshine
eclipse *m* eclipse
eco *m* echo
ecologia *f* ecology
economia *f* economy
econômico *adj* economical
economizar *v* economize
edição *f* edition
edifício *m* edifice
editar *v* edit
edredon *m* comforter
educação *f* manners
educacional *adj* educational
educado *adj* polite
educar *v* educate
efeito *m* effect
efêmero *adj* short-lived
efeminado *adj* sissy
efetividade *f* effectiveness
eficaz *adj* effective
eficiência *f* efficiency
eficiente *adj* efficient
efígie *f* effigy
efusão *f* outpouring
efusivo *adj* effusive
egoísmo *m* selfishness
egoísta *m* egoist

egoísta *adj* selfish
égua *f* mare
eixo *m* axis, axle, hub
ela *adj* her
ela *pro* she
ela mesma *pro* herself
elástico *adj* elastic
ele *pro* he
elefante *m* elephant
elegância *f* elegance
elegante *adj* elegant
eleger *v* elect
eleição *f* election
elementar *adj* elementary
elemento *m* element
eles *pro* they
eles mesmos *pro* themselves
eletricidade *f* electricity
eletricista *m* electrician
elétrico *adj* electric
eletrificar *v* electrify
eletrocutar *v* electrocute
eletrônico *adj* electronic
elevação *f* elevation
elevado *adj* towering
elevador *m* elevator
elevar *v* elevate, raise
eliminar *v* eliminate
elo *m* link
elogiar *v* praise
elogio *f* praise
eloqüência *f* eloquence

em *pre* on; in
em branco *adj* blank
em brasa *adj* red-hot
em chamas *adv* alight
em cima *adv* upstairs
em curso *adj* ongoing
em declive *adv* downhill
em favor de *adv* behalf (on)
em frente a *pre* facing
em frente a *adv* opposite
em outro lugar *adv* elsewhere
em parte *adv* partly
em partes *adv* piecemeal
em substituição *adv* instead
em terra firme *adv* ashore
em torno *pre* around
em vez de *adv* lieu
emaciado *adj* emaciated
emanar *v* emanate
emancipado *v* emancipate
emaranhar *v* entangle
embaçado *adj* blurred
embaixada *f* embassy
embaixador *m* ambassador
embalsamar *v* embalm
embaraçar *v* embarrass
embaraçoso *adj* awkward
embaralhar *v* shuffle
embarcar *v* embark, board
embelezar *v* embellish, beautify
emblema *n* emblem
embora *c* although

E

embora *adv* away
emboscada *f* setup
embriaguez *f* drunkenness
embrião *m* embryo
embrulhar *v* wrap
embrulho *m* wrapping
embutido *adj* built-in
emenda *f* amendment
emendar *v* amend
emergência *f* emergency
emergir *v* emerge
emigrante *m* emigrant
emigrar *v* emigrate
emissão *f* broadcast
emitir *v* emit
emoção *f* emotion, thrill
emocional *adj* emotional
emoldurar *v* frame
empacotar *v* pack
empanar *v* tarnish
emparelhar *v* match
empatar *v* tie
empate *m* draw, tie
empenhar *v* pawn, engage
empilhar *v* pile up
emplastrar *v* plaster
emplastro *m* plaster
empobrecido *adj* impoverished
empoeirado *adj* dusty
empreendedor *m* entrepreneur
empreender *v* undertake
empregado *m* employee

empregador *m* employer
empregar *v* employ
emprego *m* employment
emprestar *v* lend, loan
empréstimo *m* loan
empurrão *m* shove
empurrar *v* push, shove
encadernação *f* binding
encalhado *adj* stranded
encanador *m* plumber
encanamento *m* plumbing
encantador *adj* charming
encantar *v* charm
encanto *m* spell
encaracolado *adj* curly
encaracolar *v* curl
encarar *v* envisage
encarcerar *v* incarcerate, confine
encardimento *m* grime
encargo *m* charge
encarregado *m* warden
encenar *v* stage
encerramento *m* enclosure
encerrar *v* lock up
encharcar *v* soak
encher *v* fill, stuff
enchimento *m* padding
enciclopédia *n* encyclopedia
enclave *n* enclave
encobrir *v* cover up
encolher *v* shrink
encolher (ombros) *v* shrug

encompridar _v_ lengthen
encontrar _v_ find, run into
encontro _m_ encounter
encorajar _v_ encourage
encosta _f_ hillside
encruzilhada _f_ crossroads
encurtar _v_ shorten, curtail
encurvado _adj_ hunched
endereçar _v_ address
endereço _m_ address
endossar _v_ endorse
endosso _m_ endorsement
endurecer _v_ harden, stiffen
energia _f_ energy
enérgico _adj_ energetic
enevoado _adj_ foggy, hazy
enevoar _v_ blur
enfaixar _v_ bandage
ênfase _m_ emphasis
enfatizar _v_ emphasize
enfeitiçar _v_ bewitch
enfeixar _v_ cluster
enfermaria _f_ infirmary
enfermeiro _m_ nurse
enferrujado _adj_ rusty
enferrujar _v_ rust
enfiar _v_ squeeze in
enfim _adv_ lastly
enfraquecer _v_ weaken
enfrentar _v_ face up to
enfurecer _v_ enrage
enfurecer(se) _v_ anger

enganador _adj_ deceptive
enganar _v_ deceive, fool
engano _m_ deceit, swindle
enganoso _adj_ misleading
engarrafar _v_ bottle
engatinhar _v_ crawl
engenheiro _m_ engineer
engenhoso _adj_ witty
engolir _v_ swallow, gobble
engordar _v_ fatten
engraçadinho _adj_ cute
engraçado _adj_ funny
engrenagem _m_ gear
engrossar _v_ thicken
enguiçar _v_ stall
enigma _m_ riddle
enigmático _adj_ puzzling
enlameado _adj_ muddy
enlatado _adj_ canned
enlatar _v_ can
enlouquecer _v_ madden
enlutado _adj_ bereaved
enorme _adj_ huge
enquanto que _c_ whereas, while
enraizado _adj_ ingrained
enriquecer _v_ enrich
enrolado _adj_ convoluted
enrugar _v_ wrinkle
ensaiar _v_ rehearse
ensaio _m_ essay
enseada _f_ cove
ensinar _v_ teach

E

ensolarado *adj* sunny
ensopado *adj* soggy
ensurdecedor *adj* deafening
ensurdecer *v* deafen
entalhar *v* carve
então *adv* then
enteada *f* stepdaughter
enteado *m* stepson
entediado *adj* bored
entender *v* understand
entender mal *v* misunderstand
enterrar *v* bury
enterro *m* burial
entorpecido *adj* numb
entortar *v* warp
entrada *f* entrance, way in
entranha *f* bowels
entrante *adj* incoming
entrar *v* enter, get in
entre *pre* among, between
entreaberto *adj* ajar
entrega *f* delivery
entregar *v* deliver, hand in
entrelaçarer *v* intertwine
entreter *v* entertain
entrever *v* glimpse
entrevista *f* appointment, interview
entristecer *v* sadden
entroncamento *m* junction
entrouxar *v* bundle
entulho *m* rubbish

entupir *v* clog
entusiarmar(-se) *v* enthuse
entusiasmo *m* enthusiasm
enumerar *v* enumerate
envelope *m* envelope
envenenar *v* poison
envergonhado *adj* ashamed
envergonhar *v* shame
envernizar *v* varnish
enviado *m* envoy
enviar *v* send
enviar por correio *v* mail
envolver *v* involve
envolvido *adj* involved
envolvimento *m* involvement
enxaguar *v* rinse
enxame *m* swarm
enxaqueca *f* migraine
enxertar *v* graft
enxerto *m* graft
enxofre *m* sulfur
enxotar *v* chase away
epidemia *f* epidemic
epilepsia *f* epilepsy
episódio *m* episode
epístola *f* epistle
epitáfio *m* epitaph
época *f* epoch
equação *f* equation
equador *m* equator
equilibrar *n* poise
equilibrio *m* balance

equipamento *m* equipment
equipar *v* equip
equiparar *v* equate
equipe *m* staff
equivalente *adj* equivalent
equivalente a *adj* tantamount to
equivaler a *v* amount to
era *f* era
eregir *v* erect
ereto *adj* erect, upright
ermitão *m* hermit
ermo *adj* bleak
erradicar *v* stamp out
errado *adj* mistaken
errante *m* vagrant
errar *v* err, miss
erro *m* error, mistake
erudição *f* learning
erudito *adj* learned
erupção *f* eruption, rash
erva *f* herb
ervilha *f* pea
esbanjador *adj* wasteful
esbanjar *v* lavish
esboçar *v* sketch
esboço *m* groundwork
esbravejar *v* rampage
escada portátil *f* ladder
escada rolante *f* escalator
escadaria *f* staircase
escadinha *f* stepladder
escalar *v* climb

escaldar *v* scald
escalpo *m* scalp
escama *f* scale
escamar *v* scale
escandalizar *v* scandalize
escândalo *m* scandal
escapada *f* escapade
escapar *v* run away
escape *m* vent, retreat
escaramuça *f* skirmish
escarnecer *v* deride
escárnio *n* ridicule
escassez *f* scarcity
escasso *adj* sparse
escavar *v* excavate
esclarecer *v* clarify
escola *f* school
escolha *f* choice
escolher *v* choose
escolta *f* escort
escombros *m* debris
esconder *v* hide
esconder-se *v* lurk
escondido *adj* hidden
escorpião *m* scorpion
escorregadio *adj* slippery
escorregar *v* slip
escorrer *v* pour
escoteiro *m* scout
escova *f* brush
escovar *v* brush
escravatura *n* slavery

E

E

escravo *m* slave
escrever *v* write
escrita *f* writing
escrito *adj* written
escritor *m* writer
escritório *m* office
escrivaninha *f* bureau, desk
escrúpulo *m* qualm
escrúpulos *m* scruples
escrupuloso *adj* scrupulous
escrutínio *m* scrutiny
escudo *m* shield
escultor *m* sculptor
escultura *f* sculpture
escurecer *v* darken, dim
escuridão *f* darkness
escuro *adj* dark
escutar *v* listen, hear
esfera *f* sphere
esfolar *v* skin
esforçar-se *v* strive, exert
esforço *n* effort, exertion
esfregar *v* rub, scrub, scour
esfriar *v* chill, cool
esgômago *m* stomach
esgotado *adj* sold-out
esgotar *v* exhaust, wear
esgoto *m* sewage
esgueirar-se *v* sneak
esguicho *m* nozzle
esguio *adj* slender
esmagador *adj* crushing

esmagar *v* crush, mash
esmeralda *f* emerald
esôfago *m* esophagus
espaçar *v* space out
espaço *m* space
espaço aéreo *m* airspace
espaçoso *adj* spacious
espada *f* sword
espalhafatoso *adj* flashy
espalhar *v* spread
espancar *v* batter, club
Espanha *f* Spain
espanhol *m* Spaniard
espanhol *adj* Spanish
espantar *v* scare away
esparramar *v* sprawl
espasmo *m* spasm
especial *adj* special
especialidade *ff* specialty
especializado *adj* expert
especializar *v* specialize
especialmente *adv* especially
espécie *f* species
específico *adj* specific
espécime *m* specimen
espectador *m* spectator
espectral *adj* spooky
especulação *f* speculation
especular *v* speculate
espelho *m* mirror
espera *f* waiting
esperança *f* hope

esperançoso *adj* hopeful
esperar *v* wait, expect
esperma *m* sperm
esperto *adj* smart, clever
espetáculo *m* spectacle
espiar *v* spy
espiar *m* spy
espinha *f* backbone
espinho *m* thorn
espinhoso *adj* thorny
espionagem *m* espionage
espírito *m* spirit
espiritual *adj* spiritual
espirrar *v* sneeze
espirro *m* sneeze
esplêndido *adj* splendid
esplendor *m* splendor
esponja *f* sponge
espontâneo *adj* spontaneous
esporádico *adj* sporadic
esporear *v* spur
esporte *m* sport
esposa *f* wife
esposas *f* wives
espreitar *v* peep, stalk
espremer *v* squeeze
espuma *f* foam, lather
esquálido *adj* squalid
esquecer *v* forget
esquecido *adj* oblivious
esqueleto *m* skeleton
esquentar *v* heat

esquiar *v* ski
esquilo *m* squirrel
esquina *f* corner
esquivar *v* avoid, dodge
esquivar-se *v* duck
esquivo *adj* elusive
esse *adj* that
essência *f* essence, scent
essencial *adj* essential
estabelecer *v* establish
estabilidade *f* stability
estábulo *m* stable
estaca *f* stake
estação *f* station, season
estacionamento *m* parking
estacionar *v* park
estadia *f* stay
estado *m* state
estagiário *m* trainee
estágio *m* stage
estagnação *f* stagnation
estagnado *adj* stagnant
estagnar *v* stagnate
estaleiro *m* shipyard
estande *m* stall
estanho *m* tin
estante *m* bookcase, shelf
estapear *v* slap
estar alerta *v* watch out
estar de luto *v* mourn
estar en pé *v* stand up
estatística *f* statistic

E

estátua *n* statue
estatuto *n* statute
estável *adj* stable
este *adj* this
esterco *n* manure
estéril *adj* barren, sterile
esterilizar *v* sterilize
estes *adj* these
estético *adj* aesthetic
esticador *m* stretcher
estilhaço *m* splinter
estilo *m* style
estilo de vida *m* lifestyle
estima *v* esteem
estimar *v* estimate
estimulante *adjf* stimulant
estimular *v* stimulate
estímulo *m* spur, stimulus
estipular *v* stipulate
estirar *v* stretch
estóico *adj* stoic
estojo *m* case
estoque *m* stockpile
estória *f* story
estorvar *v* hinder
estorvo *m* hindrance
estraçalhar *v* mangle
estrada *f* road
estrado *m* stand
estragar *v* blemish
estrangeiro *m* foreigner
estrangular *v* strangle

estranho *adj* strange, odd
estranho *m* stranger
estratagema *f* ploy
estratégia *f* strategy
estréia *f* debut
estreito *adj* narrow
estreito *m* strait
estrela *f* star
estremecer *v* shudder
estressante *adj* stressful
estresse *m* stress
estrito *adj* strict
estrondo *m* boom, crash
estrutura *f* structure
estuário *m* estuary
estudante *m-f* student
estudar *v* study
estufa *f* stove
estupendo *adj* stupendous
estupidez *n* stupidity
estúpido *adj* stupid
estuprador *m* rapist
estuprar *v* rape
estupro *m* rape
esvaziar *v* empty
etapa *f* stage
eternamente *adv* forever
eternidade *f* eternity
eterno *adj* timeless
ética *f* ethics
ético *adj* ethical
etiqueta *f* etiquette, tag

eu *pro* I
eu mesmo *pro* myself
euforia *f* euphoria
Europa *f* Europe
europeu *adj* European
evacuar *v* evacuate
evadir *v* evade
evangelho *m* gospel
evaporar *v* evaporate
evasão *f* evasion
evasivo *adj* evasive
evento *m* event
eventualmente *adv* eventually
evidência *f* evidence
evidente *adj* evident
evitar *v* avoid, shun, avert
evitável *adj* avoidable
evocar *v* evoke
evolução *f* evolution
evoluir *v* evolve
exagerar *v* exaggerate
exaltar *v* exalt
exame *f* examination
exame geral *m* check up
examinar *v* examine
exasperar *v* exasperate
exatamente *adv* right
exatidão *f* accuracy
exato *adj* exact
exaurir *v* exhaust
exaustão *f* exhaustion
exaustivo *adj* exhausting

exceção *f* exception
exceder *v* exceed
excelência *f* excellence
excelente *adj* excellent
excêntrico *m* crank
excêntrico *adj* eccentric
excepcional *adj* exceptional
excerto *m* excerpt
excessivo *adj* excessive
excesso *m* excess
exceto *pre* except
excitação *m* excitement
excitante *adj* exciting
excitar *v* excite
exclamar *v* exclaim
excluir *v* exclude
excursão *f* excursion
excursionar *v* sightseeing
executar *v* execute, enforce
executivo *m* executive
exemplar *adj* exemplary
exemplificar *v* exemplify
exemplo *m* example
exercer *v* exert
exercício *n* exercise, drill
exercitar *v* exercise
exército *m* army
exibição *f* exhibition
exibir *v* exhibit, show off
exigente *adj* demanding
exilar *v* exile
exílio *m* exile

E

existência *f* existence
existir *v* exist
êxodo *m* exodus
exonerar *v* exonerate
exorbitante *adj* exorbitant
exorcista *m* exorcist
exortar *v* exhort
exótico *adj* exotic
expandido *adj* widespread
expandir *v* expand
expansão *f* expansion
expectativa *f* expectation
expedição *f* expedition
expelir *v* expel
experiência *f* experience
experimento *m* experiment
expiação *f* atonement
expiar *v* atone, expiate
expiração *f* expiration
expirar *v* expire
explicar *v* explain
explícito *adj* explicit
explodir *v* explode
exploração *f* exploitation
explorador *m* explorer
explorar *v* explore
explosão *f* explosion
explosivo *adj* explosive
expor *v* display
exportar *v* export
exposição *f* display
exposto *adj* exposed

expressamente *adv* expressly
expressão *f* expression
expressar *v* utter
expresso *f* express
expropriar *v* expropriate
expulsão *f* expulsion
expulsar *v* eject
êxtase *m* ecstasy
extático *adj* ecstatic
extender *v* extend
extensão *f* extension
exterior *adj* exterior
exterminar *v* exterminate
externo *adj* external, outer
extinguir *v* extinguish
extinguir-se *v* die out
extinto *adj* extinct
extirpar *v* weed
extorquir *v* extort
extorsão *f* extortion
extra *adv* extra
extração *m* draw
extradição *f* extradition
extraditar *v* extradite
extrair *v* draw, extract
extraordinário *adj* astonishing
extravagância *f* extravagance
extravagante *adj* extravagant
extraviar *v* misplace
extremamente *adv* exceedingly
extremidades *f* extremities
extremista *adj* extremist

extremo *adj* extreme
extrovertido *adj* outgoing
exultante *adj* elated
exultar *v* exult

fâ *m* fan
fábrica *f* factory
fabricante *m* maker
fabricar *v* manufacture
fábula *f* fable
fabuloso *adj* fabulous
faca *m* knife
facada *f* stab
façanha *f* exploit
faceta *f* facet
fachada *n* front
fácil *adj* easy
facilidade *f* ease
facilitar *v* facilitate
facilmente *adv* easily
factual *adj* factual
faculdade *f* faculty
fada *f* fairy
faisão *m* pheasant
faixa *f* banner
fala *f* speech

falácia *f* fallacy
falante *adj* talkative
falar *v* speak
falar mal de *v* malign
falcão *m* hawk
falecido *adj* deceased
falência *f* bankruptcy
falha *f* fault
falhar *v* fail, miss
falido *adj* broke
falir *v* bankrupt, crash
falível *adj* unreliable
falsificação *f* forgery
falsificado *adj* counterfeit
falsificar *v* falsify, fake
falso *adj* phony, untrue
falta *f* fault, lack
falta de jeito *f* clumsiness
faltar *v* lack
fama *f* fame
família *f* family
familiar *adj* familiar
faminto *adj* hungry
famoso *adj* famous
fanático *adj* fanatic
fanatismo *m* bigotry
fantasia *f* fantasy
fantasma *m* ghost
fantástico *adj* fantastic
fardo *m* bale
farinha *f* flour
farmacêutico *m* pharmacist

E
F

farmácia *f* pharmacy
faroeste *adj* western
farol *m* beacon
farsa *f* farce
farto *adj* fed up
fascinação *f* allure
fascinante *adj* alluring
fascinar *v* fascinate
fase *f* phase
fatal *adj* fatal
fatiga *f* fatigue
fato *m* fact
fator *m* factor
fatura *f* invoice
favor *m* favor
favorável *adj* favorable
favorito *adj* favorite
fazenda *f* farm
fazendeiro *m* farmer
fazer *v* do, make
fazer acordo *v* compromise
fazer amizade *v* befriend
fazer auditoria *v* audit
fazer campanha *v* campaign
fazer coçegas *v* tickle
fazer compras *v* shop
fazer entrar *v* let in
fazer escala *v* stop over
fazer fila *v* line up
fazer fronteira *v* border on
fazer genuflexão *v* genuflect
fazer lembrar *v* remind

fazer pressão *v* lobby
fazer sair *v* let out
fé *f* faith
fealdade *f* ugliness
febre *f* fever
febril *adj* feverish
fechado *adj* closed
fechamento *m* closure
fechar *v* close, shut
fedelho *adj* brat
feder *v* stink
federal *adj* federal
fedido *adj* smelly, stale
fedor *m* stench, stink
fedorento *adj* stinking
feijão *m* bean
feijão-roxo *m* kidney bean
feio *adj* ugly
feira *f* fair
feitiçaria *f* sorcery
feiticeiro *m* sorcerer
feito à mão *adj* handmade
feito em casa *adj* homemade
feixe *m* bunch
felicidade *f* happiness
feliz *adj* happy
felpudo *adj* plush
fêmea *f* female
feminino *adj* feminine
fenda *f* crevice
feno *f* hay
fenômeno *m* phenomenon

F

feriado *m* holiday
férias *f* vacation
ferida *f* wound, sore
ferido *adj* hurt
ferir *v* wound, injure
ferir com tiro *v* gun down
fermentar *v* ferment
fermento *m* ferment
ferocidade *f* ferocity
feroz *adj* fierce
ferragens *m* hardware
ferramenta *f* tool
ferreiro *m* blacksmith
ferro *m* iron
ferrolho *m* latch
ferrovia *f* railroad
ferrugem *m* rust
fértil *adj* fertile
fertilidade *f* fertility
fertilizar *v* fertilize
ferver *v* boil, simmer
fervoroso *adj* fervent
festa *f* party
festividade *f* festivity
festivo *adj* festive
fétido *adj* fetid
feto *m* fetus
feudo *m* feud
Fevereiro *m* February
fiador *m* bond, voucher
fiança *f* bail
fibra *f* fiber, staple

ficar para trás *v* fall behind
ficção *f* fiction
ficha *f* chip
fictício *adj* fictitious
fidelidade *f* allegiance
fiel *adj* faithful
fígado *m* liver
figo *m* fig
figura *f* figure
fila *f* line, queue, row
filha *f* daughter
filho *m* son
filhote *m* cub
filhote de ave *m* chick
filiação *f* affiliation
filme *m* film, movie
filosofia *f* philosophy
filósofo *m* philosopher
filtrar *v* filter
filtro *m* filter
fim *m* end, demise
fim de semana *m* weekend
final *adj* final
finalidade *f* end
finalizar *v* finalize
finança *v* finance
financeiro *adj* financial
financiar *v* fund
fingido *adj* fake
fingimento *n* sham
fingir *v* feign, pretend
finlandês *adj* Finnish

Finlândia *f* Finland
fino *adj* genteel
fio *m* yarn, thread
fiorde *m* fjord
firma *f* firm
firmar *v* fasten
firme *adj* firm, steady
firmeza *f* firmness
física *f* physics
fisicamente *adj* physically
fissura *f* cleft
fita *f* band, ribbon
fitar *v* stare
fivela *f* buckle
fixação *f* hang-up
fixar *v* fix
fixo *adj* stationary
flagelo *m* scourge
flamejante *adj* ablaze
flanar *v* loiter
flanco *m* flank
flauta *f* flute
flectir *v* flex
flertar *v* flirt
flexível *adj* flexible
floco de neve *m* snowflake
flor *f* flower
florescer *v* bloom, flourish
floresta *f* forest
fluentemente *adv* fluently
fluido *m* fluid
flutuar *v* float

fluxo *m* flow
fobia *f* phobia
foca *f* seal
focinheira *f* muzzle
foco *m* focus
fofoca *f* gossip
fofocar *v* gossip
fogão *f* stove
fogo *m* fire
fogo cruzado *m* crossfire
fogos de artifício *m* fireworks
fogueira *f* campfire
foguete *m* rocket
foice *f* sickle
folgado *adj* baggy
folha *f* leaf
folhear *v* browse
folheto *m* brochure, flier
fome *f* famine, hunger
fone de ouvido *m* earphones
fonte *f* fountain
for *pre* for
for a *adv* outside, out
fora *adv* outdoors
fora de moda *adj* old-fashioned
forasteiro *m* outsider
força *f* force, strength
forçadamente *adv* forcibly
forcado *m* fork
forçar *v* force
forjado *adj* trumped-up
forjar *v* forge

forma *f* form, shape
formação *f* upbringing
formal *adj* formal
formalidade *f* formality
formalizar *v* formalize
formalmente *adv* formally
formato *m* format
formiga *f* ant
fórmula *f* formula
fornada *f* batch
fornalha *f* furnace
fornecer *v* supply
forno *m* oven
forro *m* lining
fort *m* fort
fortalecer *v* strengthen
fortaleza *f* fortress
forte *adj* strong
fortificar *v* fortify
fortuna *f* fortune
fósforo *m* match
fóssil *m* fossil
foto *f* photo
fotocópia *f* photocopy
fotografar *v* photograph
fotografia *f* photography
fotógrafo *m* photographer
fração *f* fraction
fracassar *v* backfire, flunk
fracasso *m* failure
fraco *adj* weak, slim
frade *m* friar

frágil *adj* fragile, frail
fragilidade *f* frailty
fragmentar *v* splinter
fragmento *m* fragment
fragrância *f* fragrance
fralda *f* diaper
framboesa *f* raspberry
França *f* France
francamente *adv* frankly
francês *adj* French
franco *adj* outspoken
frango *m* chicken
franja *f* fringe, stripe
franqueza *f* frankness
franzir a testa *v* frown
fraqueza *f* weakness
frase *f* phrase
fraternal *n* brother-in-law
fraternal *adj* fraternal
fraternidade *f* fraternity
fratura *f* fracture
fraudar *v* swindle
fraude *m* fraud, scam
fraudulento *adj* fraudulent
freio *m* brake, curb
freira *f* nun
frenesi *m* frenzy
frenético *adj* frenetic
frente *m* front
frequência *f* frequency
frequentar *v* frequent
frequente *adj* frequent

F

freqüentemente *adv* often
fresco *adj* cool, fresh
frescura *f* freshness
fretar *v* charter
friagem *f* coolness
fricção *f* friction
frieza *f* coldness
frigata *f* frigate
frigideira *f* frying pan
frígido *adj* frigid
frio *adj* chilly, cold
fritar *v* fry
frito *adj* fried
frívolo *adj* frivolous
fronha *f* pillowcase
frontal *adj* front
fronteira *f* border
frota *f* fleet
frugal *adj* frugal, thrifty
frugalidade *f* frugality
frugalmente *adv* sparingly
frustração *f* frustration
frustrar *v* frustrate, foil
fruta *f* fruit
frutífero *adj* fruitful
frutos do mar *m* seafood
fuga *f* flight
fuga precipitada *f* stampede
fugir *v* break away, escape, flee
fugitivo *m* fugitive
fumaça *f* fumes
fumante *m* smoker

fumar *v* smoke
fumigar *v* fumigate
função *f* function
funcionar *v* work
funcionário *m* officer
fundação *f* foundation
fundador *m* founder
fundamental *adj* fundamental
fundamentar *v* underlie
fundição *f* foundry
fundir-se *v* merge
fundo *m* bottom, fund
fundo *adj* deep
fundos *m* funds
funeral *m* funeral
fungar *v* sniff
fungo *m* fungus
furacão *m* hurricane
furar *v* drill
furgão *f* van
fúria *f* fury
furiosamente *adv* furiously
furioso *adj* furious
furo *m* puncture
furor *m* furor
furto *m* larceny
furto em loja *m* shoplifting
fusão *f* fusion, merger
fusível *m* fuse
futebol *m* football
fútil *adj* futile
futilidade *n* futility

futilmente *adv* vainly
futuro *adj* forthcoming
futuro *m* future

G

gabar-se *v* brag
gado *m* cattle
gaguejar *v* stutter
gaiola *f* cage
gaivota *f* seagull
galante *adj* gallant
galanteio *m* courtship
galão *m* gallon
galáxia *f* galaxy
galeria *f* gallery
galgo *m* greyhound
galho *m* branch
galinha *f* hen
galo *m* cock, rooster
galopar *v* gallop
galvanizar *v* galvanize
ganancioso *adj* greedy
gancho *m* hook
gangrena *f* gangrene
gângster *m* gangster
gangue *m* gang
ganhador *m* winner

ganhar *v* earn, gain, win
ganho *m* gain
ganir *v* whine
ganso *m* goose
gansos *m* geese
garagem *m* garage
garantia *f* guarantee
garantido *adj* foolproof
garantir *v* assure, warrant
garçom *m* waiter
garçonete *f* barmaid, waitress
garfo *m* fork
garganta *f* throat
gargarejar *v* gargle
garra *f* claw
garrafa *f* bottle
garragem *m* barrage
gárrulo *adj* garrulous
gás *m* gas
gasolina *f* gasoline
gastar *v* spend
gasto *n* spending
gástrico *adj* gastric
gatilho *m* trigger
gatinho *m* kitten
gato *m* cat
gatuno *m* prowler
gaveta *f* drawer
gaze *f* gauze
geada *f* frost
gêiser *m* geyser
geladeira *f* icebox

F
G

gelado *adj* freezing
geléia *f* marmalade
geleira *m* glacier
gelo *m* ice
gema *f* yolk; gem
gêmeo *m* twin
gemer *v* moan
gemido *m* groan, moan
gene *m* gene
generalizar *v* generalize
genérico *adj* generic
gênero *m* gender
generosidade *f* generosity
genético *adj* genetic
gengibre *m* ginger
gengiva *f* gum
genial *adj* genial
gênio *m* genius
genocídio *m* genocide
genro *m* son-in-law
gentil *adj* kind
gentileza *f* kindness
genuíno *adj* genuine
geografia *f* geography
geologia *f* geology
geometria *f* geometry
geração *f* generation
gerador *m* generator
geral *m* general
gerar *v* generate
germe *m* germ
germinar *v* germinate

gerúndio *m* gerund
gestação *f* gestation
gestão *f* conduct
gesticular *v* gesticulate
gesto *m* gesture
gesto *f* motion
gigante *m* giant
gigantesco *adj* gigantic
ginásio *n* gymnasium
girafa *f* giraffe
girar *v* spin, rotate
girl *f* gal
giro *m* turn, twist
giz *m* chalk
giz de cera *m* crayon
gladiador *m* gladiator
glamouroso *adj* glamorous
glândula *f* gland
glicose *f* glucose
globo *m* globe
glóbulo *m* globule
glória *fm* glory
glorificar *v* glorify
glorioso *adj* glorious
glossário *m* glossary
glutão *m* glutton
gol *f* goal
gola *f* collar
goleiro *m* goalkeeper
golfinho *m* dolphin
golfo *m* gulf
golinho *m* sip

golpe *n* knock, hit, coup
golpear *v* beat, hit
gordo *adj* fat
gordura *f* fat
gorduroso *adj* fatty
gorila *m* gorilla
gostar de *v* enjoy, like
gosto *m* liking, taste, zest
gostoso *adj* tasteful, tasty
gota *f* drop, gout
gotejar *v* drip, trickle
governador *m* governor
governanta *f* housekeeper
governar *v* govern
governo *m* government
gozo *m* enjoyment
graça *f* grace
graças *f* thanks
gracioso *adj* graceful
graduação *f* graduation
gradual *adj* gradual
gráfico *m* chart
gráfico *adj* graphic
grama *m-f* gram, grass
gramática *f* grammar
grampeador *m* stapler
grampear *v* staple
grampo *m* staple
granada *f* grenade
grande *adj* big, large
grandeza *f* greatness
grandioso *adj* grand

granito *m* granite
granizo *m* hail
grânulo *m* pellet
grão *m* grain
grarduar-se *v* graduate
gratidão *f* gratitude
gratificante *adj* gratifying
gratificar *v* gratify
grato *adj* grateful
gratuidade *f* gratuity
gratuito *adj* free
gravação *m* recording
gravador *m* recorder
gravar *v* engrave, record
gravata *f* necktie
grave *adj* grave, serious
gravemente *adv* gravely
grávida *adj* pregnant
gravidade *f* gravity
gravidez *f* pregnancy
gravitar *v* gravitate
gravura *f* engraving
graxa *f* grease
graxa de sapato *f* shoe polish
Grécia *f* Greece
grego *adj* Greek
grelha *f* broiler
grelhar *v* broil, grill
greta *f* rift
greve *n* strike, walkout
grilo *m* cricket
grinalda *f* garland

G

gripe _f_ influenza
grisalho _adj_ gray
gritar _v_ shout, yell
gritaria _f_ shouting
grito _m_ shout, scream
Groenlândia _f_ Greenland
grosseiro _adj_ gross
grosso _adj_ thick
grossura _f_ thickness
grotesco _adj_ grotesque
grou _m_ crane
grunhir _v_ grumble
grupo _m_ group
grupo domiciliar _m_ household
gruta _f_ cave, grotto
guarda _m_ caretaker
guarda-chuva _f_ umbrella
guardanapo _m_ napkin
guardar _v_ keep
guarda-roupa _m_ wardrobe
guardião _m_ custodian
guarnecer _v_ garnish
guarnição _f_ garnish
guerra _f_ war
guerreiro _m_ warrior
guerrilheiro _m_ guerrilla
guia _m_ guidebook
guiar _v_ guide
guilhotina _f_ guillotine
guinchar _v_ screech
guincho _m_ tow truck
guisado _m_ stew

gula _f_ greed

habilidade _f_ ability, skill
habilidoso _adj_ skillful
habitante _m_ inhabitant
habitar _v_ inhabit
habitável _adj_ habitable
hábito _m_ habit
habitual _adj_ habitual
hálito _m_ breath
hambúrguer _f_ hamburger
harmonia _f_ harmony
harmonizar _v_ harmonize
harpa _m_ harp
helicóptero _m_ helicopter
hemisfério _m_ hemisphere
hemorragia _f_ hemorrhage
herança _f_ inheritance
herdar _v_ inherit
herdeira _f_ heiress
herdeiro _m_ heir
hereditário _adj_ hereditary
herege _adj_ heretic
heresia _f_ heresy
hermético _adj_ hermetic
hérnia _f_ hernia

herói *m* hero
heróico *adj* heroic
heroína *f* heroin
heroísmo *m* heroism
hesitação *f* hesitation
hesitante *adj* hesitant
hesitar *v* hesitate
hidráulico *adj* hydraulic
hidrogênio *m* hydrogen
hiena *f* hyena
hierarquia *f* hierarchy
hífen *m* hyphen
higiene *f* hygiene
hilariante *adj* hilarious, exhilarating
hino *f* anthem, hymn
hipnose *f* hypnosis
hipnotizar *v* hypnotize, mesmerize
hipocrisia *f* hypocrisy
hipócrita *adj* hypocrite
hipoteca *f* mortgage
hipótese *f* hypothesis
hispânico *adj* Hispanic
histeria *f* hysteria
histérico *adj* hysterical
história *f* history
historiador *m* historian
hodômetro *m* odometer
hoje *adv* today
hoje à noite *adv* tonight
Holanda *f* Holland

holandês *adj* Dutch
holocausto *m* holocaust
holofote *m* floodlight
homem *m* man
homenagem *m* homage
homens *m* men
homicídio *m* homicide
homília *f* homily
honestidade *n* honesty
honesto *adj* honest
honorários *m* fee
honra *m* honor
hora *f* hour
hora extra *adv* overtime
horario *m* schedule
horizontal *adj* horizontal
horizonte *m* horizon
hormônio *f* hormone
horrendo *adj* horrendous
horripilante *adj* terrifying
horrível *adj* horrible
horror *m* horror
horrorizar *v* horrify
horroroso *adj* hideous
horta *m* garden
hóspede *m* guest
hospital *m* hospital
hospitalidade *f* hospitality
hospitalizar *v* hospitalize
hostil *adj* hostile
hostilidade *f* hostility
hotel *m* hotel

H

humanidade *f* humankind
humanidades *f* humanities
humano *adj* human
humildade *f* humility
humilde *adj* humble
humildemente *adv* humbly
humilhante *adj* demeaning
humilhar *v* humiliate
humor *m* mood, humor
humorístico *adj* humorous

iate *m* yacht
iberal *adj* open-minded
içar *v* hoist
iceberg *m* iceberg
ícone *m* icon
idade *f* age
ideal *adj* ideal
idéia *f* idea
idêntico *adj* identical
identidade *f* identity
identificar *v* identify
ideologia *f* ideology
idiota *m* idiot, jerk
idiota *adj* idiotic
idolatria *f* idolatry

ídolo *m* idol
idoso *adj* elderly
ignorância *f* ignorance
ignorante *adj* ignorant
ignorar *v* ignore
igreja *f* church
igual *adj* equal
igualar *v* match
igualdade *f* equality
igualmente *adv* likewise
ilegal *adj* illegal
ilegítimo *adj* illegitimate
ilegível *adj* illegible
ileso *adj* unharmed
ilha *f* island, isle
ilícito *adj* illicit
ilimitado *adj* boundless
ilógico *adj* illogical
iluminação *f* lighting
iluminar *v* illuminate
ilusão *f* illusion
ilustração *f* illustration
ilustrar *v* illustrate
ilustre *adj* illustrious
ímã *m* magnet
imaculado *adj* spotless
imagem *f* image
imaginação *f* imagination
imaginar *v* imagine
imaturidade *f* immaturity
imaturo *adj* immature
imbatível *adj* unbeatable

imcompatível *adj* incompatible
imediatamente *adv* immediately
imensidade *f* immensity
imenso *adj* immense
imerecido *adj* undeserved
imergir *v* immerse
imersão *f* immersion
imigração *f* immigration
imigrante *m* immigrant
imigrar *v* immigrate
iminente *adj* imminent
imitação *f* imitation
imitar *v* imitate
imobilizar *v* immobilize
imoral *adj* immoral
imoralidade *f* immorality
imortal *adj* immortal
imortalidade *f* immortality
imóvel *adj* immobile, motionless, still
impaciência *f* impatience
impaciente *adj* impatient
impactar *v* impact
impacto *m* impact
ímpar *adj* odd
imparcial *adj* unbiased
impecável *adj* impeccable, flawless
impedimento *m* impediment
impedir *v* thwart
impendente *adj* impending
impenetrável *adj* watertight

impensável *adj* unthinkable
imperador *m* emperor
imperatriz *f* empress
imperdoável *adj* inexcusable
imperfeição *f* imperfection
imperial *adj* imperial
imperialismo *m* imperialism
império *m* empire
impertinência *f* impertinence
impertinente *adj* impertinent
impessoal *adj* impersonal
ímpeto *m* bounce
impetuoso *adj* impetuous
impiedoso *adj* heartless
implacável *adj* relentless
implantar *v* implant
implementar *v* implement
implicação *f* implication
implicar *v* implicate
implícito *adj* implicit
implorar *v* beg, implore
imponente *adj* imposing
impopolar *adj* unpopular
impor *v* impose
importação *f* importation
importância *f* importance
importante *adj* momentous
importar *v* import
importunar *v* harass, pester
imposição *ff* imposition
impossível *adj* impossible
imposto *m* tax

I

impotente *adj* powerless
impreciso *adj* imprecise
impressão *f* printing
impressionante *adj* impressive
impressionar *v* impress
impressora *f* printer
imprestável *adj* useless
imprevisível *adj* unpredictable
imprevisto *adj* unforeseen
imprimir *v* print
impróprio *adj* improper
improvável *adj* unlikely
improvisar *v* improvise
impulsivo *adj* impulsive
impulso *m* impulse
impunidade *f* impunity
impuro *adj* impure
imune *adj* immune
imunidade *f* immunity
imunizar *v* immunize
imutável *adj* immutable
in *pre* at
inabilidade *f* inability
inacessível *adj* inaccessible
inacreditável *adj* unbelievable
inadequado *adj* inadequate
inadmissível *adj* inadmissible
inadvertência *f* oversight
inalar *v* inhale
inamistoso *adj* unfriendly
inanimado *adj* lifeless
inapropriado *adj* inappropriate

inato *adj* innate
inauguração *f* inauguration
inaugurar *v* inaugurate
incalculável *adj* incalculable
incansável *adj* tireless
incapacitar *v* incapacitate
incapaz *adj* unable
incendiário *m* arsonist
incêndio *m* arson, blaze
incenso *m* incense
incentivo *m* incentive
incerto *adj* uncertain
incessante *adj* incessant
inchação *m* swelling
inchaço *m* lump
inchado *adj* swollen
inchar *v* swell, bloat
incidente *m* incident
incisão *f* incision
incitação *m* incitement
incitar *v* incite
inclinação *f* inclination
inclinado *adj* slanted
inclinar *v* incline, tilt
inclinar-se *v* lean
incluir *v* enclose, include
inclusive *adv* inclusive
incoerente *adj* incoherent
incomodar *v* bother, nag
incômodo *adj* bothersome
incompetência *f* incompetence
incompetente *adj* incompetent

incompleto *adj* incomplete
incomum *adj* unusual
inconsciente *adj* unconscious
inconsistente *adj* inconsistent
incontável *adj* countless
inconteste *adj* undisputed
incontinência *f* incontinence
inconveniente *adj* inconvenient
incorporação *f* annexation
incorporar *v* incorporate
incorrer *v* incur
incorreto *adj* inaccurate
incorrigível *adj* incorrigible
incremento *m* increment
incriminar *v* incriminate
incrível *adj* incredible
incrustado *adj* inlaid
inculto *adj* uneducated
incurável *adj* incurable
indagar *v* inquire
indecência *f* indecency
indecisão *f* indecision
indeciso *adj* indecisive
indefeso *adj* defenseless
indefinido *adj* indefinite
indelicadeza *f* discourtesy
indenização *f* indemnity
indenizar *v* indemnify
independente *adj* independent
indesejável *adj* undesirable
indevido *adj* undue
indicação *f* indication

indicar *v* indicate
índice *m* index
indiferença *f* indifference
indiferente *adj* indifferent
indigente *adj* indigent
indigestão *f* indigestion
indireta *m* innuendo
indireto *adj* indirect
indiscrição *f* indiscretion
indiscreto *adj* indiscreet
indiscutível *adj* indisputable
indispensável *adj* indispensable
indisposição *f* ailment
indisposto *adj* indisposed
indivisível *adj* indivisible
indizível *adj* unspeakable
indolor *adj* painless
indulgência *f* leniency
indulgente *adj* indulgent
indústria *f* industry
industrioso *adj* industrious
induzir *v* induce
ineficaz *adj* ineffective
ineficiente *adj* inefficient
inegável *adj* undeniable
inepto *adj* inept
inequívoco *adj* unmistakable
inesperado *adj* unexpected
inesquecível *adj* unforgettable
inestimável *adj* invaluable
inevitável *adj* inevitable
inexperiente *adj* inexperienced

inexplicável *adj* inexplicable
infalível *adj* infallible
infame *adj* infamous
infância *f* childhood
infantaria *f* infantry
infecção *f* infection
infeccionar *v* fester, infect
infeccioso *adj* infectious
infelicidade *f* unhappiness
infeliz *adj* unhappy
inferior *adj* inferior
inferir *v* infer
inferno *m* hell
infértil *adj* infertile
infestado *adj* infested
infidelidade *f* infidelity
infiltração *f* infiltration
infiltrar *v* infiltrate
infinito *adj* infinite
inflação *f* inflation
inflamação *f* inflammation
inflamar *v* ignite
inflamável *adj* flammable
inflar *v* inflate
inflexível *adj* inflexible
infligir *v* inflict
influência *f* influence
influente *adj* influential
influenza *f* flu
informação *f* information
informal *adj* casual
informalidade *f* informality

informante *m* informer
informar *v* inform, brief
infortúnio *m* misfortune
infração *f* breach
infreqüente *adj* infrequent
infundado *adj* groundless
infusão *f* infusion
ingenuidade *f* ingenuity
ingênuo *adj* naive
ingerir *v* ingest
Inglaterra *f* England
inglês *adj* English
ingratidão *f* ingratitude
ingrato *adj* ungrateful
ingrediente *m* ingredient
inibir *v* inhibit
iniciais *f* initials
inicial *adj* initial
inicialmente *adv* initially
iniciante *m* beginner
iniciar *v* begin, initiate
iniciativa *f* initiative
início *m* beginning
inimigo *m* enemy
injeção *f* injection
injetar *v* inject
injustamente *adv* unfairly
injustiça *f* injustice
injustificado *adj* unjustified
injusto *adj* unjust, unfair
inlimitado *adj* unlimited
inocência *f* innocence

inocentar *v* clear
inocente *adj* innocent
inofensivo *adj* harmless
inoportuno *adj* untimely
inovação *n* innovation
inoxidável *adj* rust-proof
inpecionar *v* inspect
input *m* input
inquérito *m* inquest
inquietação *m* unrest
inquietante *adj* worrisome
inquieto *adj* restless
inquilino *m* tenant
inquisição *f* inquisition
insaciável *adj* insatiable
insanidade *f* insanity
insano *adj* insane
insatisfação *adj* dissatisfied
insatisfeito *adj* disgruntled
insconsciente *adj* unaware
inscrever *v* enroll
inscrição *m* enrollment
insegurança *f* insecurity
inseguro *adj* unsafe
insensato *adj* mindless
insensível *adj* insensitive
inseparável *adj* inseparable
inserção *f* insertion
inserir *v* insert
inseto *m* bug, insect
insignificante *adj* insignificant
insinceridade *f* insincerity

insincero *adj* insincere
insinuação *m* hint
insinuar *v* insinuate, hint
insípido *adj* insipid
insistência *f* insistence
insistente *adj* pushy
insistir *v* insist
insolação *f* heatstroke
insolente *adj* insolent
insolúvel *adj* insoluble
insônia *f* insomnia
insosso *adj* bland
inspeção *f* inspection
inspetor *m* inspector
inspiração *f* inspiration
inspirar *v* inspire
inssurreição *f* insurrection
instabilidade *f* instability
instalação *f* installation
instalar *v* install
instalar-se *v* settle down
instantâneo *m* snapshot
instante *m* instant
instável *adj* unsteady
instigar *v* instigate
instilar *v* instill
instinto *m* instinct
instituição *n* institution
instituir *v* institute
instrução *n* coaching
instruir *f* instruct
instrutor *m* instructor

insuficiente *adj* insufficient

insultar *v* insult

insulto *m* insult

insunuação *f* insinuation

insuportável *adj* unbearable

insurgência *f* insurgency

intacto *adj* intact

integração *f* integration

integrar *v* integrate

integridade *f* integrity

inteiramente *adv* entirely

inteiro *adj* entire, whole

inteligente *adj* intelligent

intenção *f* intention

intensidade *f* intensity

intensificar *v* intensify

intensivo *adj* intensive

intenso *adj* intense

intercâmbio *m* interchange

interceder *v* intercede

interceptar *v* intercept

intercessão *f* intercession

interditar *v* ban

interessado *adj* interested

interessante *adj* interesting

interesse *m* interest

interesse próprio *m* self-interest

interferência *f* interference

interferir *v* interfere

interior *adj* interior, inner

interlúdio *m* interlude

intermediário *m* intermediary

interminável *adj* endless

internar *v* intern

interno *adv* indoor

interno *m* inmate

interno *adj* inside

interpretação *f* interpretation

interpretar *v* interpret

interpretar mal *v* misinterpret

intérpreter *m* interpreter

interrogar *v* interrogate

interrogatório *m* inquiry

interromper *v* interrupt

interrupção *f* interruption

intervalo *m* interval, gap

intervenção *f* intervention

intervir *v* intervene

intestino *m* intestine

intimação *f* subpoena

intimar *v* subpoena

intimidade *f* intimacy

intimidar *v* intimidate

íntimo *adj* close, intimate

intocável *adj* untouchable

intolerância *f* intolerance

intolerável *adj* intolerable

intoxicado *adj* intoxicated

intravenoso *adj* intravenous

intrépido *adj* intrepid

intricado *adj* intricate

intriga *f* intrigue

intrigante *adj* intriguing

intrínseco *adj* intrinsic

introdução *f* introduction
introduzir *v* introduce
intrometer *v* intrude
intrometido *adj* nosy
introvertido *adj* introvert
intrusão *f* intrusion
intruso *m* intruder
intuição *f* intuition
inumano *adj* inhuman
inumerável *adj* innumerable
inundação *f* flooding
inundado *adj* swamped
inundar *v* flood
inútil *adj* hopeless
invadir *v* invade
invalidar *v* invalidate
invalidez *f* disability
inválido *adj* disabled, void
invasão *f* invasion
invasor *m* invader
inveja *f* envy
invejar *v* envy
invejoso *adj* envious, jealous
invenção *f* invention
invencível *adj* invincible
inventar *v* invent
inventório *m* inventory
inverno *n* winter
inversamente *adv* conversely
inverter *v* turn over
inverter *m* reverse
investidor *m* investor

investigação *f* investigation
investigar *v* investigate
investimento *m* investment
investir *v* invest
invisível *adj* invisible
invocar *v* invoke
iodo *m* iodine
ir *v* go
ir embora *v* go away
ir mais devagar *v* slow down
ira *f* wrath
irado *adj* irate
Irlanda *f* Ireland
irlandês *adj* Irish
irmã *f* sister
irmandade *adj* brotherly
irmão *m* brother
ironia *f* irony
irônico *adj* ironic
irracional *adj* irrational, unreasonable
irreal *adj* unreal, unrealistic
irrefutável *adj* irrefutable
irregular *adj* irregular
irrelevante *adj* irrelevant
irreparável *adj* irreparable
irresistível *adj* irresistible
irreversível *adj* irreversible
irrevogável *adj* irrevocable
irrigação *f* irrigation
irrigar *v* irrigate
irrisório *adj* paltry

I

irritadiço *adj* edgy
irritante *adj* irritating, annoying
irritar *v* irritate, annoy
irromper *v* burst into
isca *f* bait
isenção *f* exemption
isentar *adj* exempt
islâmico *adj* Islamic
isolado *adj* secluded
isolamento *m* isolation
isolar *v* isolate
isqueiro *m* lighter
isto é *adv* namely
Itália *f* Italy
italiano *adj* Italian
itálico *adj* italics
itinerário *m* itinerary

J

já *adv* already, yet
jacaré *m* alligator
Janeiro *m* January
janela *f* window
janta *f* dinner
jantar *v* dine
Japão *m* Japan
japonês *adj* Japanese

jaqueta *f* jacket
jarda *f* yard
jardineiro *m* gardener
jasmim *m* jasmine
javali *m* boar, wild boar
jeans *m* jeans
joalheiro *m* jeweler
joalheria *f* jewelry store
joelho *f* knee
jogador *m* player
jogar *v* toss, throw, play
jogar fora *v* throw away
jogo *m* game, play
jóia *f* jewel
jornal *m* newspaper
jornalista *m* journalist
jovem *adj* young
jovem *m* youngster
jovial *adj* jolly
jubilante *adj* jubilant
judaísmo *m* Judaism
judeu *m* Jew
judeu *adj* Jewish
judicioso *adj* judicious
jugo *m* yoke
juiz *m* judge
julgamento *m* judgment
julgar mal *v* misjudge
julho *m* July
junco *m* reed
junho *m* June
junta *f* joint

I
J

juntar *v* add, adjoin
juntar-se *v* get together
junto *adv* together
juramento *m* oath
jurar *v* swear, vow
júri *m* jury
justamente *adv* justly
justiça *n* fairness
justiça *f* justice
justificar *v* justify
justo *adj* fair, just
juvenil *m* juvenile
juvenil *adj* youthful
juventude *f* youth

L

lá *adv* there
lã *f* wool
labaça *f* dock
lábio *m* lip
labirinto *m* labyrinth
laboratory *m* lab
labutar *v* toil
lacerar *v* maul
laço *m* tie
lacrimoso *adj* tearful
lado *m* side

lado a lado *adv* abreast
ladrão *m* burglar, thief
lagarta *f* caterpillar
lagartear *v* bask
lagarto *m* lizard
lago *m* lake
lagoa *f* pond
lagosta *f* lobster
lágrima *f* tear
laguna *f* lagoon
lama *f* mud
lamber *v* lick
lamentar *v* lament, regret
lamentável *adj* regrettable
lamento *m* lament, wail
lâmina *f* blade
lança *f* spear
lançamento *m* launch
lançar *v* hurl, launch
lance *m* move
lanche *m* refreshment
lancinante *adj* excruciating
lanterna *f* flashlight
lápide *f* gravestone
lápis *m* pencil
lapso *m* lapse, slip
laranja *f* orange
lareira *f* fireplace
largar *v* let go
largo *adj* broad
largura *f* breadth, width
laringe *f* larynx

J

L

lasca *f* chip
lascívia *f* lust
lascivo *adj* lewd
laser *m* laser
lata *f* can, canister
lata de lixo *f* bin
latejo *m* beat
lateral *adj* lateral
latido *m* bark
latir *v* bark
latitude *f* latitude
lavalouças *m* dishwasher
lavanderia *f* laundry
lavar *v* wash
lavar a seco *v* dry-clean
lavável *adj* washable
laxante *adj* laxative
lazer *m* leisure
leal *adj* loyal, staunch
lealdade *f* loyalty
leão *m* lion
lebre *f* hare
legado *m* legacy
legal *adj* lawful, legal
legalidade *f* legality
legalizar *v* legalize
legar *v* bequeath
legião *f* legion
legislação *f* legislation
legislador *m* lawmaker
legislar *v* legislate
legislatura *f* legislature

legítimo *adj* legitimate
legível *adj* legible
lei *f* law
leigo *m* layman
leilão *f* auction
leiloar *v* auction
leiloeiro *m* auctioneer
leite *f* milk
leito de morte *m* deathbed
leitor *m* reader
leitoso *adj* milky
leitura *f* reading
lema *m* motto
lembrança *m* remembrance
lembrar *v* remember
lembrete *m* reminder
leme *m* rudder
lenço *m* handkerchief
lençóis *f* sheets
lenda *f* legend
lenha *f* firewood
leniente *adj* lenient
lentamente *adv* slowly
lentes *n* eyeglasses
lentilha *n* lentil
lento *adj* slow
leoa *n* lioness
leopardo *n* leopard
lepra *n* leprosy
leproso *n* leper
ler *v* read
lerdo *adj* sluggish

lesão *n* injury
lesivo *adj* hurtful
Leste *n* east
letal *adj* lethal
letra *n* letter
letra de música *n* lyrics
leucemia *n* leukemia
levantar *v* pick up, lift
levantar-se *v* rise, get up
leve *adj* flimsy, light
levedura *f* yeast
liberação *f* liberation
liberar *v* liberate
liberdade *f* freedom
libertar-se *v* break free
libra *f* pound
lição *f* lesson
licença *f* license
licor *m* liqueur
líder *m* leader
liderança *f* leadership
liderar *v* spearhead
liga *f* league
ligação *f* liaison
ligamento *m* ligament
ligar *v* link
ligeiramente *adv* lightly, slightly
lima *f* file
limão *m* lemon
limar *v* file
limiar *m* threshold
limitar *v* limit

limitação *n* limitation
limite *n* limit
limítrofe *adj* borderline
limonada *f* lemonade
limpador *m* cleaner
limpar *v* clean
limpeza *f* cleanliness
limpo *adj* clean
lince *m* lynx
linchar *v* lynch
lindíssimo *adj* gorgeous
lingote *m* ingot
língua *f* tongue
linguagem *m* language
linha *f* rank
linha aérea *f* airline
linho *m* linen
liquidação *f* liquidation
liquidar *v* liquidate
liquidificador *m* blender
líquido *m* liquid
liso *adj* even
lista *f* list
listar *v* list
listra *f* stripe
listrado *adj* striped
litania *f* litany
literal *adj* literal
literalmente *adv* literally
literatura *n* literature
litigar *v* litigate
litígio *m* litigation

L

litoral *m* coastline
litro *m* liter
liturgia *f* liturgy
lívido *adj* livid
livraria *f* bookstore
livrar-se *v* free
livrar-se de *v* rid of
livre *adj* free
livreiro *m* bookseller
livrete *m* booklet
livro *m* book
livro escolar *m* textbook
livro-razão *m* ledger
lixa *f* sandpaper
lixeira *f* trash can
lixo *m* garbage, trash
lobo *m* wolf
local *adj* local
localização *f* location
localizado *adj* located
localizar *v* locate, spot
loção *f* lotion
locusta *f* locust
locutor *m* speaker
lógica *f* logic
lógico *adj* logical
logo *adv* shortly, soon
loiro *adj* blond, fair
loja *f* shop, store
loja de sapatos *f* shoe store
lombo *m* loin, sirloin
lona *f* canvas

longe *adv* far
longitude *f* longitude
longo *adj* long
longo prazo *adj* long-term
lontra *f* otter
lote *m* batch
lotear *v* allot
loteria *f* lottery
louça *f* crockery
loucamente *adv* madly
louco *adj* crazy
louco *m* madman
loucura *f* craziness
louro *m* parrot
louvável *adj* praiseworthy
lua *f* moon
lua-de-mel *f* honeymoon
lubrificação *f* lubrication
lubrificar *v* lubricate
lucha final *f* showdown
lúcido *adj* lucid
lucrar *v* profit
lucrativo *adj* profitable
lucro *m* profit
ludibriar *v* dupe
lufada *f* puff
lugar *m* place, site
lúgubre *adj* eerie
lula *f* squid
lume *m* fire
luminoso *adj* luminous
lunático *adj* lunatic

L

lustroso *adj* glossy
luta *f* fight, struggle
lutador *m* fighter
lutar *v* struggle, fight
luto *m* mourning
luva *f* glove
luxo *f* luxury
luxuoso *adj* luxurious
luz *f* light, flare
luz tênue *f* glimmer

má conduta *f* misconduct
maçã *f* apple
macacão *adv* overall
macaco *m* ape, monkey
maçaneta *f* handle
maçante *adj* boring
machadinha *f* hatchet
machado *m* ax
macho *m* male
maciço *adj* massive
maçom *m* mason
macular *v* defile
madame *f* madam
madeira *f* wood, lumber
madrasta *f* stepmother

maduro *adj* mature, ripe
mãe *f* mom, mother
mafioso *m* racketeering
mágica *f* magic
mágico *adj* magical
mágico *m* magician
magistrado *m* magistrate
magnata *m* tycoon
magnético *adj* magnetic
magnetismo *m* magnetism
magnificente *adj* magnificent
magnitude *f* magnitude
mago *m* wizard
magro *adj* thin, lean
Maio *m* May
maior *adj* utmost
maioridade *f* majority
mais *adj* more, most
mais *adv* moreover, plus
mais baixo *adj* lower
mais longe *adv* farther, further
mais tarde *adv* later
mais velho *m* elder
mais velho *adj* senior
majestade *f* majesty
majestoso *adj* majestic
mal *adv* poorly
malabarista *f* juggler
malária *f* malaria
malcriado *adj* naughty
maldade *f* wickedness
maldizer *v* curse

maldoso *adj* sly, spiteful
maleta *f* suitcase
malevolente *adj* malevolent
malha *f* mesh
malhar *v* work out
mal-humorado *adj* moody
malícia *n* malice
malignidade *f* malignancy
maligno *adj* malignant
malsucedido *adj* unsuccessful
maltrapilho *adj* shabby
maltratar *v* mistreat
maltrato *m* mistreatment
malvadeza *n* wickedness
malvado *adj* wicked
malventilado *adj* stuffy
mamífero *m* mammal
mamilo *m* nipple
mamute *m* mammoth
mancar *v* limp
mancha *f* stain, spot
manchado *adj* tainted
manchar *v* blot, stain
manco *adj* lame
manco *m* limp
mandar *v* rule
mandato *m* mandate
mandatório *adj* mandatory
mandíbula *f* jaw
maneira *f* manner
maneirismo *m* mannerism
manejar *v* wield

manga *f* sleeve
mangueira *f* hose
manhã *f* morning
maníaco *adj* maniac
manifestar *v* manifest
manipular *v* manipulate
manjedoura *f* manger
manobra *f* maneuver
mansão *f* mansion
manteiga *f* butter
manter *v* maintain
mantimentos *m* groceries
manual *m* handbook
manual *adj* manual
manufaturar *v* fabricate
manuscrito *m* manuscript
manutenção *m* maintenance
mão *f* hand
mão-de-obra *f* labor
mapa *m* chart, map
maquiagem *m* makeup
máquina *f* machine
mar *f* sea
maravilha *f* marvel, wonder
maravilhar *v* astound
maravilhoso *adj* wonderful
marca *f* brand, make, mark
marca registrada *f* trademark
marcador *m* marker
marcar *v* mark
marcar ponto *v* score
marcha *f* march

M

marchar *v* march
Março *m* March
maré *f* tide
mareado *adj* seasick
marechal *m* marshal
marfim *m* ivory
margarida *f* daisy
margem *m* margin
marginal *adj* marginal
marido *m* husband
marinar *v* marinate
marinha *f* navy
marinheiro *m* sailor
marinho *adj* marine
marisco *m* shellfish
marital *adj* marital
mármore *m* marble
maroto *m* rascal
marrom *adj* brown
Marte *m* Mars
martelo *m* hammer
mártir *m* martyr
martírio *m* martyrdom
marxista *m* Marxist
mas *c* but
masca *f* dough
mascar *v* chew
máscara *f* mask
masculino *adj* masculine
masoquismo *n* masochism
massa *f* bulk, mass
massacrar *v* slaughter

massacre *f* slaughter
massagear *v* massage
massagem *m* massage
mastigar *v* chew, munch
mastro *m* flagpole, mast
matador *m* killer
matadouro *m* shambles
matança *f* killing
matar *v* kill, slay
matemática *f* math
material *m* material
materialismo *m* materialism
maternal *adj* maternal
maternidade *f* maternity
mato *m* weed
matricular *v* matriculate
matrimônio *m* matrimony
maturidade *f* maturity
mau *adj* bad, evil
mau *adv* badly
mau *m* evil
mau estado *n* disrepair
mau uso *m* misuse
máxima *f* maxim
máximo *adj* maximum
mecânico *m* mechanic
mecanismo *m* mechanism
mecanizar *v* mechanize
medalha *f* medal
medalhão *m* medallion
média *f* average
mediador *n* mediator

M

mediar *v* mediate
medicação *f* medication
medicina *f* medicine
medicinal *adj* medicinal
médico *m* physician
medida *f* measurement
medieva *adj* medieval
médio *adj* medium
medíocre *adj* mediocre
mediocridade *f* mediocrity
medir *f* measure
meditação *f* meditation
meditar *v* meditate
medo *m* fear
medroso *adj* afraid
medula *f* marrow
meia *f* stocking
meia-calça *f* pantyhose
meia-irmã *f* stepsister
meia-noite *f* midnight
meigo *adj* mellow
meio *adj* half
meio *m* middle
meio a meio *adv* fifty-fifty
meio-dia *m* midday, noon
meio-irmão *m* stepbrother
meios *m* means
mel *f* honey
melancia *f* watermelon
melancolia *f* melancholy
melão *m* melon
melhor *adj* better

melhorar *v* improve
melhoria *f* improvement
melindroso *adj* squeamish
melodia *f* melody
melódico *adj* melodic
membrana *f* membrane
membro *m* member, limb
memorando *m* memo
memorável *adj* memorable
memória *f* memory; memorial
memorizar *v* memorize
menção *f* mention
mencionar *v* mention
mendigar *v* beg
mendigo *m* beggar
menear *v* wag, wiggle
meneiro *m* miner
meningite *f* meningitis
menino *m* boy, lad
menopausa *f* menopause
menor *adj* minor, lesser
menos *adj* fewer, less
menosprezar *v* look down
mensageiro *m* messenger
mensagem *m* message
mensal *adv* monthly
menstruação *f* menstruation
menta *f* mint
mental *adj* mental
mentalidade *f* mentality
mentalmente *adv* mentally
mente *f* mind

mentir *v* lie
mentira *f* lie
mentiroso *adj* liar
mentor *m* mastermind
menu *m* menu
meramente *adv* merely
mercado *m* market
mercadoria *f* goods
mercúrio *m* mercury
merecedor *adj* worthy
merecer *v* deserve, merit
mergulhador *m* diver
mergulhar *v* dive, plunge
mergulho *m* diving, plunge
meridional *adj* southern
mérito *m* merit
mês *m* month
mesa *m* table
mesada *f* allowance
mesmo *adj* same
mesmo que *c* even if
mesquinharia *n* pettiness
mesquinho *adj* mean, petty
mesquita *f* mosque
Messias *m* Messiah
mestria *f* mastery
meta *f* target
metade *f* half
metáfora *f* metaphor
metal *m* metal
metálico *adj* metallic
meteoro *m* meteor

meticuloso *adj* meticulous
metódico *adj* methodical
método *m* method
metralha *f* shrapnel
metralhadora *f* machine gun
métrico *adj* metric
metro *m* meter, subway
metrópole *f* metropolis
meu *pro* mine
meu *adj* my
mexer *v* budge
mexicano *adj* Mexican
mexido *adj* scrambled
micróbio *m* microbe
microfone *m* microphone
microondas *m* microwave
microscópio *m* microscope
migalha *f* crumb
migrante *m* migrant
migrar *v* migrate
mil *adj* thousand
milagre *m* miracle
milagroso *adj* miraculous
milênio *m* millennium
milha *f* mile
milhagem *m* mileage
milhão *m* million
milho *m* corn
miligramo *m* milligram
milímetro *m* millimeter
milionário *m* millionaire
militante *adj* militant

M

mimar *v* spoil, pamper
mimicar *v* mime
mina *f* mine
minar *v* undermine
mineral *m* mineral
minério *m* ore
minguar *v* dwindle
minha *pro* mine
miniatura *f* miniature
minimizar *v* minimize
mínimo *adj* least
mínimo *m* minimum
minissaia *f* miniskirt
ministério *m* ministry
ministro *m* minister
minoria *f* minority
minucioso *adj* nitpicking
minúsculo *adj* tiny
minuto *m* minute
míope *adj* shortsighted
miragem *f* mirage
miserável *adj* miserable
miséria *f* misery
misericórdia *f* mercy
misericordioso *adj* merciful
mission *f* mission
missionário *m* missionary
mistério *m* mystery
misterioso *adj* mysterious
místico *adj* mystic
mistificar *v* mystify
mistura *f* blend, mixture

misturador *m* mixer
misturar *v* blend, mix
misturar-se *v* mingle
mitigar *v* mitigate
mito *m* myth
mobilia *f* furnishings
mobiliar *v* furnish
mobilizar *v* mobilize
moça *f* girl
mochila *f* backpack
moda *f* fashion
modelar *v* emboss
modelo *m* design, model
moderação *f* moderation
moderado *adj* moderate
modernizar *v* modernize
moderno *adj* modern
modéstia *f* modesty
modesto *adj* modest
modificar *v* modify
modo *m* mode
módulo *m* module
moeda *f* coin, currency
moer *v* grind
mofado *adj* moldy
mofo *m* mildew
moinho *m* mill
moinho de vento *m* windmill
mola *f* spring
molar *m* molar tooth
moldar *v* shape, mold
moldura *f* frame

mole *adj* sloppy
molécula *f* molecule
molestar *f* molest
molhado *adj* wet
molho *m* sauce
molho de carne *m* gravy
momento *m* moment
monarca *m* monarch
monarquia *f* monarchy
monastério *m* monastery
monástico *adj* monastic
monge *m* monk
monitorar *v* monitor
monogamia *f* monogamy
monólogo *m* monologue
monopólio *m* monopoly
monopolizar *v* monopolize
monotonia *f* monotony
monótono *adj* monotonous
monstro *m* monster
monstruoso *adj* monstrous
montanha *f* mountain
montanhoso *adj* hilly
montar *v* assemble, ride
monte *m* stack, heap
monumental *adj* monumental
monumento *m* monument
moradia *f* dwelling
moral *f* moral
moralidade *f* morality
morango *f* strawberry
morar *v* dwell

morcego *m* bat
mordaça *f* gag
morder *v* bite
mordida *f* bite
mordiscar *v* nibble
mordomo *m* butler
morena *adj* brunette
morfina *f* morphine
morrer *v* die
morrer de fome *v* starve
morsa *f* walrus
mortal *adj* deadly
mortalha *f* shroud
mortalidade *f* mortality
morte *f* death
morteiro *m* mortar
mortificação *f* mortification
mortificar *v* mortify
morto *adj* dead
mosaico *m* mosaic
mosca *f* fly
mosquito *m* mosquito
mostarda *f* mustard
mosteiro *f* abbey
mostrar *v* show
motel *m* motel
motim *m* mutiny
motivar *v* motivate
motivo *m* motive
motocicleta *f* motorcycle
motor *m* engine, motor
motorista *m* driver

M

motosserra *f* chainsaw
móveis *m* furniture
móvel *adj* mobile
mover *v* move, shift
mover para trás *v* back up
movimentar *v* stir
movimento *f* motion
movimento *m* movement
muco *m* mucus
muçulmano *adj* Muslim
mudança *m* change, move
mudar *v* move, relocate
mudar-se *v* move out
mudo *adj* mute, dumb
muito *adj* very, much
muito bem *adv* fine
muitos *adj* many
mula *f* mule
muleta *f* crutch
mulher *f* woman
mulheres *f* women
multa *n* fine
multar *v* fine
multidão *f* crowd, mob
multiplicação *f* multiplication
multiplicar *v* multiply
múltiplo *adj* multiple
múmia *n* mummy
mundano *adj* worldly
mundial *adj* worldwide
mundo *m* world
munição *f* ammunition

município *m* borough
munições *f* munitions
murchar *v* wither
murmurar *v* murmur
murmúrio *m* murmur
músculo *m* muscle
museu *m* museum
musgo *m* moss
música *f* music
músico *m* musician
mutilar *v* mutilate
mutualmente *adv* mutually

N

nação *f* nation
nacional *adj* national
nacionalidade *f* nationality
nacionalizar *v* nationalize
naco *m* chunk
nada *f* nothing
nadadeira *m* fin
nadador *m* swimmer
nadar *v* swim
namorado *n* boyfriend
não *m* not
não lucrativo *adj* unprofitable
não prático *adj* impractical

não-fumante *m* nonsmoker
narcótico *m* narcotic
narina *f* nostril
nariz *f* nose
narrador *m* teller
narrar *v* narrate
nascer *v* be born
nascer do sol *m* sunrise
nascido *adj* born
nascimento *m* birth
natação *f* swimming
Natal *f* Christmas
nativo *adj* native
natural *adj* natural
naturalmente *adv* naturally
natureza *f* nature
naufrágio *m* shipwreck
náufrago *m* castaway
náusea *f* nausea
nauseante *adj* sickening
navalha *f* razor
nave *f* nave
navegação *f* navigation
navegador *m* browser
navegar *v* cruise
navio *m* ship
navio de guerra *m* warship
neblina *f* fog
nebuloso *adj* misty
necessário *adj* necessary
necessidade *f* need
necessitado *adj* needy

necessitar *v* need
necrotério *m* mortuary
negar *v* deny
negativa *f* denial
negativo *adj* negative
negligência *f* negligence
negligenciar *v* neglect
negligente *adj* negligent
negociação *f* negotiation
negociante *m* dealer
negociar *v* negotiate, trade
negócio *m* business
nem *c* nor
nenhum *pre* none
nenhum dos dois *adj* neither
nervo *m* nerve
nervoso *adj* nervous
nesse ínterim *adv* meantime
neto *m* grandchild
neurótico *adj* neurotic
neutralizar *v* neutralize
neutro *adj* neutral
nevada *f* snowfall
nevar *v* snow
neve *f* snow
neve com vento *f* blizzard
névoa *f* haze, mist
nicotina *f* nicotine
ninguém *pro* nobody
ninho *m* nest
níquel *m* nickel
nítido *adj* clear-cut

N

nitrogênio *m* nitrogen
nível *m* level
nivelar *v* level
nó *m* knot
nó corredio *m* noose
no entanto *c* however
nobre *adj* noble
nobreza *f* nobility
noção *f* notion
noite *f* evening, night
noite passada *adv* last night
noiva *f* bride
noivo *m* groom, fiancé
nojento *adj* foul
nome *m* name, noun
nomeação *f* appointment
nomear *v* nominate
nono *adj* ninth
nora *f* daughter-in-law
nordeste *m* northeast
norma *f* norm, standard
normal *adj* normal
normalizar *v* normalize
normalmente *adv* normally
norte *m* north
nortista *adj* northerner
Noruega *f* Norway
norueguês *adj* Norwegian
nós *pro* we, us
nossa *pro* ours
nosso *adj* our
nostalgia *f* nostalgia

nostálgico *adj* homesick
nota *f* bill
nota de rodapé *f* footnote
notação *f* notation
notar *v* notice
notário *m* notary
notável *adj* remarkable
noticiário *m* newscast
notícias *f* news
notificação *f* notification
notificar *v* notify
notório *adj* notorious
noturno *adj* nocturnal
novamente *adv* afresh
nove *adj* nine
novela *f* novel
Novembro *m* November
noventa *adj* ninety
noviço *m* novice
novidade *f* novelty
novo *adj* new
novo em folha *adj* brand-new
nóxio *adj* noxious
noz *f* walnut, nut
nu *adj* nude, naked
nuance *f* nuance
nublado *adj* cloudy
nuclear *adj* nuclear
núcleo *m* core
nudez *f* nudity
nudismo *m* nudism
nudista *m* nudist

nulo *adj* null
número *m* number
numeroso *adj* numerous
nunca *adv* never
nupcial *adj* bridal
nutrição *f* nutrition
nutrir *v* nourish
nutritivo *adj* nutritious
nuvem *f* cloud

oásis *m* oasis
obcecado *adj* single-minded
obedecer *v* obey
obediência *f* obedience
obediente *adj* obedient
obeso *adj* obese
objeção *f* objection
objetar *v* object
objetivo *m* goal
objeto *m* object
objeto de cristal *m* glassware
oblíquo *adj* oblique
oblívio *m* oblivion
obra-prima *f* masterpiece
obrigação *f* obligation
obrigado *adj* obliged

obrigar *v* oblige, compel
obrigatório *adj* obligatory
obscenidade *f* obscenity
obsceno *adj* obscene
obscuridade *f* obscurity
obscuro *adj* obscure
obsedar *v* obsess
observação *f* remark
observar *v* observe, remark
observatório *m* observatory
obsessão *f* obsession
obsoleto *adj* outdated
obstáculo *m* obstacle
obstinação *f* obstinacy
obstinado *adj* obstinate
obstruição *f* obstruction
obstruir *v* obstruct
obter *v* get, obtain
obturação *m* filling
obtuso *adj* dull
obviamente *adv* obviously
óbvio *adj* obvious
ocasião *f* occasion
ocaso *m* sunset
oceano *m* ocean
ocidental *adj* westerner
ocioso *adj* idle
oco *adj* hollow
ocorrência *f* occurrence
ocorrer *v* occur
óculos *m* glasses
óculos escuros *m* sunglasses

N O

oculto *adj* occult
ocupação *f* occupation
ocupado *adj* busy
ocupante *m* occupant
ocupar *v* occupy
ocupar-se *v* pursue
odiar *v* hate
ódio *m* hatred
odioso *adj* hateful
odisséia *f* odyssey
odor *m* odor
Oeste *m* west
ofegar *v* gasp
ofender *v* offend
ofensa *f* offense
ofensivo *adj* offensive
oferecer *v* offer, bid
oferenda *f* offering
oferta *f* offer
oficial *adj* official
oficiar *v* officiate
oficina *n* workshop
ofuscar *v* daze, overshadow
oitavo *adj* eighth
oitenta *adj* eighty
oito *adj* eight
olá *e* hello
óleo *m* oil
olhada *f* look
olhadela *f* glance
olhar *v* look
olhar de cima *v* overlook

olhar de relance *v* glance
olhar fixamente *v* gaze
olhar para *v* look at
olho *m* eye
Olimpíada *f* Olympics
oliva *f* olive
olmo *m* elm
ombro *m* shoulder
omelete *f* omelet
omissão *f* omission
omitir *v* leave out, omit
onça *f* ounce
onda *f* wave
onda de calor *f* heat wave
ondulação *f* ripple
ondulado *adj* wavy
ônibus *m* bus
onipotente *adj* almighty
ontem *adv* yesterday
onze *adj* eleven
opaco *adj* opaque
opção *f* choice, option
opcional *adj* optional
ópera *f* opera
operação *f* operation
operar *v* operate
opinião *f* opinion, view
ópio *m* opium
oponente *m* opponent
opor *v* oppose
oportunidade *f* opportunity
oportuno *adj* timely

oposição *f* opposition
oposto *adj* opposite
opressão *f* oppression
opressivo *adj* burdensome
oprimido *adj* downtrodden
oprimir *v* oppress
optar por *v* opt for
óptico *adj* optical
óptico *m* optician
opulência *f* opulence
opulento *adj* wealthy
oração *f* clause, prayer
oráculo *m* oracle
oralmente *adv* orally
orangutango *m* orangutan
órbita *f* orbit
orçamento *m* budget
ordem *m* order
ordem de prisão *m* warrant
ordenação *f* ordination
ordenar *v* ordain
orelha *f* ear
orfanato *m* orphanage
órfão *m* orphan
organismo *m* organism
organista *m* organist
organização *f* organization
organizar *v* organize
órgão *m* organ
orgulho *f* pride
orgulhoso *adj* proud
orientação *f* orientation

orientado *adj* oriented
oriental *adj* eastern
oriental *m* easterner
oriente *m* orient
origem *f* source, origin
original *adj* original
originalmente *adv* originally
originar *v* originate
orla *f* fringe
ornamental *adj* decorative
ornamento *m* ornament
orquestra *f* orchestra
ortografia *f* spelling
orvalho *m* dew
oscilar *v* fluctuate, waver
osso *m* bone
ostentar *v* flaunt
ostentoso *adj* ostentatious
ostra *f* oyster
otimismo *m* optimism
otimista *adj* optimistic
ótimo *adj* fine
ou *c* or
ouro *m* gold
ousadia *f* boldness
ousado *adj* bold
Outono *m* autumn, fall
outorgar *v* bestow
outro *adj* another, other
Outubro *m* October
ouvido *m* hearing
ouvinte *m* listener

ouvir *v* hear
ovação *f* ovation
oval *adj* oval
ovário *m* ovary
ovelha *f* sheep
overdose *f* overdose
ovo *m* egg
oxigênio *m* oxygen

P

pá *f* shovel, spade
paciência *f* patience
paciente *adj* patient
pacote *m* package, parcel
pacto *m* pact
padaria *f* bakery
padeiro *m* baker
padrão *m* standard, pattern, model
padrasto *m* stepfather
padre *m* father
padrinho *m* best man
padronizar *v* standardize
pagamento *m* payment
pagão *adj* pagan
pagar *v* defray, pay
pagável *adj* payable

pagem *f* page
painel *m* board
país *m* country
paisagem *m* landscape
paixão *f* passion
palácio *m* palace
paladar *f* palate
palavra *f* word
paletó *m* suit
palha *f* straw
palhaço *m* clown
palheiro *m* haystack
palidez *f* paleness
pálido *adj* pale
palito de dente *m* toothpick
palma *f* palm
palmada *f* smack
palpável *adj* palpable
pálpebra *f* eyelid
palpite *m* hunch, suggestion
pâncreas *m* pancreas
panela *f* pan
panfleto *n* pamphlet
pânico *m* panic
pano *m* cloth
panorama *f* panorama
pântano *m* swamp, bog
pantera *f* panther
pantufa *f* slipper
panturrilha *f* calf
pão *m* bread
Papa *m* Pope

papado _m_ papacy
papai _m_ dad
papel _m_ paper
papelada _f_ paperwork
papelão _m_ cardboard
papelaria _f_ stationery
papoula _f_ poppy
par _f_ couple, pair
par _adj_ even
para _pre_ for, to
para a frente _adv_ onwards
para baixo _adv_ down, downstairs
para cada _adv_ apiece
para cima _adv_ uphill, upwards
para dentro _adv_ inwards
para leste _adj_ eastbound
para leste _adv_ eastward
para o sul _adv_ southbound
para trás _adj_ backward
parábola _f_ parable
pára-brisa _f_ windshield
pára-choque _m_ bumper
parada _f_ parade, stop
paradeiro _m_ whereabouts
paradoxo _f_ paradox
parafusar _v_ screw
parafuso _m_ screw
parágrafo _m_ paragraph
paraíso _m_ paradise
paralelo _m_ parallel
paralisar _v_ paralyze
paralisia _m_ paralysis

parâmetros _m_ parameters
paranóico _adj_ paranoid
pára-quedas _m_ parachute
pára-quedista _m_ paratrooper
parar _v_ halt, stop
parasita _f_ parasite
parceiro _m_ partner
parceria _f_ partnership
parcial _m_ partial
parcialidade _f_ bias
parco _adj_ spare
pardal _m_ sparrow
parecer _v_ look, seem
parecer-se com _v_ resemble
parecido _adj_ alike
parede _f_ wall
parente _m_ relative
parentes _m_ folks
parentesco _m_ kinship
parêntese _m_ bracket
parêntesis _m_ parenthesis
paridade _m_ parity
parlamento _m_ parliament
paróquia _f_ parish
paroquial _adj_ parochial
paroquiano _m_ parishioner
parque _m_ park
parte _f_ part, share
parteira _f_ midwife
participação _f_ participation
participar _v_ participate
particípio _m_ participle

P

partícula *f* particle
particular *adj* particular
partida *f* departure, match
partidário *n* supporter
partidário *m* partisan
partido *m* party
partilhar *v* share
partir *v* depart, leave
Páscoa *f* Easter
pasmar *v* amaze
pasmo *adj* dazed
passado *adj* former, past
passageiro *m* passenger
passagem *m* fare
passante *m* passer-by
passaporte *m* passport
passar *v* pass
passar a ferro *v* iron
passar os olhos *v* look through
passar por *v* go through
pássaro *m* bird
passatempo *m* hobby
passe *m* pass
passear *v* stroll
passeio *m* outing
passeio de carro *m* drive
passivo *adj* passive
passo *m* step
passo a passo *adv* step-by-step
pasta *f* paste
pastar *v* graze
pasteurizar *v* pasteurize

pastinaca *f* parsnip
pasto *m* graze, pasture
pastor *m* pastor, shepherd
pastoral *adj* pastoral
pata *f* paw
patente *f* patent
patente *adj* patent
paternalmente *adj* fatherly
paternidade *f* paternity
patético *adj* pathetic
patim *m* skate
patinar *v* skate
patinar no gelo *v* ice skate
patinete *m* scooter
pátio *m* patio
pato *m* duck
patrão *m* master
patriarca *m* patriarch
patrimônio *m* patrimony
patriota *m* patriot
patriótico *adj* patriotic
patrocinador *m* sponsor
patrocinar *v* patronize
patrocínio *m* patronage
patrono *m* patron
patrulha *f* patrol
pausa *f* break
pavão *m* peacock
pavilhão *m* pavilion
pavimento *m* pavement
pavio *m* string
pavor *f* fright

pavoroso *adj* dreadful

paz *f* peace

pé *m* foot, feet

peça *f* piece, play

pecado *m* sin

pecador *adj* sinful

pecador *m* sinner

pecar *v* sin

pedaço *m* bit, chunk

pedágio *m* toll

pedagogia *f* pedagogy

pedal *m* pedal

pedante *adj* pedantic

pé-de-cabra *m* crowbar

pedestre *m* pedestrian

pedir *v* ask

pedir carona *m* hitchhike

pedir desculpa *v* apologize

pedra *f* stone, rock

pedra angular *f* cornerstone

pedregulho *m* gravel, pebble

pedreira *f* quarry

pedreiro *m* bricklayer

pegada *f* footprint

pegajoso *adj* sticky

peito *m* chest, breast

peixe *m* fish

peixe-espada *m* swordfish

pela presente *adv* hereby

pele *m* skin

pelicano *m* pelican

pelo *m* fur

pelotão *m* platoon

peludo *adj* hairy, furry

pena *f* feather, pity

penalidade *f* penalty

penalizar *v* penalize

penalty *m* penalty

pendente *adj* pending

pêndulo *m* pendulum

pendurar *v* hang

penedo *m* boulder

peneirar *v* sift

penetrar *v* penetrate

penhasco *m* cliff

penhor *m* pledge

penhorar *v* gage, pawn

penhorista *f* pawnbroker

penicilina *f* penicillin

península *f* peninsula

penitência *f* penance

penitente *m* penitent

pensão *f* pension

pensar *v* think

pentágono *m* pentagon

pente *m* comb

penteado *m* hairdo

pentear *v* comb

penumbra *f* dusk

pepino *m* cucumber

pequeno *adj* little, small

pêra *f* pear

perceber *v* perceive

percentagem *m* percentage

P

percepção *f* perception
percoço *m* neck
perda *f* loss
perdão *m* pardon
perdedor *m* loser
perder *v* lose, miss
perdido *adj* stray
perdiz *f* partridge
perdoar *v* forgive, pardon
perdoável *adj* forgivable
perecer *v* perish
perecível *adj* perishable
peregrinação *f* pilgrimage
peregrino *m* pilgrim
perene *adj* perennial
perfeição *f* perfection
perfeito *adj* perfect
perfil *m* profile
perfumado *adj* fragrant
perfume *m* perfume
perfuração *f* perforation
perfurar *v* perforate, pierce
pergaminho *m* parchment
pergunta *f* question
perguntar *v* ask, question
perguntar-se *v* wonder
perigo *m* danger, peril
perigoso *adj* dangerous
perímetro *m* perimeter
período *m* period, term
periquito *m* parakeet
perjúrio *m* perjury

permanecer *v* remain
permanente *adj* permanent
permear *v* permeate
permissão *m* permission
permitir *v* allow, permit
permutar *v* barter, swap
perna *f* leg
pernicioso *adj* pernicious
pérola *f* pearl
perpetrar *v* perpetrate
perpétuo *adj* everlasting
perseguição *f* chase
perseguir *v* chase, haunt
perseverar *v* persevere
persistência *f* persistence
persistente *adj* persistent
persistir *v* persist
personalidade *f* personality
personificar *v* personify
perspectiva *f* perspective
perspicaz *adj* shrewd
perspiração *f* perspiration
perspirar *v* perspire
persuadir *v* persuade
persuasão *f* persuasion
persuasivo *adj* persuasive
pertencer *v* belong, pertain
pertences *f* belongings
pertinente *adj* pertinent
perto de *pre* near, close to
perturbação *f* disruption
perturbador *adj* disturbing

perturbar *v* perturb, disturb
peruca *f* wig
perverso *adj* perverse
perverter *v* pervert
pervertido *adj* pervert
pesadelo *m* nightmare
pesado *adj* heavy
pesar *m* weigh, regret
pesar mais *v* outweigh
pescador *m* fisherman
peso *m* weight
pesquisa *f* research
pesquisar *v* research
pêssego *m* peach
pessimismo *m* pessimism
pessimista *adj* gloomy
pessoa *f* person
pessoal *m* personnel
pessoas *f* people
pestanejo *m* wink
peste *f* pest
pesticida *m* pesticide
pétala *m* petal
petição *f* request, petition
petrificado *adj* petrified
petróleo *m* petroleum
piada *f* joke
pianista *m* pianist
piano *m* piano
picada *f* sting
picadinho *m* mincemeat
picante *adj* spicy

picar *v* sting, prick, chop
picar fininho *v* mince
pico *m* peak, summit
piedade *f* piety
piedoso *adj* pious
pijama *f* pajamas
pilar *f* pillar
pilha *f* battery
pilhar *v* pillage, sack
piloto *m* pilot
pílula *f* pill
pimenta *f* pepper
pimentão *m* bell pepper
pinça *f* tweezers
pinçada *f* nip
pinçar *v* nip
pincel *m* paintbrush
pingar *v* drip
pingente *m* pendant
pingüim *m* penguin
pinheiro *m* pine
pintar *v* paint
pintor *m* painter
pintura *f* painting
piolhento *adj* lousy
piolho *m* lice, louse
pioneiro *m* pioneer
pior *adj* worse
piorar *v* worsen
pipa *f* kite
pirado *adj* nutty
pirâmide *f* pyramid

P

pirata *m* pirate
pirataria *f* piracy
pires *m* saucer
pirralho *adj* brat
pisar *v* tread
piscar *v* blink, wink
piscina *f* pool
pisotear *v* trample
pista *f* clue, tip
pistola *f* pistol
pistoleiro *m* gunman
pitoresco *adj* picturesque
placa *f* plate
plácido *adj* placid
planalto *m* plateau
planar *v* glide
planejar *v* devise, plan
planeta *m* planet
planície *f* plain
plano *adj* flat
plano *m* plan
planta *f* plant
plantar *v* plant
plástico *m* plastic
plataforma *f* platform
platina *f* platinum
plausível *adj* plausible
playground *m* playground
plenamente *adv* fully
pleno verão *m* midsummer
plural *m* plural
plutônio *m* plutonium

pneu furado *m* blowout
pneumonia *f* pneumonia
pó *m* powder
pobre *m* poor
pobreza *f* poverty
poço *m* well
podar *v* prune
poder *v* can
poder *m* power
poderoso *adj* mighty, powerful
podre *adj* rotten
podridão *f* rot
poeira *m* dust
poema *m* poem
poesia *f* poetry
poeta *m* poet
polar *adj* polar
polegada *f* inch
polegar *m* thumb
pólen *m* pollen
polícia *f* cop, police
policial *m* policeman
polidez *f* politeness
poligamia *f* polygamy
polígamo *adj* polygamist
polimento *m* polish
polir *v* polish
política *f* policy
político *m* politician
pólo *m* pole
polonês *adj* Polish
Polônia *f* Poland

polpa *f* pulp
poltrona *f* armchair
poluição *f* pollution
poluir *v* pollute
polvo *m* octopus
pólvora *f* gunpowder
pomar *f* orchard
pomba *f* dove
pombo *m* pigeon
pomposidade *f* pomposity
ponderar *v* ponder
ponta *f* tip
ponta do dedo *f* fingertip
ponta do pé *f* tiptoe
pontada *f* pang
ponte *m* bridge
pontífice *m* pontiff
ponto *m* dot, point, stitch
ponto culminante *m* highlight
ponto de vista *m* viewpoint
pontual *adj* punctual
pontudo *adj* pointed
popa *f* stern
população *f* population
popular *adj* popular
popularizar *v* popularize
por *pre* through, per
pôr *v* set, put
por baixo *pre* underneath
por causa de *pre* because of
por cento *adv* percent
por de lado *v* put aside

pôr de pé *v* stand
pôr em perigo *v* endanger
pôr focinheira *v* muzzle
por quê *adv* why
por um triz *adv* narrowly
porão *m* basement
porção *f* portion
porcelana *f* porcelain
porco *m* pig, hog
porco-espinho *m* porcupine
pôr-do-sol *m* sundown
poro *m* pore
poroso *adj* porous
porque *c* because
porta *f* door
portador *m* bearer
portanto *adv* therefore
portão *m* gate
portátil *adj* portable
pórtico *m* porch
porto *m* harbor, port
Portugal *f* Portugal
português *adj* Portuguese
posar *v* pose
pose *m* pose
posição *f* position
posicionar *v* deploy
positivo *adj* positive
posse *m* asset
posses *m* assets
possessão *f* possession
possibilidade *f* possibility

P

possibilitar *v* enable
possível *adj* possible
possuir *v* possess, own
postagem *m* postage
poste *m* post
poste de luz *m* streetlight
postergar *v* postpone
posteridade *f* posterity
posterior *adj* later
posto *m* rank, post
potável *adj* drinkable
pote *m* jar, pot
potencial *adj* potential
potente *adj* potent
potro *m* colt
pouco *adv* little
pouco a pouco *adv* little by little
poucos *adj* few
pouquinho *m* little bit
povoar *f* populate
praça *f* square
prado *m* meadow
praga *f* plague
pragmatista *adj* pragmatist
praia *f* shore, beach
prancha *m* board
pranto *m* crying
prata *f* silver
prataria *f* silverware
prateiro *m* silversmith
prática *f* practice
praticar *v* practice

prático *adj* practical
prato *m* plate, dish
prazer *m* pleasure
prazo final *m* deadline
precário *adj* precarious
precaução *f* precaution
precedente *m* precedent
precedente *adj* preceding
preceder *v* precede
preceito *m* precept
precioso *adj* precious
precipício *m* precipice
precipitação *f* rainfall
precipitar *v* precipitate
precipitar-se *v* scramble
precisão *f* precision
preciso *adj* accurate
preço *m* cost, price
precoce *adj* precocious
preconceito *m* prejudice
precussor *m* precursor
predecessor *m* predecessor
predicamento *m* predicament
predição *f* prediction
predileção *f* predilection
prédio *f* building
predisposto *adj* predisposed
predizer *v* predict
predominar *v* predominate
preencher *v* fill
pré-estréia *m* preview
prefabricar *v* prefabricate

P

prefácio _m_ preface
prefeito _m_ mayor
prefeitura _f_ city hall
preferência _f_ preference
preferir _v_ prefer
prefixo _m_ prefix
prega _f_ pleat
pregador _m_ preacher
pregar _v_ preach
pregueado _adj_ pleated
preguiça _f_ laziness
preguiçoso _adj_ lazy, slob
pre-histórico _adj_ prehistoric
prejudicar _v_ harm, hurt
prejudicial _adj_ harmful, injurious
preliminar _adj_ preliminary
prelúdio _m_ prelude
prematuro _adj_ premature
premeditação _f_ premeditation
premeditar _v_ premeditate
premer _v_ press
premiar _v_ award
prêmio _m_ award, prize
premissa _f_ premise
premonição _f_ premonition
prender _v_ arrest
prenúncio _m_ foretaste
preocupação _f_ worry
preocupante _adj_ troublesome
preocupar _v_ preoccupy
preocupar-se _v_ worry
preparação _f_ preparation

preparado _m_ concoction
preparar _v_ prepare
preparar-se para _v_ brace for
preposição _f_ preposition
pre-requisito _m_ prerequisite
prerogativa _f_ prerogative
presa _f_ prey
prescrever _v_ prescribe
prescrição _f_ prescription
presença _f_ presence
presente _m_ treat, gift
preservar _v_ preserve
presidência _f_ presidency
presidente _m_ president
presidir _v_ preside
preso _adj_ attached
pressa _f_ haste
pressagiar _v_ foreshadow
presságio _m_ omen
pressão _f_ pressure
pressionar _v_ pressure
pressupor _v_ presuppose
pressuposição _f_ presupposition
prestação _f_ installment
prestar atenção _v_ heed
prestar contas _v_ account for
prestar serviço _v_ service
prestígio _m_ prestige
presumir _v_ presume
presunção _f_ presumption
presunçoso _adj_ conceited
presunto _m_ ham

pretender dizer *v* drive at
pretensão *f* pretension
pretenso *adj* would-be
pretexto *m* pretense
preto *adj* black
prevalecente *adj* prevalent
prevalecer *v* prevail
prevenção *f* prevention
prevenir *v* prevent
preventivo *adj* preventive
prever *v* foresee
previdência *f* foresight
primacia *f* primacy
primavera *f* spring
primeiro *adj* first, prime
primeiro plano *m* foreground
primitivo *adj* primitive
primo *m* cousin
primoroso *adj* exquisite
princesa *f* princess
principal *adj* leading, main
principalmente *adv* mainly
príncipe *m* prince
princípio *m* principle
prioridade *f* priority
prioritário *adj* prior
prisão *f* prison
prisioneiro *m* prisoner
prisma *m* prism
privação *f* deprivation
privacidade *f* privacy
privado *adj* private

privar *v* deprive
privilégio *m* privilege
proa *f* prow
probabilidade *f* likelihood
problema *m* problem
problemático *adj* problematic
procastinar *v* procrastinate
procedimento *m* procedure
processar *v* sue, process
processo *m* lawsuit, proceedings
procissão *f* procession
proclamação *f* proclamation
proclamar *v* proclaim
procriar *v* procreate
procuração *m* proxy
procurar *v* look for
prodência *n* prudence
prodígio *m* prodigy
prodigioso *adj* prodigious
pródigo *adj* lavish
produção *f* production
produtivo *adj* productive
produto *m* product
produzir *v* produce
proeminente *adj* prominent
proeza *f* feat
profanar *v* desecrate
profano *adj* profane
profecia *f* prophecy
professar *v* profess
professor *m* professor
profeta *m* prophet

proficiência *f* proficiency
proficiente *adj* proficient
profissão *m* profession
profissional *adj* professional
profundidade *f* depth
profundo *adj* profound
programa *m* program
programador *m* programmer
programar *v* schedule
progredir *v* progress
progressivo *adj* progressive
progresso *m* progress
proibição *f* prohibition
proibido *adj* unlawful
proibir *v* forbid
projetar *m* project
projétil *m* projectile
projeto *m* project, design
prólogo *m* prologue
prolongado *adj* protracted
prolongar *v* prolong
promessa *f* promise
prometer *v* pledge, vow
promíscuo *adj* promiscuous
promoção *f* clearance
promover *v* promote
pronome *m* pronoun
prontidão *f* readiness
pronto *adj* prompt, ready
pronunciar *v* pronounce
propaganda *f* advertising
propagar *v* propagate

propelir *v* propel
propensão *f* penchant
propenso *adj* prone
propor *v* propose
proporção *f* proportion
propósito *m* purpose
proposta *f* proposal, proposition
propriedade *f* property
próprio *adj* own
prosa *f* prose
proscrito *adj* outcast
prosperar *v* thrive
prosperidade *f* prosperity
próspero *adj* prosperous
prosseguir *v* proceed
próstata *f* prostate
prostrado *adj* prostrate
proteção *n* protection
protegir *v* protect
proteína *f* protein
protestar *v* protest
protesto *f* protest
protetor solar *f* sun block
protocolo *m* protocol
protótipo *m* prototype
protuberância *n* bulge
prova *f* proof
provação *f* ordeal
provado *adj* proven
provar *v* prove, taste
provável *adv* likely
provável *adj* probable

P

prover *v* provide
provérbio *m* proverb
providência *f* providence
província *f* province
provisório *adj* provisional
provocação *f* provocation
provocar *v* provoke
proximidade *f* proximity
próximo *adj* next
prudente *adj* prudent
pruriente *adj* prurient
pseudônimo *m* pseudonym
psicologia *f* psychology
psicopata *m* psychopath
psiquiatra *m* psychiatrist
psiquiatria *f* psychiatry
psíquico *adj* psychic
puberdade *f* puberty
publicação *n* publication
publicador *m* publisher
publicamente *adv* publicly
publicar *v* publish
publicidade *n* publicity
público *adj* public
pudim *m* pudding
pueril *adj* childish
pulga *f* flea
pulmão *m* lung
pulo *m* skip, leap
púlpito *m* pulpit
pulsação *f* throb
pulsar *v* pulsate, throb

pulso *m* pulse
pulverizar *v* pulverize
pungente *adj* poignant
punhado *m* handful
punhal *m* dagger
punho *m* cuff, fist, hilt
punição *m* punishment
punir *v* punish
punível *adj* punishable
pupila *f* pupil
purê *n* puree
pureza *f* purity
purgatório *m* purgatory
purificação *f* purification
purificar *v* cleanse, purify
puro *adj* pure
pus *f* pus
pútrido *adj* putrid
puxar *v* pull

quadrado *adj* square
quadril *f* hip
quadro-negro *f* blackboard
qual *adj* which
qualidade *f* quality
qualificado *adj* eligible

P
Q

qualificar *v* qualify
qualquer *adj* any
qualquer coisa *pro* anything
qualquer lugar *c* wherever
qualquer pessoa *pro* anybody
qualquer um *pro* anyone
qualquer um *adj* whatever
quando *adv* when
quantia *f* amount
quantia total *f* lump sum
quantidade *f* quantity
quarenta *adj* forty
Quaresma *f* Lent
Quarta-feira *m* Wednesday
quartel *m* barracks, quarters
quartel-general *m* headquarters
quartilho *m* pint
quarto *adj* fourth
quarto *m* room, quarter
quase *adv* almost, nearly
quatro *adj* four
que *adj* what
que vicia *adj* addictive
quebra-cabeças *m* puzzle
quebradiço *adj* brittle
quebrado *adj* broken
quebrar *v* break, shatter
quebrável *adj* breakable
queda *f* drop, fall
queijo *m* cheese
queimadura *f* burn
queimar *v* burn

queixa *n* complaint, gripe
queixo *m* chin
quem *pro* who
quente *adj* hot
querelar *v* quarrel
querer *v* want
querido *adj* darling
querido *m* sweetheart
questionário *m* questionnaire
quieto *adj* quiet
quietude *f* quietness
quilate *m* carat
quilograma *m* kilogram
quilômetro *m* kilometer
quilowatt *m* kilowatt
química *f* chemistry
químico *adj* chemical
químico *m* chemist
Quinta-feira *m* Thursday
quinto *adj* fifth
quinze *adj* fifteen
quiosque *m* kiosk
quociente *m* quotient

Q

R

rã _f_ frog
rabanete _m_ radish
rabino _m_ rabbi
rabiscar _v_ scribble
rabo _m_ tail
rabugento _adj_ grouchy
raça _f_ race, breed
ração _f_ ration
rachadura _f_ crack
rachar _v_ slit, crack
raciocinar _v_ reason
raciocínio _m_ reasoning
racional _adj_ rational
racionalizar _v_ rationalize
racionar _v_ ration
racismo _m_ racism
racista _adj_ racist
radar _m_ radar
radiação _f_ radiation
radiador _m_ radiator
radical _adj_ radical
rádio _f_ radio
rainha _f_ queen
raio _m_ beam, ray, radius
raiva _f_ anger, rabies
raiz _f_ root, stem
rajada _f_ gust, blast
ramificação _f_ ramification
ramificar _v_ branch out

ramo _m_ bough, limb
rampa _f_ ramp
rancho _m_ ranch
rancor _m_ grudge, rancor
rangido _m_ creak
ranhura _f_ groove
rapidamente _adv_ quickly
rápido _adj_ fast, quick
raposa _f_ fox
raptar _v_ abduct
rapto _f_ abduction
raquete _n_ racket
raramente _adv_ rarely, seldom
raro _adj_ scarce, rare
rascunhar _v_ draft
rascunho _m_ draft
rasgar _v_ rip, tear
raso _adj_ shallow
raspar _v_ scrape
rastejar _v_ trail, creep
rastelo _m_ rake
rasto _m_ track
rastrear _v_ trace, track
rastro _m_ trail
ratificação _f_ ratification
ratificar _v_ ratify
rato _m_ rat, mouse
ratos _m_ mice
ravina _f_ ravine
razão _f_ reason
razoável _adj_ reasonable
reabastecer _v_ replenish**

reação *f* reaction
reagir *v* react
real *adj* actual, royal
realçar *v* enhance
realeza *f* royalty
realidade *f* reality
realismo *m* realism
realização *f* attainment
realizar *v* achieve
realmente *adv* really
reaparecer *v* reappear
rebaixar *v* demean
rebanho *m* flock
rebelar-se *v* rebel
rebelde *m* rebel
rebelião *f* rebellion
rebentar *v* burst
rebitagem *adj* riveting
rebitar *v* rivet
rebocar *v* tow
reboque *m* trailer
rebotalho *m* junk
recado *m* errand
recaída *f* relapse
recapitular *v* recap
recapturar *v* recapture
recarregar *v* recharge
recebedor *m* payee
receber *v* receive
receita *f* recipe
recém-casado *adj* newlywed
recém-chegado *m* newcomer

recém-nascido *m* newborn
recente *adj* recent
recentemente *adv* newly
recepção *f* reception
recepcionista *f* receptionist
receptivo *adj* receptive
recessão *f* recession
recesso *m* recess
rechear *v* pad
rechecar *v* double-check
recheio *m* filling
rechinante *adj* squeaky
rechonchudo *adj* chubby
recibo *m* receipt
reciclar *v* recycle
recife *m* reef
recinto *m* compound
recipiente *m* container
recíproco *adj* reciprocal
recital *m* recital
recitar *v* recite
reclamação *f* claim
reclamar *v* claim, complain
recluso *m* recluse
recobrar *v* regain, recoup
recolher *v* gather
recomendar *v* recommend
recompensa *f* reward
recompensar *v* reward
reconciliar *v* reconcile
reconhecer *v* recognize
reconsiderar *v* reconsider

R

reconstruir v rebuild
recordação m memento
recordar v recollect
recorrência f recurrence
recorrer v resort
recortar v cut out
recorte de jornal m clipping
recostar v recline
recreação f recreation
recriar v recreate
recruta m recruit
recrutamento m recruitment
recrutar v recruit
recuar v fall back
recuperação m recovery
recuperar v recover
recuperar-se v get over
recurso m recourse
recusa f refusal
recusar v refuse
redação f wording
rede f net, network
rédea f bridle, rein
redecorar v refurbish
redemoinho n whirlpool
redenção f redemption
redimir v redeem
redobrar v redouble
redondo adj round
redundante adj redundant
reduzir v reduce
reeleger v reelect

reembolsar v reimburse
reembolso m refund
reentrada f reentry
refazer v redo, remake
refeição f meal
refém m hostage
referência f reference
referendar v countersign
referir-se a v refer to
refinado adj ladylike
refinanciar v refinance
refinar v refine
refinaria f refinery
refletir v reflect
refletor m spotlight
reflexão f reflection
reflexivo adj reflexive
reflexo m reflection
refluir v ebb
reforçar v reinforce
reforço n reinforcements
reforma f reform
reformar v reform
refrear v restrain
refrescante adj refreshing
refrescar v refresh
refrigerar v refrigerate
refugiado m refugee
refúgio m refuge
refugo m refuse
refutar v refute, rebut
regar v water

R

regatear *v* haggle
regateio *m* bargaining
regeneração *f* regeneration
regente *m* regent
região *f* region
regime *m* regime
regimento *m* regiment
régio *adj* regal
regional *adj* regional
registrar *v* register
regozijar *v* rejoice
regra *f* rule
regressar *v* move back
régua *m* ruler
regulação *f* regulation
regulamento *m* rule
regular *v* regulate
regularidade *f* regularity
rehabilitar *v* rehabilitate
rei *m* king
reide *m* raid
reimpressão *f* reprint
reimprimir *v* reprint
reinar *v* reign
reino *m* kingdom, realm
reiterar *v* reiterate
rejeição *f* denial
rejeição *m* rejection
rejeitar *v* reject
rejuvenecer *v* rejuvenate
relacionamento *f* relationship
relacionar-se *v* get along

relatar *f* recount
relatar *v* report
relativo *adj* relative
relatório *m* report
relaxamento *f* relaxation
relaxante *adj* relaxing
relaxar *v* relax
relegar *v* relegate
relevante *adj* relevant
relgularmente *adv* regularly
relicário *m* shrine
religião *f* religion
religioso *adj* religious
relíquia *f* relic
relocação *f* relocation
relógio *m* watch, clock
relojoeiro *m* watchmaker
relutante *adj* reluctant
reluzir *v* gleam
remanescente *m* remnant
remar *v* row, paddle
remediar *v* remedy
remédio *m* remedy
remendar *v* darn, mend
remendo *m* patch
remessa *f* consignment
remetência *f* remittance
remetente *m* sender
remeter *v* remit
remissão *f* remission
remo *m* oar
remoção *f* removal

R

remodelar *v* remodel
remorso *m* remorse
remoto *adj* remote
removedor *m* cleanser
remover *v* remove
remuneração *f* pay
remunerar *v* remunerate
rena *f* reindeer
renascimento *m* rebirth
render *v* surrender
render-se *v* give in
rendimento *m* income
renegar *v* disclaim, disown
renovação *f* renovation
renovar *v* renew
renunciar *v* renounce
renunciar a *v* relinquish
reorganizar *v* reorganize
reparação *f* reparation
reparar *v* repair
repartir *v* give away
repatriar *v* repatriate
repelir *v* rebuff, repel
repentino *adj* sudden
repetição *f* repetition
repetir *v* repeat, recur
repleto *adj* replete
réplica *f* replica
replicar *v* replicate
repolho *m* cabbage
repórter *m* reporter
repousado *adj* restful

repousar *v* repose
repouso *m* repose
repreender *v* chide, rebuke
repreensão *f* scolding
represa *f* reservoir, dam
represália *f* reprisal
representar *v* represent
repressão *f* repression
reprimir *v* repress, stifle
reprodução *f* reproduction
reproduzir *v* reproduce
reprovação *m* reproach
reprovar *v* reproach
réptil *m* reptile
república *f* republic
repudiar *v* repudiate
repugnante *adj* repugnant
repulsa *f* rebuff
repulsa *n* repulse
repulsivo *adj* repulsive
reputação *f* reputation
requerer *v* require
requerimento *m* requirement
rerrôneo *adj* erroneous
reserva *f* reservation
reservado *adj* low-key
reservar *v* reserve
resfolegar *v* wheeze
resgatar *v* ransom, rescue
resgate *m* rescue
residência *f* residence
residir *v* reside

resíduo *m* residue
resignação *f* resignation
resignar *v* resign
resiliente *adj* resilient
resinoso *adj* balmy
resistência *f* resistance
resistente *adj* hardy, sturdy
resistir *v* resist, hold out
resmungar *v* grouch
resolução *f* resolution
resoluto *adj* resolute
resolver *v* resolve
respectivo *adj* respective
respeitar *v* respect
respeito *n* respect, awe
respeito próprio *m* self-respect
respeitoso *adj* respectful
respiração *f* breathing
respirar *v* breathe
responder *v* answer, reply
responsável *adj* responsible
responsivo *adj* responsive
resposta *f* answer, reply
ressaltar *v* stick out
ressecar *v* parch
ressentimento *m* resentment
ressentir *v* resent
ressonante *adj* resounding
ressunção *f* resumption
ressurgir *v* resurface
ressurreição *f* resurrection
ressuscitar *v* resuscitate

restante *adj* remaining
restauração *f* restoration
restaurante *m* restaurant
restaurar *v* restore
restituição *f* restitution
resto *m* remainder
restos *n* remains
restringir *v* restrict, curb
resultado *m* result
resumir *v* resume, abridge
resumo *m* outline
retaguarda *f* rear
retalhar *v* whittle
retaliação *f* retaliation
retaliar *v* retaliate
retangular *adj* rectangular
retângulo *m* rectangle
retardado *adj* retarded
retenção *f* retention
reter *v* withhold, retain
retido *adj* pent-up
retificar *v* rectify
retirada *f* withdrawal
retirar-se *v* retreat, retire
retiro *m* retirement
reto *m* rectum
reto *adj* straight
retocar *v* touch up
retornar *v* return
retorno *m* return, retrieval
retraído *adj* withdrawn
retrair *v* withdraw

R

retratar *v* recant, portray

retrato *m* portrait, picture

retroativo *adj* retroactive

retroceder *v* recede

réu *m* defendant

reumatismo *m* rheumatism

reunião *f* reunion, meeting

reunir *v* rejoin

revelação *f* revelation

revelador *adj* revealing

revelar *v* disclose, reveal

rever *v* review

reverência *f* reverence

reversível *adj* reversible

reverso *m* reverse

reverter *v* revert

revés *m* setback

revidar *v* hit back

revisão *f* review, revision

revisar *v* revise

revista *f* magazine

reviver *v* revive

revogação *f* repeal

revogar *v* repeal

revoltante *adj* revolting

revoltar *v* revolt

revolver *v* revolve

revólver *v* revolver

revulsão *f* revulsion

rezar *v* pray

riacho *m* creek

ribombar *v* rumble

rico *adj* rich

ricochetear *v* rebound

ridicularizar *v* ridicule

ridículo *adj* ridiculous

rifa *f* raffle

rifle *m* rifle

rígido *adj* rigid, stiff

rigor *m* rigor

rigoroso *adj* stringent

rim *m* kidney

rima *f* rhyme

ringue *m* ring

rinoceronte *m* rhinoceros

rio *m* river

riqueza *f* wealth

rir *v* laugh

risada *f* laugh, laughter

riscar *v* scratch

risco *m* hazard, risk

risível *adj* laughable

ritmo *m* pace, rhythm

rito *m* rite

rival *m* rival

rivalidade *f* rivalry

rixa *f* feud

robusto *adj* burly, robust

roçar *v* graze

rochoso *adj* rocky

roda *f* wheel

rodar *v* swivel

rodear *v* encircle

rodovia *f* highway

roedor *m* rodent
roer *v* gnaw
rojão *m* firecracker
rolar *v* roll
roldana *f* pulley
rolha *f* cork
rolo *m* scroll
romã *f* pomegranate
romance *m* romance, affair
romancista *m* novelist
romper *v* sever, rupture
rompimento *m* severance
roncar *v* snore
ronco *m* snore
rondar *v* prowl
rosa *f* rose
rosado *adj* rosy, pink
rosário *m* rosary
rosca *f* thread
roscar *v* thread
rosnar *v* growl
rosto *m* face
rota *f* route
rotação *f* rotation
rotina *f* routine
rótula *f* kneecap
rótulo *m* label
roubar *v* steal, rob
roubo *m* burglary, theft
rouco *adj* hoarse, husky
roupa de baixo *f* lingerie
roupa de cama *f* bedding

roupa interior *f* underwear
roupas *f* clothes, clothing
rouxinol *m* nightingale
rua *f* street, lane
rubi *m* ruby
ruborizar *v* blush
rude *adj* rude, impolite
rudeza *f* rudeness
rudimentar *adj* rudimentary
ruga *ff* crease, wrinkle
rugido *m* roar
rugir *v* roar
ruído *m* noise, uproar
ruido sudo *m* rumble
ruidosamente *adv* loudly
ruidoso *adj* noisy
ruína *f* downfall, ruin
ruir *v* collapse, topple
rum *m* rum
rumar para *v* stand for
rumo a *pre* towards
rumo oeste *adv* westbound
rumor *m* rumor
ruptura *f* rupture, break
rural *adj* rural
Rússia *f* Russia
russo *adj* Russian
rústico *adj* rustic

R

S

sábado *m* Saturday
sabedoria *f* wisdom
saber *v* know
sabio *m* scholar
sábio *adj* wise
sabor *m* flavor
saborear *v* relish, savor
sabotagem *m* sabotage
sabotar *v* sabotage
sacerdócio *m* priesthood
sacerdote *m* priest
sacerdotisa *f* priestess
saciar *v* quench
saco *m* bag, sack
sacolejar *v* jolt
sacramento *m* sacrament
sacrifício *m* sacrifice
sacrilégio *m* sacrilege
sacudir *v* shake, convulse
sádico *mf* sadist
safira *n* sapphire
sagrado *adj* sacred
saia *f* skirt
saída *f* way out, exit
sair *v* go out
sair a caminho *v* set off
sair juntos *v* date
sal *f* salt
sala de aula *f* classroom

sala de estar *f* living room
sala de jantar *f* dining room
salada *f* salad
salão *m* saloon
salão de baile *m* ballroom
salário *m* salary, wage
salgado *adj* salty
salgueiro *m* willow
salientar-se *v* protrude
saliente *adj* outstanding
saliva *f* saliva
salmão *m* salmon
salpicar *v* sprinkle, splash
salsa *f* parsley, sauce
salsicha *f* sausage
saltar *v* leap, jump, hop
saltitar *v* skip
salto *m* leap, jump
salvação *f* salvation
salvador *m* savior
salvaguarda *f* safeguard
salvar *v* save, salvage
salva-vidas *m* lifeguard
sanção *f* sanction
sancionar *v* sanction
sandália *f* sandal
sanduíche *m* sandwich
sangrar *v* bleed
sangrento *m* bleeding
sangrento *adj* bloody, gory
sangue *f* blood
sanguessuga *f* leech**

sanguinário *adj* bloodthirsty
sanidade *f* sanity
sanitário *m* lavatory
santidade *f* sanctity
santificar *v* sanctify
santo *adj* holy
santo *m* saint
santuário *m* sanctuary
são *adj* sane
sapatear *v* stamp
sapato *m* shoe
sapo *m* toad
saque *m* sack
saquear *n* loot, plunder
sarampo *m* measles
sarcasmo *m* sarcasm
sarcástico *adj* sarcastic
sarda *f* freckle
sardento *adj* freckled
sardinha *f* sardine
sargento *m* sergeant
sarjeta *f* gutter
satânico *adj* satanic
satélite *m* satellite
sátira *f* satire
satisfação *f* satisfaction
satisfatório *adj* satisfactory
satisfazer *v* satisfy
saturar *v* saturate
saudações *m* greetings
saudar *v* greet
saudável *adj* healthy

saúde *f* health
sazonal *adj* seasonal
script *m* script
se *c* if, whether
seca *f* drought
secador *m* dryer
seção *f* section
secar *v* dry, wipe
seco *adj* dried, dry
secredo *m* secrecy, secret
secretamente *adv* secretly
secretário *m* secretary
secreto *adj* undercover
século *m* century
secundário *adj* secondary
seda *f* silk
sedação *f* sedation
sedar *v* sedate
sedento *adj* thirsty
sedução *f* seduction
seduzir *v* seduce
segmento *m* segment
segregação *f* segregation
segregar *v* segregate
seguidor *m* follower
seguir *v* follow
seguir de perto *v* tail
Segunda-feira *m* Monday
segundo *m* second
segurança *f* safety
segurar *v* secure, insure
seguridade *f* security

S

seguro *m* insurance
seguro *adj* safe, secure
seio *m* breast, bosom
seis *adj* six
seita *f* sect
seiva *f* sap
selar *v* stamp, seal
seleção *f* selection
selecionar *v* select
selo *m* stamp
selva *f* jungle
selvagem *adj* savage, wild
selvageria *f* savagery
sem *pre* without
sem base *m* baseball
sem chumbo *adj* unleaded
sem costura *adj* seamless
sem culpa *adj* blameless
sem fala *adj* speechless
sem filhos *adj* childless
sem fio *adj* cordless, wireless
sem fundo *adj* bottomless
sem gosto *adj* tasteless
sem manga *adj* sleeveless
sem moral *adj* amoral
sem móveis *adj* unfurnished
sem nuvens *adj* cloudless
sem rumo *adv* adrift
sem saída *f* dead end
sem semente *adj* seedless
sem sentido *adj* meaningless, pointless

sem um tostão *adj* penniless
sem valor *adj* worthless
semana *f* week
semanalmente *adv* weekly
semear *v* sow
semelhança *f* resemblance
semente *f* seed
semestre *m* semester
seminário *m* seminary
sempre *adv* always
sempre que *adv* whenever
sem-teto *adj* homeless
Senado *m* senate
senador *m* senator
senão *adv* otherwise
senha *f* password
senhor *m* sir, lord, mister
senhora *f* lady
senhoria *m* lordship
senhorio *m* landlord
senhorita *f* miss
senil *adj* senile
sensação *f* sensation
sensato *adj* sensible
sensitivo *adj* sensitive
senso *m* sense
sensual *adj* sensual
sentado *adj* seated
sentar *v* sit
sentença *f* sentence
sentenciar *v* sentence
sentido *m* meaning

sentimental *adj* sentimental
sentimento *m* feeling
sentimentos *m* feelings
sentinela *f* sentry
sentir *v* feel, sense
sentir saudade *v* long for
separação *f* separation
separadamente *adv* apart
separado *adj* separate
separar *v* separate, split
separar-se *v* break up
separável *adj* detachable
seqüencia *f* sequence, sequel
sequestrador *m* kidnapper
seqüestrador *m* hijacker
seqüestrar *v* hijack, kidnap
sequestro *m* kidnapping
ser *m* being
ser *v* be
ser humano *m* human being
ser levado *v* drift
ser possível *v* may
sereia *f* mermaid
serenata *f* serenade
serenidade *f* serenity
sereno *adj* serene
seriamente *adv* earnestly
série *f* string, series
seriedade *f* seriousness
seringa *f* syringe
sério *adj* serious
sermão *m* sermon

serpente *f* serpent, snake
serralheiro *m* locksmith
serrar *v* saw
serrote *f* saw
serviço *m* service
servir *v* serve
servo *m* servant
sessão *f* session, sitting
sessenta *adj* sixty
seta *f* arrow
sete *adj* seven
Setembro *m* September
setenta *adj* seventy
sétimo *adj* seventh
setor *m* sector
seu *adj* your
seu *pro* yours
severamente *adv* harshly
severidade *f* severity
severo *adj* severe, harsh
sexo *m* sex
Sexta-feira *m* Friday
sexto *adj* sixth
sexualidade *f* sexuality
si mesmo *pre* oneself
sibilar *v* hiss
sidra *f* cider
sífilis *f* syphilis
significância *f* significance
significante *adj* significant
significar *v* mean, signify
significativo *adj* meaningful

S

sílaba *f* syllable

silenciar *v* silence

silêncio *m* silence

silencioso *adj* silent

silhueta *f* silhouette

sim *adv* yes

simbólico *adj* symbolic

símbolo *m* symbol

simetria *f* symmetry

similar *adj* alike, similar

similaridade *f* similarity

simpatia *f* sympathy

simpatizar *v* sympathize

simples *adj* plain, simple

simplesmente *adv* plainly, simply

simplicidade *f* simplicity

simplificar *v* simplify

simular *v* simulate

simultâneo *n* simultaneous

sinagoga *f* synagogue

sinal *f* sign, signal, token

sinceridade *f* sincerity

sincero *adj* sincere

sincronizar *v* synchronize

sinfonia *f* symphony

singular *adj* singular

sinistro *adj* grim, sinister

sínodo *m* synod

sinônimo *m* synonym

síntese *f* synthesis

sintoma *m* symptom

sirene *f* siren

sistema *m* system

sistemático *adj* systematic

site *m* site

sitiar *v* siege

situação *f* situation

situado *adj* situated

slogan *m* slogan

só *adj* single

soar *v* sound

sob *pre* beneath

sob medida *adj* custom-made

soberania *f* sovereignty

soberano *adj* sovereign

soberbo *adj* superb

sobra *f* leftovers

sobrancelha *n* eyebrow

sobre *pre* on, upon

sobrecarga *f* surcharge

sobrecarregar *v* burden

sobremesa *f* dessert

sobrenome *m* last name

sobrepeso *adj* overweight

sobrepor *v* overlap

sobressair *v* stand out

sobressaltado *adj* jumpy

sobretudo *m* overcoat

sobrevivência *f* survival

sobrevivente *m* survivor

sobreviver *v* survive, outlive

sobrinha *f* niece

sobrinho *m* nephew

sóbrio *adj* sober

S

socar *v* punch
socialismo *m* socialism
socialista *adj* socialist
socializar *v* socialize
sociável *adj* sociable
sociedade *f* society
soco *m* punch
soda *f* soda
sofá *m* sofa
sofrer *v* suffer
sofrimento *m* suffering
sogra *f* mother-in-law
sogro *m* father-in-law
sol *m* sun
sola *f* sole
solapar *v* sap
solar *adj* solar
solavanco *m* bump
soldado *m* soldier
soldador *m* welder
soldar *v* solder, weld
solene *adj* solemn
soletrar *v* spell
solicitar *v* solicit
solidão *f* loneliness
solidariedade *f* solidarity
sólido *adj* solid
solitário *adj* solitary, lonesome
solitário *adv* lonely
solitário *m* loner
solo *m* ground
soltar *v* release

solteiro *m* bachelor
solteirona *f* spinster
solto *adj* loose
solução *f* solution
soluçar *v* sob
soluço *m* hiccup, sob
solúvel *adj* soluble
solvente *adj* solvent
solver *v* solve
som *m* sound
soma *f* sum
somar *v* sum
sombra *f* shade, shadow
sombrio *adj* somber
sondar *v* probe
soneca *f* nap
sonhar *v* dream
sonho *m* dream
sono *m* sleep
sonolento *adj* drowsy
sopa *f* soup
soprar *v* blow
sórdido *adj* nasty
soro *m* serum
sorrir *v* smile
sorriso *f* smile
sorte *n* luck
sortido *adj* assorted
sortimento *m* assortment
sortudo *adj* lucky
sorver *v* sip
sorvete *m* ice cream

S

sotaina *f* cassock
sótão *m* attic
soviético *adj* soviet
sozinho *adj* alone
suar *v* sweat
suave *adj* smooth
suavemente *adv* softly
suavidade *f* smoothness
suavizar *v* soften
subir *v* go up
subjugar *v* subdue
sublime *adj* sublime
sublinhar *v* underline
submergir *v* submerge
submerso *adj* sunken
submeter *v* submit
submeter-se *v* undergo
submisso *adj* submissive
sub-norma *adj* substandard
subornar *v* bribe, buy off
suborno *m* bribe, bribery
subproduto *m* by-product
subscrever *v* subscribe
subscrição *f* subscription
subseqüente *adj* subsequent
subsidiar *v* subsidize
subsidiário *adj* subsidiary
subsídio *m* subsidy
subsistir *v* subsist, linger
substância *f* substance
substancial *adj* substantial
substituir *v* replace

substituto *m* substitute
subterrâneo *adj* underground
subtítulo *m* subtitle
subtração *f* subtraction
subtrair *v* deduct, subtract
subúrbio *m* suburb
subvenção *f* grant
suceder *v* succeed
sucesso *m* hit, success
sucessor *m* successor
suco *m* juice
suculento *adj* succulent
sucumbir *v* succumb
sudeste *m* southeast
sudoeste *m* southwest
Suécia *f* Sweden
sueco *adj* Swedish
suéter *m* sweater
suficiente *adv* enough
suficiente *adj* sufficient
sufocante *adj* stifling
sufocar *v* suffocate, choke
sugerir *v* suggest
sugestão *f* suggestion
sugestivo *adj* suggestive
Suíça *f* Switzerland
suicídio *n* suicide
suíço *adj* Swiss
sujar *v* soil
sujeição a *f* liability
sujeira *f* dirt, filth
sujeitar *v* subject

S

sujeito *m* subject, guy
sujo *adj* dirty, soiled
sul *m* south
sulgo *m* furrow
sulista *m* southerner
sumário *m* summary
suntuoso *adj* sumptuous
suor *m* sweat
superar *v* surpass
superestimar *v* overrate
superfície *f* surface
supérfluo *adj* superfluous
superior *adj* superior
superioridade *f* superiority
superlotado *adj* overcrowded
supermercado *m* supermarket
superpotência *f* superpower
superstição *f* superstition
supervisão *f* supervision
supervisar *v* supervise
suplantar *v* supersede
suplicar *v* entreat, plead
supondo que *c* supposing
supor *v* assume, suppose
suportar *v* back, bear
suportável *adj* bearable
suporte *v* support
suposição *f* assumption
supostamente *adv* allegedly
suposto *adj* so-called
supremacia *f* supremacy
supremo *adj* supreme

suprimento *m* supplies
suprimir *v* suppress
surdez *f* deafness
surdo *adj* deaf
surfar *v* surf
surgir *v* arise
surpreender *v* surprise
surpresa *n* surprise
surra *n* spanking, beating
surrar *v* spank
suscetível *adj* susceptible
suspeição *f* suspicion
suspeitar *v* suspect
suspeito *m* suspect
suspeitoso *adj* suspicious
suspenção *f* suspension
suspender *v* suspend
suspense *m* suspense
suspensório *m* suspenders
suspirar *v* sigh
suspiro *m* sigh
sussurrar *v* whisper
sustentar *v* sustain
sustento *m* sustenance
suster *v* uphold
susto *m* scare
sutiã *f* bra
sutil *adj* subtle
sutura *f* stitch
suturar *v* stitch
suvenir *m* souvenir

S

T

tabaco *m* tobacco
tabela de horário *f* timetable
tablete *f* tablet
taça *f* cup
tacha *f* tack
tachinha *f* thumbtack
tal *adj* such
tala *f* splint
talão de cheques *f* checkbook
talento *m* talent, wit
talentoso *adj* gifted
talhada *f* slice
talhar *v* hack, slash
talho *m* slash, gash
talo *m* stalk
talvez *adv* perhaps
tamanho *m* size
também *adv* also, too
tambor *m* drum
tamborete *m* stool
tampa *f* cap, lid
tampão *mf* plug
tampouco *adv* neither
tangente *f* tangent
tangerina *f* tangerine
tangível *adj* tangible
tanque *m* tank
tapa *f* slap, tap
tapar *v* plug

tapeçaria *f* tapestry
tapete *m* rug
tapinha *f* pat
taquigrafia *f* shorthand
tarântula *f* tarantula
tarde *f* afternoon
tarefa *f* homework, task
tarefa doméstica *f* chore
tarifa *f* tariff
tarifa aérea *fm* airfare
tartamudear *v* stammer
tártaro *m* tartar
tartaruga *f* tortoise, turtle
tática *f* tactics
tático *adj* tactical
tato *m* tact, touch
taverna *f* tavern
taxa *f* duty
taxi *m* cab
tchau *e* bye
tear *m* loom
teatro *m* theater
tecer *v* weave
tecido *m* fabric
tecido *adj* woven
teclado *m* keyboard
técnica *f* technique
técnico *adj* technical
técnico *m* technician
tecnologia *f* technology
tédio *m* boredom, tedium
tedioso *adj* dull, tedious

teia *f* web

teia de aranha *f* spider web

teimoso *adj* stubborn

tela *f* canvas

telefonar *v* phone, ring

telefone *m* telephone

telefone celular *m* cell phone

telegrama *m* wire, telegram

telepatia *f* telepathy

telescópio *m* telescope

televisão *f* television

televisionar *v* televise

telha *f* tile

tema *m* theme

temer *v* dread

temerário *adj* reckless

temeroso *adj* startled

temido *adj* dreaded

temor *m* awe

temperamento *m* temper

temperatura *f* temperature

tempero *m* spice

tempestade *f* storm

tempestuoso *adj* stormy

templo *m* temple

tempo *m* weather, time

temporada *f* season

temporário *adj* temporary

tenacidade *f* tenacity

tencionar *v* intend

tendência *f* tendency

tenente *m* lieutenant

tênis *m* tennis

tenor *m* tenor

tenro *adj* tender

tensão *f* tension

tensionar *v* strain

tenso *adj* tense, uptight

tentação *f* temptation

tentáculo *m* tentacle

tentador *adj* tempting

tentar *v* tempt, try

tentativa *f* attempt

tentativo *adj* tentative

tênue *adj* faint, feeble

tênuo *adj* tenuous

teologia *f* theology

teólogo *m* theologian

teoria *f* theory

tépido *adj* lukewarm

ter *v* have

ter alucinação *v* hallucinate

ter que *v* have to

ter recursos *v* afford

ter sede *v* thirst

terapia *f* therapy

Terça-feira *m* Tuesday

terceiro *adj* third

terminar *v* end

término *m* completion

terminologia *f* terminology

termômetro *m* thermometer

termostato *m* thermostat

terno *adj* gentle

ternura *f* tenderness

terra *f* earth, land, soil

terra natal *f* homeland

terraço *m* terrace

terreiro *m* farmyard

terremoto *m* earthquake

terreno *m* terrain

terrestre *adj* terrestrial

território *m* territory

terrível *adj* awful

terror *m* terror

terrorismo *m* terrorism

terrorista *m* terrorist

tese *f* thesis

tesoura *f* scissors

tesoureiro *m* treasurer

tesouro *m* treasure

testa *f* forehead

testamento *m* testament

testar *v* test

teste *m* test

testemunha *m* testimony

testificar *v* testify

teto *m* ceiling, roof

texto *m* text

textura *f* texture

tia *f* aunt

tigela *f* bowl

tigre *m* tiger

tijolo *m* brick

timão *m* helm

time *m* team

timidez *f* shyness

tímido *adj* bashful, shy

tímpano *m* eardrum

tingir *v* dye

tinta *f* ink

tintura *f* dye

tio *m* uncle

típico *adj* typical

tipificar *v* type

tipo *m* type

tira *f* stripe, shred, strip

tirania *f* tyranny

tirano *m* tyrant

tireóide *f* thyroid

tiritar *v* shiver

tiro *m* shot

tiroteio *m* gunfire

títere *m* puppet

título *m* heading, title

toalha *f* towel

toalha de mesa *f* tablecloth

toca *f* burrow, den

tocar *v* play, touch

tocha *f* torch

toco *m* butt, stub

todo *adj* every, all

todo dia *adj* everyday

todo o mundo *pro* everybody

toga *f* gown

toicinho *m* bacon

toldo *m* awning

tolerância *f* tolerance

T

tolerante *adj* broadminded

tolerar *v* tolerate

tolerável *adj* tolerable

tolo *m* fool

tolo *adj* silly

tom *n* tune, tone

tomar *v* take

tomar as rédeas *v* rein

tomar conta *v* mind

tomar cuidado *v* beware

tomar emprestado *v* borrow

tomar lugar *v* preempt

tomate *m* tomato

tombar *v* tumble

tonelada *f* ton

tônico *adj* tonic

tonteira *f* dizziness

tonto *adj* dizzy

topar com *v* bump into

tópico *m* topic

topo *m* top

toque *m* touch

toque de recolher *m* curfew

torção *f* twist

torcer *v* twist

torcido *adj* twisted

tormentar *v* torment

tormento *m* torment

tornar-se *v* turn up, become

torneio *m* tournament

torneira *f* faucet

torniquete *m* clamp

tornozelo *m* ankle

toronja *f* grapefruit

torrada *f* toast

torradeira *f* toaster

torre *m* turret

torrente *m* torrent

tórrico *adj* torrid

torta *f* pie

torta de frutas *f* tart

tortuoso *adj* winding

tortura *f* torture

torturar *v* torture

tosquiar *v* shear

tosse *f* cough

tossir *v* cough

tostar *v* toast

total *adj* total

totalidade *f* totality

totalitário *adj* totalitarian

totalmente *adj* altogether

totalmente *adv* quite

toucinho *m* lard

tourada *f* bull fight

toureiro *m* bull fighter

touro *m* bull

tóxico *adj* toxic

toxina *f* toxin

trabalhador *m* worker

trabalhar *v* work

trabalho *m* work, job

traça *f* moth

tração *f* traction

T

traçar *v* trace
tradição *f* tradition
tradutor *m* translator
traduzir *v* translate
tráfico *m* traffic
tragar *v* engulf
tragédia *f* tragedy
trágico *adj* tragic
traição *f* treason
traiçoeiro *adj* treacherous
traidor *m* traitor
trair *v* betray
traje *m* outfit
trajetória *f* trajectory
trama *f* scheme, plot
tramar *v* plot, frame
trampolim *m* springboard
tranca *f* lock, bolt
trancar *v* lock, bolt
tranco *m* jolt
tranqüilidade *f* tranquility
tranqüilizar *v* reassure
tranqüilo *adj* peaceful
transação *f* transaction
transbordar *v* overflow
transcender *v* transcend
transcorrer *v* elapse
transcrever *v* transcribe
transe *m* trance
transferência *f* transfer
transferir *v* transfer
transformação *f* transformation

transformar *v* transform
transformar-se *v* mutate
transfusão *f* transfusion
transgredir *v* trespass
transição *f* transition
trânsito *m* transit
transitório *adj* transient
transmitir *v* transmit
transparente *adj* transparent
transpirar *v* exude
transplantar *v* transplant
transportar *v* transport
transtornado *adj* distraught
transtornar *v* bewilder
trapacear *v* cheat
trapaceiro *m* cheater
trapo *m* rag
traquéia *f* windpipe
traseiro *adj* rear
trasseiro *m* pillow
tratado *m* treaty
tratamento *m* treatment
tratar *v* handle
tratar de *v* deal with
trator *m* tractor
traumático *adj* traumatic
traumatizar *v* traumatize
travado *adj* deadlock
travessia *f* crossing
travesso *adj* mischievous
travessura *f* mischief
trazer *v* bring

T

trecho *m* stretch
trégua *f* respite, truce
treinador *m* coach
treinamento *m* training
treinar *v* coach, train
trem *m* train
tremendo *adj* tremendous
tremor *m* tremble, tremor
tremular *v* flicker
trêmulo *adj* shaky
trenó *m* sleigh
três *adj* three
treze *adj* thirteen
triângulo *m* triangle
tribo *m* tribe
tribulação *f* tribulation
tribunal *f* courthouse
tributo *m* tribute
tricotar *v* knit
trigo *m* wheat
trilhar *v* thresh
trilho *m* rail
trimestral *adj* quarterly
trimestre *m* trimester
trincheira *f* trench
trinta *adj* thirty
tripé *m* tripod
triplo *adj* triple
tripulação *m* crew
triste *adj* sad
tristeza *f* sadness
triunfante *adj* triumphant

triunfo *m* triumph
trivial *adj* trivial
trocar *v* switch, change
troçar *v* scoff
troféu *m* trophy
trombar *v* slam
trombeta *f* trumpet
trombose *f* thrombosis
tronco *m* stem, trunk
trono *m* throne
tropa *f* troop
tropeçar *v* stumble
tropeço *m* blunder
tropical *adj* tropical
trópico *m* tropic
trouxa *f* bundle
trovão *f* thunder
trovejar *v* boom
truque *m* trick
truta *f* trout
tu *pro* you
tubarão *m* shark
tuberculose *f* tuberculosis
tudo *pro* everything
tudo bem *adv* okay
tulipa *m* tulip
tumba *f* tomb
tumor *m* tumor
túmulo *m* grave
tumulto *m* tumult, turmoil
tumultuoso *adj* tumultuous
túnel *m* tunnel

T

túnica *f* tunic
turbina *f* turbine
turbulência *f* turbulence
turco *adj* Turk
turfa *f* turf
turismo *m* tourism
turista *m* tourist
turno *m* shift
Turquia *f* Turkey
tutano *m* bone marrow
tutor *m* tutor

U

uivar *v* howl
uivo *m* howl
úlcera *f* ulcer
ultimamente *adv* lately
ultimato *m* ultimatum
último *adj* last, latter
ultraje *n* outrage
ultrapassar *v* overstep
ultrassom *n* ultrasound
um *a* a, an
um *adj* one
um ou outro *adj* either
um pouco *adv* somewhat
uma vez *adv* once

uma vez que *c* once
umbigo *m* belly button
umedecer *v* moisten
umidade *f* humidity
úmido *adj* damp
unanimidade *f* unanimity
undécimo *adj* eleventh
ungir *v* anoint
ungüento *m* ointment
unha *f* fingernail
unha do pé *f* toenail
união *f* union, unity
unicamente *adv* solely
único *adj* unique, sole
unidade *f* unit
unificação *f* unification
unificar *v* unify
uniforme *adj* even
uniforme *m* uniform
uniformidade *f* uniformity
unilateral *adj* unilateral
unir *v* join, unite
universal *adj* universal
universidade *f* university
universo *m* universe
urbano *adj* urban
urgência *f* urgency
urgente *adj* urgent
urgir *v* urge
urina *f* urine
urinar *v* urinate
urna *f* urn

urso *m* bear
usar *v* use
uso *m* use, usage
usual *adj* usual
usuário *m* user
usurpar *v* usurp, encroach
utensílio *m* utensil
útero *m* uterus
útil *adj* helpful, useful
utilidade *f* usefulness
utilizar *v* utilize
uva *f* grape
uva passa *f* raisin

vaca *f* cow
vacância *f* vacancy
vacilar *v* vacillate, falter
vacina *f* vaccine
vacinar *v* vaccinate
vácuo *m* gap
vadiar *v* hang around
vagabundo *m* wanderer
vagão *m* wagon
vagar *v* roam, wander
vagem *f* green bean
vago *adj* fuzzy, vague

vaidade *f* vanity
vala *f* ditch
vale a pena *adj* worthwhile
vale postal *m* money order
valentão *adj* bully
valente *adj* valiant
valentia *f* hardness
validade *f* validity
validar *v* validate
válido *adj* valid
valioso *adj* valuable
valor *m* worth, value
valsa *f* waltz
válvula *f* valve
vampiro *m* vampire
vandalismo *m* vandalism
vandalizar *v* vandalize
vândalo *m* vandal
vangloriar-se *v* boast
vanguarda *f* forefront, lead
vantagem *f* advantage
vão *adj* vain
vapor *m* steam
vaporizar *v* vaporize
vara *f* stick
variado *adj* varied
variar *v* vary
variável *adj* variable
variedade *f* variety
varíola *f* smallpox
vários *adj* several, various
varrer *v* sweep

vasculhar *v* ransack
vaso *m* flowerpot, vase
vassoura *f* broom
vasto *adj* vast
vazamento *m* leakage
vazar *v* leak
vazio *m* emptiness
vazio *adj* empty
veado *m* deer
vegetação *f* vegetation
vegetal *v* vegetable
vegetariano *sdj* vegetarian
veia *f* vein
veículo *m* vehicle
vela *f* candle, sail
vela de ignição *f* spark plug
velejar *v* sail
velhaco *adj* cunning
velhice *f* old age
velho *adj* old
velocidade *f* speed
veloz *adj* speedy
velozmente *adv* speedily
veludo *m* velvet
vencedor *m* winner
vencer *v* vanquish
venda *f* blindfold, sale
vendaval *m* gale
vendedor *m* seller
vender *v* sell
veneno *m* poison, venom
venenoso *adj* poisonous

venerar *v* venerate
ventilação *f* ventilation
ventilador *m* fan
ventilar *v* ventilate, air
vento *m* wind
ventoso *adj* windy
ventre *m* womb
ver *v* see, behold
verão *m* summer
verbalmente *adv* verbally
verbo *m* verb
verdade *f* truth
verdadeiro *adj* truthful
verde *adj* green
verdura *m* vegetable
veredicto *m* verdict
vergonha *f* shame
vergonhoso *adj* shameful
verificação *f* verification
verificar *v* verify
verme *m* worm
vermelho *adj* red
verniz *m* varnish
verruga *f* mole, wart
versado *adj* versed
versão *f* version
versátil *adj* versatile
verso *m* verse
versus *pre* versus
vértebra *f* vertebra
vesícula biliar *f* gall bladder
vespa *f* wasp

véspera *f* eve
vestes *m* vest
vestiário *m* locker room
vestíbulo *m* hallway, lobby
vestido *m* dress
vestígio *m* vestige, relic
vestimenta *f* garment
vestir *v* wear, dress
vestuário *m* apparel
vetar *m* veto
veterano *m* veteran
veterinário *m* veterinarian
véu *m* veil
vezes *f* times
viaduto *m* viaduct
viagem *m* journey, trip
viajante *m* traveler
viajar *v* travel
viajem por mar *n* voyage
viável *adj* feasible
víbora *f* viper
vibração *f* vibration
vibrante *adj* vibrant
vibrar *v* vibrate
vice *m* vice
viciado *adj* addicted
vício *f* addiction
vicioso *adj* vicious
viçoso *adj* lush
vida *f* life
vida *adj* lifetime
vidro *m* glass

viga *f* beam
vigarista *m* con man
vigésimo *adj* twentieth
vigia *f* guard
vigiar *v* watch
vigilância *f* surveillance
vigilante *adj* watchful
vigília *n* vigil
vigoroso *adj* vigorous
vila *f* village
vilão *m* villain
vinagre *m* vinegar
vinco *m* crease
vínculo *m* bond, link
vinda *f* coming
vindicar *v* vindicate
vindicativo *adj* vindictive
vindouro *adj* upcoming
vingança *f* revenge
vingar *v* revenge
vinha *f* grapevine, vine
vinhedo *m* vineyard
vinho *m* wine
vinte *adj* twenty
violão *f* guitar
violar *v* violate
violência *f* violence
violento *adj* violent
violeta *adj* purple
violinista *m* violinist
violino *m* fiddle, violin
vir *v* come

virar *v* turn, capsize
virgem *f* virgin
virgindade *f* virginity
vírgula *f* comma
viril *adj* virile, manly
virilha *f* groin
virilidade *f* virility
virtualmente *adv* virtually
virtude *f* virtue
virtuoso *adj* virtuous
virulento *adj* virulent
vírus *m* virus
visão *f* vision, sight
visão geral *f* overview
visar *v* aim
visibilidade *f* visibility
visita *f* visit
visitante *m* visitor
visitar *v* visit
visível *adj* visible
vislumbre *m* glimpse
vista *f* view
visto que *c* since
vistoso *adj* dashing
visual *adj* visual
visualizar *v* visualize
vital *adj* vital
vitalidade *f* vitality
vitamina *f* vitamin
vitela *f* veal
vítima *f* victim
vitimar *v* victimize

vitória *f* victory
vitorioso *adj* victorious
viúva *f* widow
viúvo *m* widower
viva *v* cheer
vivaz *adj* vivacious
viver *v* live
viver à altura de *v* live up
viver à custa de *v* live off
vívido *adj* vivid
vivo *adj* alive
vizinhança *nf* vicinity
vizinho *m* neighbor
vizinho *adj* next door
voar *v* fly
voar alto *v* soar
vocabulário *m* vocabulary
vocábulo *m* term
vocação *f* vocation
você mesmo *pro* yourself
voga *f* vogue
vogal *f* vowel
volátil *adj* volatile
vôleibol *m* volleyball
volta *f* lap
voltagem *m* voltage
voltar *v* come back
voltar *f* comeback
volume *m* volume
volumoso *adj* bulky
voluntário *m* volunteer
vomitar *v* vomit

vômito *m* vomit
vontade *f* will
vôo *m* flight
votação *f* voting, poll
votar *v* vote
voto *m* vote
vovô *m* granddad
voz *f* voice
vulcão *m* volcano
vulgar *adj* vulgar
vulgaridade *f* vulgarity
vulnerável *adj* vulnerable

xadrez *m* chess
xarope *m* syrup
xerez *m* sherry

zangado *adj* cross
zebra *f* zebra
zelador *m* caretaker
zeloso *adj* zealous
zero *m* zero
zigoma *f* cheekbone
zinco *m* zinc
zíper *f* zipper
zombador *n* scornful
zombar *v* mock, scoff
zombaria *f* mockery
zona *f* zone
zona rural *f* countryside
zoologia *f* zoology
zoológico *m* zoo
zumbido *m* buzz
zumbir *v* buzz

Word to Word® Bilingual Dictionary Series

Language - Item Code - Pages ISBN #

Albanian - 500X - 306 pgs
ISBN - 978-0-933146-49-5

Amharic - 820X - 362 pgs
ISBN - 978-0-933146-59-4

Arabic - 650X - 378 pgs
ISBN - 978-0-933146-41-9

Bengali - 700X - 372 pgs
ISBN - 978-0-933146-30-3

Burmese - 705X - 310 pgs
ISBN - 978-0-933146-50-1

Cambodian - 710X - 348 pgs
ISBN - 978-0-933146-40-2

Chinese - 715X - 340 pgs
ISBN - 978-0-933146-22-8

Farsi - 660X - 328 pgs
ISBN - 978-0-933146-33-4

French - 530X - 320 pgs
ISBN - 978-0-933146-36-5

German - 535X - 326 pgs
ISBN - 978-0-933146-93-8

Gujarati - 720X - 334 pgs
ISBN - 978-0-933146-98-3

Haitian-Creole - 545X - 322 pgs
ISBN - 978-0-933146-23-5

Hebrew - 665X - 316 pgs
ISBN - 978-0-933146-58-7

Hindi - 725X - 320 pgs
ISBN - 978-0-933146-31-0

Hmong - 728X - 294 pgs
ISBN - 978-0-933146-31-0

Italian - 555X - 362 pgs
ISBN - 978-0-933146-51-8

All languages are two-way: English-Language / Language-English. More languages in planning and production.

Japanese - 730X - 346 pgs
ISBN - 978-0-933146-42-6

Korean - 735X - 374 pgs
ISBN - 978-0-933146-97-6

Lao - 740X - 319 pgs
ISBN - 978-0-933146-54-9

Pashto - 760X - 348 pgs
ISBN - 978-0-933146-34-1

Polish - 575X - 358 pgs
ISBN - 978-0-933146-64-8

Portuguese - 580X - 322 pgs
ISBN - 978-0-933146-94-5

Punjabi - 765X - 358 pgs
ISBN - 978-0-933146-32-7

Romanian - 585X - 354 pgs
ISBN - 978-0-933146-91-4

Russian - 590X - 298 pgs
ISBN - 978-0-933146-92-1

Somali - 830X - 320 pgs
ISBN- 978-0-933146-52-5

Spanish - 600X - 346 pgs
ISBN - 978-0-933146-99-0

Swahili - 835X - 274 pgs
ISBN - 978-0-933146-55-6

Tagalog - 770X - 294 pgs
ISBN - 978-0-933146-37-2

Thai - 780X - 330 pgs
ISBN - 978-0-933146-35-8

Turkish - 615X - 348 pgs
ISBN - 978-0-933146-95-2

Ukrainian - 620X - 337 pgs
ISBN - 978-0-933146-25-9

Urdu - 790X - 322 pgs
ISBN - 978-0-933146-39-6

Vietnamese - 795X - 324 pgs
ISBN - 978-0-933146-96-9

Order Information

To order our Word to Word® Bilingual Dictionaries or any other products from Bilingual Dictionaries, Inc., please contact us at (951) 296-2445 or visit us at **www.BilingualDictionaries.com**. Visit our website to download our current Catalog/Order Form, view our products, and find information regarding Bilingual Dictionaries, Inc.

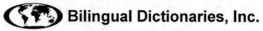 **Bilingual Dictionaries, Inc.**

PO Box 1154 • Murrieta, CA 92562 • Tel: (951) 296-2445 • Fax: (951) 461-3092
www.BilingualDictionaries.com

Special Dedication & Thanks

Bilingual Dicitonaries, Inc. would like to thank all the teachers from various districts accross the country for their useful input and great suggestions in creating a Word to Word® standard. We encourage all students and teachers using our bilingual learning materials to give us feedback. Please send your questions or comments via email to support@bilingualdictionaries.com.